an introduction to:

THE ART OF THEATRE

A comprehensive text — past, present, and future

MARSH CASSADY

MERIWETHER PUBLISHING
A division of Pioneer Drama Service, Inc.
Denver, Colorado

Meriwether Publishing
A division of Pioneer Drama Service, Inc.
PO Box 4267
Englewood, CO 80155

www.pioneerdrama.com

Editor: Theodore O. Zapel
Assistant editor: Audrey Scheck
Cover design: Jan Melvin

Library of Congress Cataloging-in-Publication Data

Cassady, Marsh, 1936-
    An introduction to—the art of theatre : a comprehensive text—past, present, and future / by Marsh Cassady.
      p. cm.
    Includes bibliographical references.
    ISBN 978-1-56608-117-7 (pbk.)
    1. Theater. I. Title. II. Title: Art of theatre.
    PN2037.C28 2006
    792--dc22

                              2006023624

        4   5   6   14   15   16

Contents

Preface

My main concern in writing *An Introduction to: The Art of Theatre* was to present a readable and interesting text. To my way of thinking, many textbooks, whatever ground they cover, are too academic. Although I have experience in many facets of theatre — acting, directing, design, and university teaching — I consider myself primarily a writer. Thus, for me, the major criterion for any book is its readability, and I feel that the readability of this book sets it apart.

Although the text covers traditional ground, I have tried to offer different perspectives in a few somewhat neglected areas. For example, as a writer, one of my major interests is playwriting, which often seems to be ignored or treated summarily in the largest number of introductory theatre texts. Of course, only so much material is practical to include for a beginning course.

No one can disagree that theatre is a collaborative art. Certainly it requires teamwork among the various artists. More than that, theatre is a collaboration of those with a myriad of different lifestyles, religions, ethnic or racial backgrounds, and experiences. Due in part to this collaboration and the contributions of many people, theatre is constantly evolving.

Another reason for change in the theatre experience is new technology. Thus, in this text I touch upon recent developments in theatre and drama, such as multimedia productions featuring the Internet and computer programs developed for set design. Theatre continues to evolve in other ways as well.

Of course, an introductory book cannot deal in depth with any one subject. By the very fact of choosing to include or not to include historical facts, for instance, a writer becomes an editor and a censor. An author of a textbook can only hope, if he or she is conscientious, to include that which is most enlightening, most captivating, and most valuable.

What I hope to have accomplished with this text is to instill in you a strong interest in theatre. In addition, I hope to encourage you to further investigate the wide range of minority contributions to American theatre, important historical developments that are mentioned only in passing due to space and time limitations, individual theatre artists and what their work includes, and the collaborative effort required to bring a production to fruition.

One of the main goals of any introductory text is to spark an interest in and appreciation of the subject. This is the reason for including cuttings from books and journals by and about practicing theatre artists. It is why I include a number of excerpts from different plays, ranging from classic to contemporary, and why I address theatre criticism.

This book is divided into three parts in such a way that you immediately become acquainted with the ideas of what theatre and drama are and what they entail. This is the purpose of the first two chapters, which define theatre and drama and show how plays are structured. Chapter 3 discusses style and genre, using illustrations and examples to better explain the material. I believe this is important because it is unique or unusual details that provide interest and involvement.

Throughout all these chapters are excerpts from plays that characterize movements, styles, and general beliefs. Chapter 4 then explains how and where various types of theatre are produced. Here you are given a look at theatre architecture and space, the physical theatre. I have included this chapter because I have found that many students have not had the opportunity to experience plays in more than one or two types of environments. Often they have viewed productions only at proscenium theatres.

Part II explains how various theatre artists work, including the playwright, the actor, the director, the designers, and supporting artists, as well as the sorts of backgrounds these artists have. I have tried to show that there are many different approaches in theatre, but I stress that theatre requires a collaborative effort. Although the artists in a production express their own unique creativity, all the elements of a theatrical production must mesh. Seeing that they do is the responsibility of one person, most often the director.

No matter what the job in theatre, the preparation is exacting. Chapter 8, which deals with designers and supporting artists, explains this preparation, from the designing of light and sound plots to preparing production or prompt books.

The business and house staffs of a theatre, including the technicians, are necessary to the success of any theatre or individual production. For this reason, in Chapter 9 I talk about the roles and responsibilities of the producer, the stage manager, and those other business people who work "behind the scenes" in educational, professional, and community theatre. Finally, this section concludes with a chapter on theatre criticism, not because I imagine a great number of beginning theatre students will become theatre critics, but rather to show you that with the knowledge you have gained, you can apply standards of judgment to any theatrical production, just as professional theatre critics do.

Part III covers theatre from ancient times to the present. Years back, when I was taking my first courses in theatre, there was little mention of Eastern theatre, except to say that it did exist. Yet, as I explain in the text, Asian theatre has greatly influenced American theatre, and, therefore, it is important to know its roots as well as those of Western theatre.

The instructor, of course, is free to "pick and choose," as he or she sees fit. Those who wish to devote little time to theatre history may simply refer students to the new timeline at the end of the book, rather than spending time on the history chapters.

Each chapter within a section is complete in itself, so that those instructors who, for instance, wish to deal with directing before discussing acting, certainly will find the text amenable to such switching.

At the end of each of the fifteen chapters is a summary. These by no means cover or include all that is important to each chapter, but simply provide overall highlights as study aids. Second, at the end of each chapter are questions for in-class discussion. These are for the purpose of helping students think through and apply the material they have learned.

Available also is a teacher's guide with suggestions for further discussion and research.

Acknowledgments

I owe a great debt of gratitude to two people who gave immeasurable help in writing *An Introduction to: The Art of Theatre*. The first is my wife, Pat Cassady (1936–1978), who coauthored with me the text that many years later became the starting point for this book. The second is Jim Kitchen for his help with the research for the history section and for his editorial suggestions.

Part 1
THEATRE, DRAMA, AND PLACE

Chapter 1

WHAT ARE THEATRE AND DRAMA?

Theatre is imagination. It is emotion and intellect. It is art. It has form, but that form moves and changes as constantly as clouds in a stormy sky. Through theatre we gain enlightenment and bring order and change to our environment. Theatre embraces all the world's cultures and perspectives, answers questions, predicts our tomorrows, and mirrors our today. It enhances individuality, yet brings us closer to one another. It enriches our lives and frees our creativity. Like all art forms, it expands our awareness and appreciation of life.

> Most important, the theater serves as a kind of public imagination, or a place where imaginations can meet. Where you can glimpse a little bit of what it might be like to be someone else. I think that's enormously valuable, and the worse things get in the wide world, the more important that becomes.[1]

Perhaps the oldest of the arts, theatre closely approximates life. Characters on-stage experience emotions we all experience. They become entangled in the same uncomfortable situations, and they react in much the same way we do. Even stage settings can be near replicas of real life.

Modern and Primitive Theatre

Although theatre is one of the oldest of the arts, its earliest form probably bore little resemblance to what most of us think of as theatrical entertainment. More likely, it began as nonverbal reenactments of human beings struggling against their environment — such as in hunting for prey or battling another tribe.

As cultures became more refined, theatre became more elaborate. Language developed; plays were recorded. The first of

---

1. Kenneth Lonergan, "Yes, Theater Is Important," *New York Times*, February 23, 2003, http://www.nytimes.com/.

which we have knowledge dates back to around 3000 BC in Egypt, although we cannot know whether such "drama" ever was performed. Since the ancient Greeks admired Egyptian culture, Greek theatre — from which most of our present theatre practices evolved — most certainly had roots in Egyptian theatre practices. Religious in nature, the earliest Greek plays consisted of little more than men in robes standing in a semicircle around an altar and chanting hymns of praise to Dionysus, the god of wine and fertility.

Despite differences, primitive and modern theatre serve similar purposes. Both relieve a sense of "otherness" — the isolation each of us feels in never fully knowing or understanding anyone else. These feelings of separation may be instinctive due to evolution and the awareness of self that developed as a result. Yet "otherness" is not inherent in newborn infants, who perceive their surroundings and different people as a part of themselves, which, it is theorized, was the case with primitive human beings.

As children develop, however, they realize that they are isolated and that others are different entities, often unfamiliar and therefore frightening.

As they developed self-awareness and a feeling of ethnocentricity or community, primitive people felt this same sort of strangeness or alienation because each tribe or settlement (outside their own) was, in effect, a different country. Probably there was little mingling with other tribes, so it was natural to fear them. In their enactments, primitive people attempted to deal with the "otherness" of their gods and of neighboring tribes so as to confirm their own tribe's identity and power.

Today, various people still believe in the inherent superiority of their own groups or cultures, which often accounts for wars and feelings of racial and ethnic prejudice. Yet, when we take time to acquaint ourselves with these others, and to approach them openly, we often find they aren't so different from ourselves. Theatre is one means of discovering information about other people and cultures.

A number of plays deal with the concept of hate through "otherness" or through feelings of racial or ethnic superiority. Examples are Athol Fugard's *Master Harold and the Boys* (as well as other plays about apartheid as it was practiced in South Africa), written in the 1980s; Lorraine Hansberry's *A Raisin in the Sun* (about an African-American family wanting to move into an all-white neighborhood), written in 1959; and Mary Burrill's *Aftermath* (the story of a young man returning from meritorious duty as an American soldier to find that in his absence his father was lynched), published in 1919. A more recent example is Rebecca Gilman's *Spinning into Butter,* which concerns racism on a college campus. The hugely successful musical *Hairspray,* which opened in New York in 2002, deals with the same sort of thing.

In any theatrical performance, the audience deals with the idea of "otherness." The modern theatergoer attempts to cope with it by seeking to understand it. The audience watches the "others" on-stage, witnessing their struggles and conflicts at a safe distance, separated from them by an "invisible wall," which — in most types of performance — neither actor nor audience will cross.

Theatre Compared with Other Art Forms

Any fine art, such as theatre, painting, sculpture, dance, or music, communicates a message. If the art and its creators are honest, the message that is communicated is truth — at least as perceived by the artists involved. Unlike a game of football or basketball, a work of art is more deliberate in its planning and its results. Thus, unless something unexpected happens, a ballet, a painting, or an opera follows a particular plan that realizes a particular effect.

To a greater degree than many other arts, theatre is specific in its communication. A symphony communicates feelings and beauty through sound, using intricate arrangements of melody and harmony. Theatre's sound is **dialog,** or the characters' conversations, which conveys more exact content than does music alone. In other words, a musical phrase is less specific than a spoken one. Although it is true that music can stir us to excitement, spoken lines can define a more specific reason for that excitement.

Theatre is not only more specific than nonverbal art, it is more encompassing than a novel, a poem, or a painting — not necessarily in what it tells, but because it combines so many elements in the telling. It is one of the most unlimited forms of art. Despite a certain framework — the three-act structure, for instance — theatre is limitless in what it can convey.

Finally, theatre is more personally involving and arouses a direct aesthetic response in both audience and artist.

We can distinguish theatre from many of the other arts in that a performance exists for a limited period of time. A particular production can never be witnessed again once the final line has been delivered or the final action has been performed. In this respect, theatre differs from painting or literature or architecture. Works in these arts can be enjoyed again and again in exactly the same state.

Of course, a play can be presented time and time again, but each performance will differ from any other. The director, the designers, and the actors of one production have a different interpretation of the play than do any other artists. One actor's appearance, movement, and voice vary from those of any other actor who takes the same role. Stages differ in size. **Properties** (objects the actors carry or use in the play) and costumes vary from production to production. The third night of a production's run will not be the same as the first night or the second. This is because the actors continue to grow in their roles. They experiment; they attempt to find out what will work best. Audiences affect the actors and their performances. As a result, they change their responses, playing differently to each specific audience.

Theatre is unique in that it directly imitates human experiences by allowing spectators to identify with characters who are represented as real. Members of the audience can put themselves in the characters' places and feel as the characters do. Thus, theatre satisfies our **mimetic instinct** (the human need or desire to imitate, which provides much of our learning; see page 11). It resembles life as it actually is lived or could be lived.

Theatre also interprets life. That is, the playwright, the actors, the director, and the designers all add their backgrounds and experiences to a production. They judge; they overlook; they point out specific traits to the exclusion of others. They select and, through this choice, add their own personalities or their perceptions of the world, interpreting events and actions in the play from differing viewpoints. Each of the individuals involved contributes something personal to the total production.

Theatre encompasses many other art forms — architecture in the setting, sculpture in three-dimensional forms and the creative use of lights and shadow, dance in the **blocking** (the planned movement of actors in the play), painting in the setting and makeup, literature in the words, and music in songs and the flow of the language.

Theatre as Imitation and Ritual

How did such a complex art form arise? Theatre probably had its beginnings in two basic human traits: the mimetic instinct and the need for ritual.

The Mimetic Instinct

Just as primitive people portrayed what was important in their lives, modern theatre artists most often begin by communicating what they have learned from the world around them. In other words, they imitate. Usually the imitation is only a starting point, and the playwright, director, actors, and designers allow their imaginations free rein.

Psychologists state that each of our new experiences is built upon something we already know. We relate a new situation to our awareness of the past and thus build memories and experiences. We have certain expectations, which are only slightly altered by new surroundings or new people. We use our past, then, as a point of departure in learning or in creativity.

Essentially, theatre artists use the same technique, but they need not be bound by what is — only by what could be.

Theatre artists explore and, through their art, present a wide range of thoughts and feelings. Theatre can be a vehicle of learning for both artist and audience. It can broaden cultural and humanistic horizons. It can give us confidence by showing us we are like others, and it can help us explore our individual selves.

Ritual

As people began to understand that forces outside their control, such as weather, dominated certain aspects of their lives, they began to believe in the power of supernatural beings. Consequently, they tried to please the gods through dance and movement. They believed that if they performed a certain ritual, a pattern of events often highly stylized and invariable, the weather would become warmer, or there would be rain to grow crops. As time went on, the rituals became more formal. The people added costumes, specific movements, and music. At first the entire tribe might participate, and the supernatural forces were the audience. Later, only certain members of the tribe participated. Now the rest of the community, in addition to the gods, was the audience.

Primitive people used ritual for other reasons, too. A portrayal of the hunt with the successful killing of game was a kind of magic to assure that the hunt would be successful. Then a dance could be performed after the hunt to show how it went. This dance probably was more for communication and entertainment than for pleasing the gods; but in such behavior primitive people still combined ritual and imitation.

Theatre in Everyday Life

The tribal organization is the origin of society. The articulation of its needs is the origin of theatre. Song and music and dance in which purpose and poetry were one and in which the entire community participated were devised as school and language and the source of common strength. The subsequent history of the theatre is an effort to recapture this initial unity at a complex level of civilization. In this sense, the history of the theatre is the history of man, for the stage deals with man's conflict with himself and the external world.[2]

Through thousands of years, theatre and "tribal organization" or government have continued to change, just as styles of painting, architecture, and sculpture change. However, basic human nature has not changed. In our own lives we join in **rituals**, we **pretend**, we **imitate**, and we **play roles**.

Everyday Ritual

Just as primitive people dressed in special costumes and masks in enacting rituals for entertainment and to please the gods, so do we. Today we participate in parades; we dress more formally to attend religious services; we belong to social organizations that have badges and passwords. At sporting events, we have rituals in the singing of the national anthem, the introduction of the players, and the halftime show. Although loosely constructed, these rituals follow a pattern.

This type of behavior is closely allied to theatre. For example, a show is rehearsed and presented more than once. Organized ritual is rehearsed through repetition and performed over and over. Although audience participation in theatre rituals generally is less direct, rituals such as that of communion in the Christian church do involve the audience. The drinking of wine and eating of unleavened bread (and the symbols they represent) involve both actors and audience — the clergy and the congregation.

---

2. Allan Lewis, *The Contemporary Theatre* , (New York: Crown Publishers, Inc , 1962), 1.

Pretending

Children play a game in which those on one side try to find and "shoot dead" those on the other side before they themselves are "killed." In playing this game, the children assume roles (as actors), follow certain loosely drawn rules (the format of the play), and treat themselves or the players as the audience. When one side has "eliminated" the other, the game ends. Like the portrayal of the hunt in primitive times, this game is similar to theatre. It includes performers, a play, a space, and an audience. And, like many children's games of "pretend," this one involves imitation (the mimetic instinct), communication, and entertainment. Theatre involves the same things.

We are forced to pretend or "make-believe" in social situations. We "enjoy" a party, "like" somebody's new outfit, or pretend to be interested in subjects that hold little interest for us. Often, we do these things to avoid hurting someone's feelings or, less nobly, to help us reach a later goal. If we are "interested" in a professor's theories about World War II, then maybe he or she will look upon us more favorably when grades are due. Regardless of our motives for pretending, however, playing "make-believe" places us in actors' roles.

Imitation

Like pretending, imitation helps us achieve certain goals. A baby cries, and the mother rushes to the crib to change its position or to feed it. Later the child imitates the first cry, and the mother comes once more. The baby has learned that imitating a certain action elicits a certain response.

Most important, as children, we gain much of our knowledge by imitating others. We learn to speak by imitating those around us. We see how others behave in social situations and imitate them. The basic instinct for imitation continues throughout our lives. We watch someone seated near us at a formal dinner to see which piece of silverware to use. We do what we think is expected of us, based on what we did or saw others do in similar situations. In other words, we use the same instinct in everyday living that the actor and dramatist use in creating characters for a play.

Role Playing

Imitation often takes the form of role playing, in which we assume roles to gain a certain response. Usually, in everyday situations, there are no memorized lines or formally rehearsed parts. Yet, when first assumed, the role of parent or grandparent

13

may seem alien and thus difficult. Yet each time we play the role, we gain practice for the next time. We use a certain vocabulary in particular situations, and later, under similar circumstances, we refine and improve this vocabulary. In playing the role of job applicant, for instance, we may rehearse answers to anticipated questions. Role playing in everyday life and acting in a stage production are both forms of theatre, although the latter generally is much more polished.

At various times or in different sets of circumstances, we allow different aspects of our personalities to surface. We follow different, relatively established patterns of behavior from situation to situation.

Because the image of ourselves that we want to project to others varies, we are not always the "same" people. We speak in different ways to the dean of our school or to our boss from the way we speak to friends. Further, we don't play just one role. At school, a professor may play the role of theatre instructor. He or she may be, for instance, a parent, a co-worker and friend, a shopper, and a competitor on a bowling team. Different actions and conversational styles go along with the changes in role. Even our clothing contributes to the roles we play. Imagine wearing gym shorts and a T-shirt to a wedding.

We find the theatrical all around us. Children "show off" to gain attention. We tend to dramatize certain situations to gain sympathy. We tell a long tale about the minor traffic accident in which we were involved. We are theatrical in creating caricatures of people with whom we have had an argument. Our voices become unpleasant and exaggerated, maybe with a hint of truth, when we relate what the other person said and how we were wronged.

> YOU: Well, you know what Mark's always been like.
> FRIEND: What do you mean?
> YOU: Oh, come on. Remember when he had the party and didn't invite either of us?
> FRIEND: I guess so.
> YOU: You guess so. *(Your voice becomes mocking and sarcastic, in supposed imitation of MARK.)* "Oh, well, I thought you were going to be out of town," he said.
> FRIEND: Both of us were out of town, weren't we?
> YOU: But that isn't the point!
> FRIEND: Oh?

YOU: He's so two-faced! *(Your voice becomes mocking again, in supposed imitation of MARK.)* "Oh, I didn't want to hurt your feelings," he said, "but, my God, you know how small my apartment is." Small, my foot.

FRIEND: Why are you so angry?

YOU: Me, angry? Not at a jerk like that. I wouldn't give him the satisfaction.

Theatre in Evolution

Clearly, life and theatre have much in common. An important similarity is that neither stands still. Theatre has always been in a state of change. Romanticism was a revolt against the rigid rules of earlier neoclassicism. Realism and naturalism were revolts against the artificial sentimentalism that romanticism became. (See Chapter 3 for a further discussion of the "isms.")

During the 1960s there was a move in theatre (and in society, as well) toward freedom of expression and dress. Forbidden topics became the subjects for plays. Nudity, often for its own sake, became the usual rather than the exceptional. Language had few taboos. We began to see such productions as the rock musical *Hair* (by Gerome Ragni, James Radi, and Galt MacDermot), a protest against the "establishment," and *Oh! Calcutta!*, an erotic production by Kenneth Tynan.

Many such productions depended on shock value to attract patrons. When the shock faded, the theatre again experienced change. Part of this change was the nostalgia movement of the early 1970s, with the revivals of early plays and musicals. Nostalgia was strong in the musical *Grease* (by Jim Jacobs and Warren Casey), which tried to recapture the 1950s. Theatre was rebelling against current plays, but as yet had developed no widely accepted ideas that were entirely new.

Yet each change in theatre is important. It not only mirrors the times; it leads the way to emerging attitudes. The changes in the 1960s broke many taboos, thus giving playwrights the freedom to explore previously unapproachable themes. The abandonment of inhibitions opened the way for such plays as David Storey's *The Changing Room* (1971), acted partially in the nude — not for the sake of nudity, but to present realistically the environment of a locker room. The play emphasizes the refusal of human beings to accept a defeatist attitude toward life, symbolized by the sport of rugby. In the eighties and nineties, it also allowed plays to deal with previously prohibited subjects and themes, such as homosexuality.

15

Examples are Fierstein's *Torch Song Trilogy* (1981) and McNally's *Love! Valour! Compassion!* (1994). In fact, writer-director John Fisher was quoted in 2000 as saying, "I can put anything on-stage now. Thirty years ago I couldn't have been the kind of theater person I am today."[3]

Universality

Just as many plays from earlier periods have little meaning for us now, many currently being written are certain to mean little to future generations. For a play to have lasting value, except as a museum piece or as a reflection of the time and place in which it was written, it must possess **universality**; that is, it must be relevant for all people at all times. Obviously, this is an overstatement, as nothing will have meaning for every individual. If someone were to present a Shakespearean drama to a primitive tribe, the production would not convey much. Nevertheless, some plays have themes that move audiences many years after the playwrights have written them.

Universality deals with common feelings and beliefs. It enables us to empathize with a character in a play or with the circumstances of the characters. Thornton Wilder's *Our Town* deals with life, love, death, and the hereafter, as experienced by the people of a small town around the beginning of the last century. The play concentrates on George, son of the town's physician, and Emily, daughter of the newspaper editor. The character of the Stage Manager acts as narrator. The two young people are seen going to high school together, falling in love over ice cream sodas at the drugstore, getting married, and suffering as Emily dies in childbirth. In a touching third act, the two young people are reunited briefly after Emily has found out how painful a return to life can be, because the living take all of life for granted. According to Wilder:

> Every action which has ever taken place — every thought, every emotion — has taken place only once, at one moment in time and place. "I love you," "I rejoice," "I suffer," have been said and felt many billions of times, and never twice the same. Every person who has ever lived has lived an unbroken succession of unique occasions. Yet the more one

---

3. Steve Winn, "Anything But a Drag: Gay theater takes new directions and more risk," *San Francisco Chronicle*, January 9, 2000.

is aware of this individuality in experience (innumerable! innumerable!) the more one becomes attentive to what these disparate moments have in common, to repetitive patterns. As an artist (or listener or beholder) which "Truth" do you prefer — that of the isolated occasion, or that which includes and resumes the innumerable? Which truth is more worth telling? Every age differs in this. Is the Venus de Milo "one woman"? Is the play Macbeth the story of "one destiny"? The theatre is admirably fitted to tell both truths.[4]

We have little trouble identifying with the characters in *Our Town*, because their experiences of growing up, living together as families, and dealing with death are similar to our own. Wilder reinforces the universal belief that each of us should learn to appreciate and notice others.

Many plays that have survived from earlier periods contain universal themes simply because our drives and motives are the same as they were thousands of years ago. *Agamemnon* (458 BC), by the Greek playwright Aeschylus, involves unfaithfulness. Clytemnestra takes a lover while her husband Agamemnon is away at war. He returns home with the captured princess Cassandra, and Clytemnestra murders both of them. Unfaithfulness is treated in many modern plays. In Arthur Miller's *Death of a Salesman*, for example, Biff discovers his father, Willy, in a hotel room with a woman.

Death of a Salesman
Arthur Miller

Willy Loman, a traveling salesman, has always felt that social success or "being well-liked" is the key to financial success. When the play opens, Willy is sixty-three and no longer able to sell. He is at the point of hallucinating and talking to himself; for him the past and the present intermingle. Through flashbacks (scenes from the past) we learn how Willy's world has fallen apart. He always viewed

4. Thornton Wilder, *Three Plays by Thornton Wilder*, (New York: Harper and Row, 1957; reprinted by Bantam, 1958), ix-x.

himself as the ideal father and husband. His image shatters when Biff, the older of his two sons, finds him in a hotel room with a woman. Willy had led Biff to believe that social popularity and success on the football field were more important than education, and he pampered both sons. The younger son, Happy, has patterned his life after Willy's and views success as his father does. After Willy finally asks his boss for an in-town selling job and is fired instead, Biff forces him to realize that both of them are failures. Because his insurance is paid up, Willy feels he still can be a success by killing himself and leaving the insurance money to his family. He goes to the garage to start his car, and his wife, Linda, foresees what will happen. Even though she loves him for what he is, she is powerless to stop him.

Theatre is an imitation of what we ourselves experience. It imitates but heightens life's experiences. It offers new insights into our feelings. It has relevance for us both as individuals and as part of the human race. We understand our own motives more fully when we see them portrayed on the stage. Certainly, most of us never will become murderers, yet we recognize that under certain circumstances — attacks against us or our families, for instance — we may be capable of killing another human being. Thus we can understand and sympathize with Hamlet when he expresses the desire to avenge his father's death.

Figure 1-1: Production shot of *Hamlet*

18

When *Hamlet* opens, Claudius has become the ruler of Denmark by killing Hamlet's father and marrying his mother. This scene from Act III shows how strongly Hamlet despises his father's murderer.

Now might I do it pat, now he is praying;
And now I'll do't. And so he goes to heaven;
And so am I revenged. That would be scann'd:
A villain kills my father; and for that,
I, his sole son, do this same villain send
To heaven.
O, this is hire and salary, not revenge.
He took my father grossly, full of bread;
With all his crimes broad blown, as flush as May;
And how his audit stands who knows save heaven?
But in other circumstance and course of thought,
'Tis heavy with him: and am I then revenged,
To take him in the purging of his soul,
When he is fit and season'd for his passage?
No!
Up, sword; and know thou a more horrid hent:
When he is drunk asleep, or in his rage,
Or in the incestuous pleasure of his bed;
At gaming, swearing, or about some act
That has no relish of salvation in 't;
Then trip him, that his heels may kick at heaven.
And that his soul may be as damn'd and black
As hell, whereto it goes.

Hamlet, Prince of Denmark
William Shakespeare

Because "the times are out of joint," sin has corrupted the royal court. Claudius, Hamlet's uncle, has secretly murdered Hamlet's father and married his mother, Gertrude. Sworn by his father's ghost to vengeance, Hamlet must first make certain that Claudius indeed is guilty. He does so by hiring a band of players (actors) to reenact the murder. Claudius betrays himself during the performance.

Hamlet suspects Polonius of being a part of the conspiracy. He now suspects Polonius's daughter, Ophelia, as well — even though formerly Hamlet had courted her. Ophelia is deeply in love with Hamlet.

Inadvertently, Hamlet kills Polonius, after which he is exiled and Ophelia goes mad. Laertes, Polonius's son and a former friend of Hamlet, challenges Hamlet to a fencing match. He puts poison on his sword point with the approval of the king. Gertrude dies after consuming a poisoned drink that Claudius had prepared for Hamlet. Hamlet kills Claudius; Laertes kills Hamlet. But Laertes himself dies by the poisoned rapier.

Figure 1-2:
The Odd Couple

Comedy, as well as tragedy and other genres of drama, imitates life. Yet the imitation involves **exaggeration**, a heightening of the ordinary. One way of achieving this is through characterization. At least since Greek and Roman times, comedy has involved **stock characters**, those that are types rather than individuals. In creating such characters, a playwright takes certain traits we can observe in friends or relatives and heightens them. We all have known finicky people and hypochondriacs. Neil Simon combined these two traits and exaggerated them to create the character of Felix in *The Odd Couple*, a play about a compulsively neat man sharing an apartment with a sloppy one after both are separated from their wives. (You may be acquainted with the film based on the play or with reruns of the television series starring Jack Klugman as Oscar and Tony Randall as Felix.) The two men moving in together sets up immediate conflict.

What Is Drama?

Even though certain elements have characterized theatre since its beginning, no one can seem to agree on what constitutes **drama**, or the written play. According to French theatre critic Ferdinand Brunetiére, there should be no rules — only conventions that vary from person to person, piece to piece, and time to time.

Nearly all we can assume for certain is that a play is the basic plan for communicating with an audience. A script, whether written in detail or only a bare outline, gives the performer a jumping-off place.

In most cases, a script begins with a writer, who records, refines, and finally shares the work with other theatre artists. Most often dramatists begin the work alone, in touch only with their imaginations and creativity.[5] Each has a different perspective, a different way of beginning. Even documentary plays are both more and less than the history they portray. The playwright, by choosing and eliminating, is editing and adding a perspective. This is true even with documentary drama such as Moisés Kaufman's *The Laramie Project* based on the murder in 1998 of college student Matthew Shepherd. The play consists of monologs given by actors representing area residents over a period of a year and a half. The two hundred interviews are distilled into two hours or so of playing time.

What, then, constitutes a good idea for a play? The only judgment of value relates to how well the playwright succeeds in transferring a vision to paper and how well the written script translates into a production. And even this is subjective, depending on how the viewer perceives the presentation, as seen in the two reviews of the musical *Wicked*, which opened on Broadway late in 2003.

---

5. Some playwrights, of course, collaborate, and sometimes an entire company of players will develop a play. See Chapter 5 for a more complete discussion of the playwriting process.

> Remember the last time an original Broadway musical made you laugh, cry and think — in the right places, and for the right reasons? I would have to go back to the 1970s and '80s ... But it's safe to say that [*Wicked*] is the most complete, and completely satisfying, new musical I've come across in a long time.[6]

Compare this review with the one that follows:

> Two of the producers of the musical *Wicked* bear the name Platt, which (in German) means flat, and one the name Stone, which (in English) means heavy. Why not also one called Long, although it is too much to ask for one called Boring, all of which apply to the show.[7]

A general belief is that, unlike other forms of literature, a play is not a complete piece of art simply because someone wrote and revised it. Except for "closet drama" — expressly written to be read and not performed — a play requires the collaboration of the other theatre artists to bring it fully to life. Tennessee Williams, author of such plays as *The Glass Menagerie* and *A Streetcar Named Desire*, calls the script "hardly more than an architect's blueprint of a house not yet built ... The color, the grace and levitation, the structural pattern in motion, the quick interplay of live beings, suspended like fitful lightning in a cloud, these things are the play, not words on paper, nor thoughts and ideas of an author ..."[8]

In other words, a production is a total experience in which the play or the script is but one element, albeit an essential one. This means that theatre is a total and integrated experience and must be grasped in whole rather than in part in order to appreciate its full impact.

Playwright Terrence McNally, who wrote such plays as *The Lisbon Traviata* and *Love! Valour! Compassion!*, feels much the same. "Reading a play," he says, "is like looking at a map. The journey is the rehearsal process. The destination is the production. I'm too impatient to get to Oz to be a good play reader. I want to be there."[9]

---

6. Elysa Gardner "Something 'Wicked' comes to Broadway,"*USA TODAY*, October 30, 2003, http://www.usatoday.com/life/theater/2003-10-30-wicked_x.htm.

7. John Simon, "Ding-Dong," *New York Magazine*, November 10, 2003, http://nymag.com/nymetro/arts/theater/reviews/n_9454/index.html.

8. Tennessee Williams, Afterword to *Camino Real, Where I Live: Selected Essays* (New York: New Directions, 1978, reprinted from the first published version of Camino Real, New Directions, 1953), 69.

9. Terrence McNally, "Introduction," *Fifteen Short Plays*, (Lyme, N.H.: Smith and Kraus, Inc., 1994), ix.

Of course, if we read a play and are able to visualize a setting and actors, the script can appeal to us emotionally and aesthetically. Playwright Jeffrey Sweet says, "there is no necessary correlation between" how well a script reads and how well it plays.[10] To be fully appreciated, the script needs the atmosphere of a theatre and the technical aspects of a performance. When the set designer adds a visual interpretation, when the actors analyze and impersonate the characters, and when the director integrates the total production, only then does a script fully communicate the playwright's intention.

In contrast to what most playwrights seem to believe, dramatist Edward Albee, whose work includes such plays as *Who's Afraid of Virginia Woolf?* and *Three Tall Women*, contends that: "Plays — good ones, at any rate — are literature, and the pervasive notion that a play comes to full life only on-stage speaks either of an inability to realize a production through reading or a flawed play."[11]

A Theory of Drama

According to the Greek philosopher Aristotle in *The Poetics* (c. 330–320 BC), the earliest treatise we have on the theory of drama, a tragedy should have a beginning, a middle, and an end; that is, it should be complete in itself. It should contain everything necessary to an audience's understanding of it. Further, the incidents should exhibit a cause-and-effect relationship. In other words, a dramatic question should be asked early on, and the rest of the play should answer this question. In *Death of a Salesman*, for instance, the question might be: How far will Willy Loman go in trying to prove himself successful? The ultimate answer is that he will decide to end his own life. All the action and conflict (the struggle between the protagonist and antagonist) should relate to the dramatic question.

Although Aristotle was discussing tragedy, what he says can be applied to drama as a whole. A play, then, is based in life, but is vastly different, since life has no real beginnings and endings except birth and death. Most often, these are not the stuff of drama. Most of us are born quietly and die quietly. At times we may struggle toward a goal, but after we achieve it or fail to, our lives continue mundanely and anticlimactically.

---

10. Jeffrey Sweet, *The Dramatist's Toolkit: The Craft of the Working Playwright*, (Portsmouth, N.H.: Heinemann, 1994), 1-2.

11. Edward Albee, "Introduction," *Selected Plays by Edward Albee*, (Garden City, N.Y.: Nelson Doubleday, Inc., "Introduction" ©1987 by Edward Albee), vii.

Since the sixteenth century, when Aristotle's writings on drama became widely known, his work has continued to influence dramatic theorists and playwrights. Yet there are those who disagree with his views. These critics say that if a writer too closely follows Aristotle's definition, the resulting play will be artificial. Most probably would concur, however, that an audience needs a sense of ending.

The Elements of Drama

A playwright, like a painter, generally works within a certain structure. The painter can choose colors, brushstrokes, and composition, but has to apply pigment to a surface. No matter how big or how small a canvas, the surface still is a limiting space. The successful artist does not view the canvas as restrictive, however. Similarly, drama and, hence, theatre has a basic structure, within which exists freedom to experiment, to establish new methods, and to present new concepts.

Aristotle described six elements as essential for tragedy: **plot, character, thought, dialog, melody,** and **spectacle**.

1. **Plot**, the most important element of a play according to Aristotle, is the framework. Within it occurs the scope of the action.

2. **Character** is the major ingredient for the advancement of the action. The characters most often are the controlling force in a play; through their speech and behavior, the ongoing action is revealed. In similar circumstances, each reacts individually. Each also is typical. Characters need individuality to come across as believable, yet similarity to others in order to arouse feelings of **empathy** or identification. A play should affect the audience personally through an appeal to the emotions. It has to provide situations, characters, and events with which audiences can identify and through which they can learn. Each of these has to be different enough to maintain interest but familiar enough to illustrate a general truth.

3. **Thought** (or intellect) refers to the playwright's ideas. Like the characters, the play itself should be both specific and general — the story of an individual, but with universal appeal.

4. **Dialog** (or diction) refers to the speech of each character. It should suit the characters and help establish the tone of the play, as well as the changing tempos of the scenes.

5. **Melody**, which may originally have referred to dancing, now is taken by most critics to refer to the rhythm and flow of the language, which should reflect the emotional content of the situation.

6. **Spectacle**, the least important element according to Aristotle, is the scenery and background — as well as all the other visual elements, those things over which the playwright has the least control.

Yet, according to playwright Ruth Wolff:

[T]he greatest reality of a play doesn't reside in the plot, the words, or the description of action. The truth of the play, its highest existence, is in something outside all these. It is a construct that exists only in the audience's mind; it is the invisible thing that they build out of the air that wafts above and between what's spoken and what's acted; it is the ineffable, the puzzle, the wonder, the fragile thing that playwrights do not write but intend. The true play exists on the level of what the viewer is thinking about what is happening. This mystical airy creation, the unwritten thing, is what one is actually creating when creating a play script. One has to be constantly and uninterruptedly in tune with it, or its magic wavelength, as one writes, or it does not exist.[12]

Aesthetic Distance

There should be a balance between empathy and objectivity or **aesthetic distance** — the detachment that allows us to appreciate the beauty of a work. In some cases, of course, the performers encourage audience participation. In children's theatre, the actors may want the spectators to warn the hero of impending doom or to boo the villain. There have been experiments of bringing audience members to the stage or going into the seating area to talk with them in an attempt to break down the barriers. Sometimes this works; often, however, it fails because it disturbs the balance between involvement and detachment. No matter how affecting the characters or the situation, an audience has to participate on two opposite levels. Otherwise, they view the action as life and try to intervene.

---

12. Ruth Wolff. "Solitude: The Playwright's Life," *The Dramatist*, May/June, 2000, 32.

Theatre Conventions

Theatre is built upon **conventions** — devices the actors, the playwright, the designers, or the director use to expedite the production. An audience willingly accepts and expects such devices as a type of shorthand.

As nineteenth-century poet and critic Samuel Taylor Coleridge said, literature in general involves "the willing suspension of disbelief." Those involved in the production of a play attempt to create an illusion of reality through the use of expected devices or conventions, and the audience completes the illusion by accepting as real what it sees and hears.

Although these conventions serve a number of purposes, many relate to the need to be selective. They imply rather than becoming explicit. In old-fashioned melodramas, for instance, we know immediately who the villain is because he dresses in black and twists the ends of his moustache.

Acting Conventions

An audience willingly accepts any number of acting conventions, from performers projecting their voices to be heard throughout the seating area to rarely turning their backs on the audience in a **proscenium** (picture-frame) theatre. In a large theatre, actors use broader gestures than people normally do in everyday life. They exaggerate so the audience has no trouble interpreting their physical actions.

Writing Conventions

Most playwriting conventions heighten and condense. These devices include the soliloquy, the aside, the monolog, and the flashback, all of which are ways of presenting **exposition** or background information (a convention in itself) and characters' emotions.

A **soliloquy** shows a character thinking aloud, revealing innermost thoughts while alone on-stage in much the same way we talk to ourselves sometimes when no one else is with us. Soliloquies present thoughts and emotions succinctly. Without conventions such as this, we would have to observe the characters in many more circumstances to understand them. A good example of a soliloquy is Hamlet's "To be or not to be" speech.

The **aside**, popular in late nineteenth- and early twentieth-century melodramas, allows a character to talk only to the audience so that the other characters on-stage "cannot hear" what is said. In many instances, during an aside the other characters "freeze."

A **monolog** is a long speech delivered either to the audience or to other characters. In *Our Town*, the stage manager often speaks directly to the theatergoers. In Eugene O'Neill's *Long Day's Journey into Night*, Edmund has a long speech in which he tells his father his feelings about the sea:

> You've just told me some high spots in your memories. Want to hear mine? They're all connected with the sea. Here's one. When I was on the *Squarehead* square rigger, bound for Buenos Aires. Full moon in the Trades. The old hooker driving fourteen knots. I lay on the bowsprit, facing astern, with the water foaming into spume under me, the masts with every sail white in the moonlight, towering high above me. I became drunk with the beauty and singing rhythm of it, and for a moment I lost myself — actually lost my life. I was set free! I dissolved in the sea, became white sails and flying spray, became beauty and rhythm, became moonlight and the ship and the high dim-starred sky! I belonged without past or future, within peace and unity and a wild joy, within something greater than my own life, or the life of Man, to Life itself! To God, if you want to put it that way. Then another time, on the American Line, when I was lookout on the crow's nest in the dawn watch. A calm sea, that time. Only a lazy ground swell and a slow drowsy roll of the ship. The passengers asleep and none of the crew in sight. No sound of man. Black smoke pouring from the funnels behind and beneath me. Dreaming, not keeping lookout, feeling alone, and above, and apart, watching the dawn creep like a painted dream over the sky and sea which slept together. Then the moment of ecstatic freedom came. The peace, the end of the quest, the last harbor, the joy of belonging to a fulfillment beyond man's lousy, pitiful, greedy fear and hopes and dreams! And several other times in my life, when I was swimming far out, or lying alone on a beach, I have had the same experience. Became the sun, the hot sand, green seaweed anchored to a rock, swaying in the tide. Like a saint's song of beatitude. Like the veil of things as they seem drawn back by an unseen hand. For a second you see — and seeing the secret, are the secret. For a second there is meaning! Then the hand lets the veil fall and you are alone, lost in the fog again, and you stumble on toward nowhere, for no good reason.

27

(He grins wryly.) It was a great mistake, my being born a man. I would have been much more successful as a seagull or a fish. As it is, I will always be a stranger who never feels at home, who does not really want and is not really wanted, who can never belong, who must always be a little in love with death!

A **flashback** is a scene that occurred in the past, before the play's opening scene. Often the audience members are asked to imagine that they can see what a character is thinking as the remembered scene appears on-stage. Miller's *Death of a Salesman* contains a number of flashbacks involving the **protagonist** (central character) Willy Loman. In one of these, as he talks with his wife, Willy remembers with guilt an affair he had. In his imagination, he moves into this scene, which occurs in a hotel bedroom.

An audience knows that events progress faster on the stage than they do in real life. **Dramatic time**, as opposed to chronological time, means that on-stage people express their thoughts more explicitly and concisely than people do in everyday life. The term *dramatic time* refers to the amount of time represented by a play; an hour on-stage may represent any amount of actual time, although more time usually is represented as having passed than the actual two hours or so it takes to present a play. Dialog usually is free of the extraneous and distracting details that are common in ordinary conversations.

In Sophocles' *Oedipus Rex*, for example, we learn all the events that preceded the action of the play from Oedipus's infancy to marrying his mother; yet the action takes place in less than a day's time.

Oedipus Rex
Sophocles, c. 425 BC

The people of Thebes, stricken by a terrible plague, gather in prayer. King Oedipus assures them he is doing what he can to find what is causing it. He has sent his brother-in-law Creon to the oracle at Delphi to find out what to do. Creon returns and says that once the murderer of the former king, Laius, is found and exiled, the plague will end. Oedipus consults the prophet Teiresias, who tells him that Oedipus himself is the man who killed Laius. Oedipus protests, and Teiresias further warns that the king is unclean because he is guilty of incest. Alone with his wife, Jocasta, Oedipus tells her he fears that he may indeed be his father's murderer because once he did kill a man who tried to force him off a roadway. He says that he once had a prophecy from Delphi that he would murder his father and marry his mother. Jocasta comforts him, saying that Laius was murdered by a band of robbers. As proof, she summons an old herdsman, the last survivor of the fight in which Laius died. Instead of confirming Jocasta's story, the herdsman admits that Oedipus is the murderer. He also recognizes Oedipus as Jocasta's son, whom he had saved as a baby. Upon hearing the news, Jocasta kills herself and Oedipus puts out his eyes. He appears blinded before the citizens of Thebes and asks to be exiled in fulfillment of the curse placed on the killer of Laius.

An audience will accept almost any character or event if the proper framework is developed. In *Motel* van Itallie uses papier-mâché characters who are grotesque caricatures of human beings. Andrew Lloyd Webber, in the musical *Cats*, uses characters whom the audience is asked to accept as felines. In Kushner's *Angels in America*, an angel descends to earth. Shakespeare uses ghosts and witches.

Theatregoers are willing to accept such devices once a framework or a world has been established in which they can exist. Only when the author deviates from that framework does a play become unbelievable. For instance, if van Itallie suddenly introduced flesh-and-blood characters into *Motel*, the perspective would be skewed, and the play would become unbelievable.

Production Conventions

Modern audiences accept many conventions connected with the physical production. The entire concept of a **setting** is a convention. The living room on-stage is made up of a series of **flats** (painted canvas frames) positioned to bring about a certain effect. The audience knows, of course, that nobody's living room is arranged like the one on-stage. In a real house, furniture is closer together to conserve space. In contrast, a room on-stage is much larger than those in most homes.

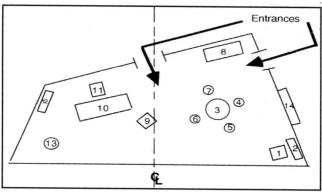

Figure 1-3: Set diagram

Often properties, or **props**, only represent objects. The diamond ring is costume jewelry, the letter a blank sheet of paper. The lighting is not sunlight or moonlight. Stage lights cast fewer shadows than lamps in living rooms. Actors wear heavy makeup, certainly more than the average person on the sidewalk.

Yet all these things are agreed upon and accepted beforehand, as part of the unspoken audience-theatre contract.

Summary

Theatre, one of the oldest of the arts, communicates a message often more specifically than other arts. It is more encompassing than many of the others and many times is more personally involving. Unlike many other arts, theatre exists in performance for only a limited time and can never again be presented in exactly the same way. It is unique in that it directly imitates human experience by allowing spectators to identify with characters who are represented as real. Therefore it needs to possess universality. Theatre probably had its beginnings in two basic human traits, the mimetic instinct and the need for ritual.

In writing about theatre, Aristotle said he believed a tragedy should be complete in itself and should contain everything necessary to its understanding. He defined what he believed to be its six basic elements: plot, character, thought, dialog, melody, and spectacle.

Theatre employs many conventions or writing, acting, and production shortcuts as a way to expedite performances.

Questions for Discussion

1. In what ways does theatre approximate life?
2. How is theatre more specific in its communication than are some other art forms?
3. How can theatre help us understand ourselves?
4. What is the relationship of imitation and ritual to theatre?
5. What is the meaning of the statement: "Theatre differs from static arts in that it is temporal?"
6. How does theatre differ from other art forms?
7. In what ways is theatre a combination of art forms?
8. In what ways is theatre a part of our everyday lives?
9. Why does theatre continually evolve?
10. How does the concept of universality apply to theatrical productions?
11. Why is a printed script often not considered an art form in itself?
12. What are drama's essential ingredients?
13. What are the six elements, according to Aristotle, that a drama should contain? How is each important?
14. What are theatrical conventions? What purpose do they serve?

Chapter 2
DRAMATIC STRUCTURE

Like all art, theatre attempts to present truth as the artists see it, yet truth is elusive and subjective. The playwright, the director, the actors, and the designers collaborate in communicating their own form of reality through dramatic structure and style.[1] As Eric Bentley said: "Would art exist at all if men did not desire to live twice? You have your life; and on the stage you have it again."[2]

The Story Play

When we think of a story, we think of being entertained. Both in theatre and in fiction, stories involve people in situations with which we can identify. The story play is an attempt to "make things right" — to re-create a balance in life.

Throughout history the story play, also called the **cause-to-effect play**, has been written and produced more than any other type.

A story play has a plot — a type of structure — that relies on conflict. Yet neither the plot nor the structure itself is the story, which is much more inclusive, encompassing everything that has happened in the world (or universe) of the play before, during, and after the events of the plot. We know, for example, that Mary, the mother in O'Neill's *Long Day's Journey into Night*, had a long history of drug abuse caused by a quack physician prescribing morphine and that this abuse started long before the action of the play opens. We know that her husband James, the father, is a talented actor who for years has been caught up in acting a role in a second-rate play, and that no one has been willing to cast him in any other role. These are "realities" of the story and have a direct bearing on the plot. Yet they are not a part of the action.

---

1. Style will be discussed in Chapter 3.
2. Eric Bentley, *The Life of the Drama*, (New York: Atheneum, 1964), 9.

Frame of Reference

A play cannot exist as an isolated entity that springs into being out of nothingness. And when a story play ends, the characters and the setting — in our imaginations, at least — don't suddenly fade into wisps of trailing fog. A **framework** or **frame of reference** prescribes all the conditions of the world and universe of the play. Most of these conditions are never mentioned because they don't directly affect the action. The audience assumes, however, when given certain conditions, that others are in effect. For instance, if the setting is a typical middle-class home in Pittsburgh and the time is the present, the audience can assume that everything else about the world/universe of the play is typical of the world/universe in which we all live.

If the framework is alien so that the play is set in a different culture, a distant time, or in an entirely different world, the playwright has to make sure the audience knows everything about that "universe" that has bearing on the action.

Once a framework is established — no matter how magical or extraordinary — a playwright cannot change it and hope to keep an audience's attention. The play most often answers certain questions: What is happening? When is it happening? Where is it happening?

The answers — the **exposition** — provide background necessary to understanding the play. Most exposition is presented through the dialog. Some is conveyed through sets, lighting, costuming, and sometimes makeup (see Chapter 9). However, the exposition should not intrude upon the progress of the play. In fact, an audience should receive any necessary information without being aware that they are receiving it; it should seem a natural part of the presentation. Unless it were done for effect, the following would come across as intrusive and ludicrous since it is completely unnatural for people to speak this way:

JOHN: Well, here we are, the first day of our vacation, and we forgot to ask the Thompsons to water our plants while we're gone.

MARSHA: Yes, and, like we discussed, we should have asked them to collect any papers left on our porch.

JOHN: Oh, well, since this is the first vacation we've taken in the last eight years, we should just try to forget such things and enjoy our two weeks together.

MARSHA: Yes, as you know, I think it's terrible that the office never let you have time off until now.

JOHN: We've discussed that, Marsha. At first, we didn't have enough employees to keep things going, and then ...

On the other hand, consider the following from Act I of Oscar Wilde's *The Importance of Being Earnest*:

ALGERNON: How are you, my dear Earnest? What brings you up to town?

JACK: Oh, pleasure, pleasure! What else should bring one anywhere? Eating as usual, I see, Algy!

ALGERNON: *(Stiffly)* I believe it is customary in good society to take some slight refreshment at five o'clock. Where have you been since last Thursday?

JACK: *(Sitting down on the sofa)* In the country.

ALGERNON: What on earth do you do there?

JACK: *(Pulling off his gloves)* When one is in town one amuses oneself. When one is in the country one amuses other people. It is excessively boring.

ALGERNON: And who are the people you amuse?

JACK: *(Airily)* Oh, neighbours, neighbours.

ALGERNON: Got nice neighbours in your part of Shropshire?

JACK: Perfectly horrid! Never speak to one of them.

ALGERNON: How immensely you must amuse them! *(Goes over and takes a sandwich.)* By the way, Shropshire is your county, is it not?

JACK: Eh? Shropshire? Yes, of course. Hallo! Why all these cups? Why cucumber sandwiches? Why such reckless extravagance in one so young? Who is coming to tea?

ALGERNON: Oh! Merely Aunt Augusta and Gwendolen.

JACK: How perfectly delightful!

ALGERNON: Yes, that is all very well; but I am afraid Aunt Augusta won't quite approve of your being here.

JACK: May I ask why?

ALGERNON: My dear fellow, the way you flirt with Gwendolen is perfectly disgraceful. It is almost as bad as the way Gwendolen flirts with you.

JACK: I am in love with Gwendolen. I have come up to

town expressly to propose to her.

ALGERNON: I thought you had come up for pleasure? ... I call that business.

JACK: How utterly unromantic you are!

ALGERNON: I really don't see anything romantic in proposing. It is very romantic to be in love. But there is nothing romantic about a definite proposal. Why, one may be accepted. One usually is, I believe. Then the excitement is all over. The very essence of romance is uncertainty. If ever I get married, I'll certainly try to forget the fact.

Wilde presents the information in an entertaining and seemingly effortless way. First, we can surmise that Jack and Algernon are fairly close friends since Jack has apparently dropped in unexpectedly. Second, we learn about the social standing of the two. We know that Algernon is soon going to serve tea to Gwendolen and his aunt. We learn that Jack probably loves Gwendolen and the feelings are reciprocated. We learn something about the men's views. Seeds are planted for future events and conflicts, such as a scene between Aunt Augusta and Jack.

Rather than having Jack simply talk about being in the country, Wilde brings out the information through lighthearted bickering that maintains our interest. Algernon is somewhat accusatory in asking where Jack has been. Then, through his line "What on earth do you do there?" we can infer that he doesn't particularly like the country. We can tell that the play will be a drawing room comedy, and so we are not to take the characters and situation seriously. We can see that the theme probably will have something to do with romance or love.

A story play involves a clash of wills or forces within the universe that has been established: Which of the two will win — the protagonist or the antagonist? In most plays it's the "good guy" versus the "bad guy," and usually it's the protagonist who we want to win. Most of the time we identify with this person; we empathize and sympathize.

The protagonist most often is an individual, though in rare cases it is a group of people, such as the weavers in Gerhart Hauptmann's play *The Weavers*, based on a revolt by Silesian weavers in 1844. The antagonist, on the other hand, can be another person, a group of people, or a nonindividualized force.

Conflict and Opposition

There are four general types of conflict or opposition:

1. protagonist against another person
2. protagonist against self
3. protagonist against society
4. protagonist against the forces of nature or fate

An example of the first type of opposition is Anthony Shaffer's *Sleuth*, a two-character melodrama in which the characters constantly try to outwit each other and gain the upper hand. Shaffer's play relies a great deal on deception and one-upmanship. Although a play pitting one person against another may have a simple plot that doesn't go deeply into character, that isn't always the case.

A number of well-known plays use the theme of protagonist against self. In Miller's *Death of a Salesman*, for example, Willy tries to live up to his own definition of success. And in Sophocles' *Oedipus Rex*, Oedipus struggles against his own sense of pride to prove that he is not his father's killer.

A protagonist against society or a particular segment of society is one of the most common types of opposition. Dramatist Henrik Ibsen, for instance, often structured his plays around such circumstances — for example, *An Enemy of the People*, in which Stockman battles an entire town when he wants to close the polluted baths — the villagers' main source of income.

Plays that pit the protagonist against a force such as nature or fate often come across as overly melodramatic. This is because it is difficult to make nature or fate a convincing antagonist since the protagonist is struggling against forces over which he can have no control. For instance, a farmer battling a drought which destroys his crops would not provide much of a plot unless the conflict between the farmer and the drought were only superficial. That is, the drought may be a way for the character to test his or her own mettle, so that the major conflict is between the character and self. Yes, the drought may defeat any such character financially. But under such circumstances, one person may become stronger or more determined to make a go of it. Another may simply give up.

Elements of Plot

Plot involves an **inciting incident, rising action**, a **turning point**, a **climax**, and the **denouement** or **falling action**, all following a linear pattern, the Aristotelian model. A number of **minor crises** occur during the rising action. Each provides further complication which seemingly is solved through a series of **minor climaxes**, but which actually serve only to intensify the rising action. The play begins when the antagonist in some way interferes with the evenness of the protagonist's life.

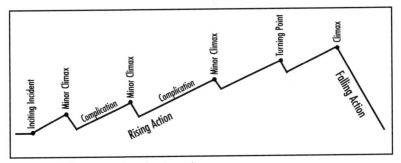

Figure 2-1: The progression of a story play.

Some plots have many more minor complications or crises than others. A play with a very simple plot is *The Fantasticks*, Off-Broadway's longest-running musical ever with 17,162 performances over a run of more than forty-one years. The fathers of Matt and Luisa want their offspring to fall in love and marry, which they do, and so a happy ending seems assured. However, at the beginning of the second (and final) act, Matt and Luisa become dissatisfied, feeling the need to experience life before settling down. The rest of the act shows that they do separate for a time, but eventually they reunite. In contrast, Shaffer's *Sleuth* has many more complications, each resulting in a minor climax in which one of the two characters seems to be winning, only to be outwitted by the other. In effect, the plot can be referred to as a fencing match in which two participants are closely matched.

Sometimes, the turning point and the climax are the same; sometimes not. The turning point is where the action can go no further without something irrevocable happening. The climax is where the irrevocable actually occurs. In Joan Schenkar's satire, *The Universal Wolf*, Grandmother decides to kill Little Red Riding Hood, which is the turning point. Before she actually kills her, which is the climax, she sings her to sleep with a lullaby. Only then does she repeatedly stab Little Red Riding Hood with knitting needles. However, if Grandmother had decided she couldn't stand to be around Little Red Riding Hood one second more and had killed her immediately, the turning point and climax would have been the same.

A play's climax begins to reveal the answer to the question asked when the problem was introduced; the denouement completes the answer by tying up the loose ends. It explains more fully how and why a thing happened, or sometimes shows the effects of the resolution on the characters. In a comedy, the audience wants to enjoy the protagonist's triumph; in a tragedy, the audience wants to come to terms with their feelings. For example, "The Requiem," the final scene of *Death of a Salesman*, shows how Willy's suicide affects the other characters.

Plays often include scenes in which there appears to be no direct conflict between the protagonist and the antagonist. Yet if the play is well written, the conflict is inherent; it relates to what already has been shown. For example, one character may be describing to another what is bothering her — what has caused the central problem and conflict. In so doing, she may begin to glimpse a possible solution or clarify her own thoughts about the situation, foreshadowing and thus building tension and suspense about whether she will succeed in her plan.

Everything that occurs in a story play has to be relevant to the advancement of the plot, to the protagonist's attempt to reach his or her goal. This dramatic action relates to the struggle between the protagonist and the antagonist, and often results in a direct clash between the two.

Character

Each character in a play has a goal, sometimes referred to as his or her superobjective. In Beth Henley's one-act play *Am I Blue?*, John and Ashbe meet for the first time in a bar, from which they are then evicted for being underage. Ashbe invites John to her apartment in New Orleans, where she offers him hot Kool-Aid and green marshmallows. Her father is out of town, and her mother lives in Atlanta.The superobjective seems to be for the two characters to become friends. However, each has a more fundamental goal — to be accepted socially. Both are misfits who react differently to their situations. Ashbe refuses to conform, while John will do almost anything to be accepted.

Central Problems

There are many ways in which the action in a play can progress; that is, there are various types of central problems affected by the introduction of the dramatic question[3] or inciting incident. These include:

3. See Chapter 1, page 23 for a definition of dramatic question.

1. The need for revenge. An example is Hamlet's wanting to get back at his uncle for killing Hamlet's father.
2. Being lured by money, sex, or fame. In Marlowe's *The Tragical History of Dr. Faustus*, the title character sells his soul to the devil and then tries to get out of the bargain.
3. The need to escape from an intolerable situation. In Schenkar's *The Universal Wolf*, Grandmother murders Little Red Riding Hood because she cannot stand the girl's "attitude" or "voice" or "smile."
4. Arriving at a crossroads and not knowing which choice to make. In Wendy Kesselman's *My Sister in This House*, Lea must choose between pleasing her sister Christine, with whom she works as a maid, or pleasing her mother. Lea still has feelings for the mother; Christine is certain their mother has exploited them.
5. Testing the limits of self or others. In William Gibson's *The Miracle Worker*, Helen Keller and her teacher Annie Sullivan push each other nearly to the breaking point.

Many plays also have one or more subplots (those of lesser importance or subordinate to the central action). Shakespeare's comedies, for instance, often have subplots that deal with love or intrigue. In *As You Like It*, the story that frames the play is that of the wicked Duke Frederick wresting power from his brother, who finds refuge in the Forest of Arden. However, the play's major focus is the love story of Rosalind and Orlando, along with two other love stories.

Scenes as Structure

Usually, a play is divided arbitrarily into acts, which then may be divided into scenes. Act I, Scene 1, may occur in the afternoon, Scene 2 in the evening, and Scene 3 the following morning.

Theatre artists, however, often think of scenes as **motivational units**, in which the protagonist wants to reach a goal. A motivational unit is made of the minor inciting incidents and minor climaxes that comprise the rising action. Each of these slightly alters the direction the central character takes in attempting to overcome the antagonist.

In this excerpt from Act II, Scene 1 of Martin Sherman's *Bent*, which takes place in a concentration camp in Nazi Germany, Horst's goal is to protect Max by telling him how to behave as he and Horst perform the useless task of moving heavy rocks back and forth from one corner of an enclosure to another.

MAX: It's supposed to drive us crazy.

HORST: These are heavy!

MAX: You get used to it.

HORST: What do you mean, drive us crazy?

MAX: Just that. It makes no sense. It serves no purpose. I figured it out. They do it to drive us crazy.

HORST: They probably know what they're doing.

MAX: But it doesn't work. I figured it out. It's the best job to have. That's why I got you here.

HORST: What? *(Puts down his rock.)*

MAX: Don't stop. Keep moving. *(HORST picks up the rock and moves it.)* A couple more things. That fence.

HORST: Yes.

MAX: It's electric. Don't touch it. You fry.

HORST: I won't touch it.

MAX: And over there — that pit.

HORST: Where?

MAX: There.

HORST: Oh yes. It smells awful.

MAX: Bodies.

HORST: In the pit.

MAX: Yes. Sometimes we have to throw them in.

HORST: Oh. Well, it will break the routine. What do you mean you got me here?

MAX: Don't walk so fast.

HORST: Why?

MAX: You'll tire yourself. Pace it. Nice and slow.

HORST: Okay. This better?

MAX: Yeah.

HORST: What do you mean you got me here?

MAX: I worked a deal.

HORST: I don't want to hear. *(Silence.)* Yes, I do. What the hell is this? You got me here? What right do you have —

MAX: Careful.

HORST: What?

MAX: You're dropping the rock.

HORST: No, I'm not. I'm holding it, I'm holding it. What

right do you have —

MAX: You were at the stones?

HORST: Yes.

MAX: Was it harder than this?

HORST: I guess.

MAX: People get sick?

HORST: Yes.

MAX: Die?

HORST: Yes.

MAX: Guards beat you if you didn't work hard enough?

HORST: Yes.

MAX: *(Proudly)* So?

HORST: So? So what?

MAX: So it was dangerous.

HORST: This isn't?

MAX: No. No one gets sick here. Look at all those guys moving rocks over there. *(Points off.)* They look healthier than most. No one dies. The guards don't beat you, because the work is totally nonessential. All it can do is drive you crazy.

HORST: That's all?

MAX: Yes.

HORST: Then maybe the other was better.

MAX: No, I figured it out! This is the best work in the camp, if you keep your head, if you have someone to talk to.

On the other hand, a **French scene** begins and ends with the entrance or exit of an important character, since the direction of a scene is almost always certain to change when a new element is introduced or an old one subtracted.

Within each scene are "beats," or points of emphasis such as occur in poetry or music. With each new "beat" the action somehow intensifies, though it does not really change direction. A beat occurs each time a character gets the upper hand. The beats are easy to follow in this dialog from the short comedy, *The Merissa Clementine Show*.

MERISSA: In this day of quickie divorces, to what do you attribute the longevity of your marriage?

CHARLIE: *(Laughing)* Letting the little lady know who's boss.

MAUDE: *(Acting the martyr)* See what I've put up with for sixty-five years. I'm sick of it, let me tell you.

CHARLIE: It was a joke, for God's sake. Look how you fly off the handle at nothing.

MAUDE: I don't know what I saw in you. If I'd listened to Mama —

CHARLIE: *(Mimicking her)* "If I'd listened to Mama." Why listen to Mama when you turned out to be just like her?

MERISSA: Stop! Think of the years you spent together. How much you love each other.

MAUDE: Love? What a joke.

Wine in the Wilderness
Alice Childress

The action occurs during a 1964 race riot in Harlem. Bill Jameson is painting a triptych. Two of the panels are finished — the first, an innocent child, and the second, a regal black woman who symbolizes "Wine in the Wilderness" or "Mother Africa." The third will be a lost woman, defeated and with nothing of substance in her life. Friends, Cynthia and Sonny-man, call to say they have found a perfect model for the final panel. When they bring her (Tommy) to the apartment, she says her own place has been destroyed in a fire resulting from the riot. Later, when Bill wants to paint her in her wig and mismatched clothes, a result of not being allowed back into her apartment, she objects.

He is patronizing, telling her she's just like most black women, eager to create a matriarchal society that robs men of their masculinity. He plays the intellectual, quizzing her about black people and white sympathizers throughout recent history.

When she spills an orange drink on herself, he gives her an African wrap. The phone rings, and she hears Bill telling the caller about the magnificent woman in his painting, "the finest" in the world. Tommy thinks he's talking about her.

Bill asks her to put on the wig again. She doesn't want to. As she is posing, he asks her to tell about herself, which she does. She also tells him some black history he doesn't know — things about which she is not the least bit pretentious. Bill has become enchanted by her transformation, but now can't recapture the image of her he wanted to paint.

The next morning while Bill is showering, an elderly black man (Oldtimer) explains to Tommy the idea behind the triptych. She's furious. She lashes out at Bill and Cynthia and Sonny-man. She tells Oldtimer he is a fool for letting middle-class people treat him as though he's invisible. She says that when whites call Negroes nigger, they mean both the educated, like you, and the uneducated like me.

Bill comes to realize that his vision was wrong and that his painting of "Mother Africa" does not actually represent the black women of America. He says that Tommy really is the "Wine in the Wilderness" because she (as well as her family) has survived slavery and race riots and still holds her head high.

Because a play is selective (See Chapter 1), you can think of it in terms of an analogy. The actions are universal; they relate to all (or most) of us, or we wouldn't be interested. Although they deal with specific characters doing specific things, they stand for something larger. Consider the following which occurs near the end of *Wine in the Wilderness*. Oldtimer has just told Tommy that she is the subject for the "messed up chick" in Bill's triptych. Bill, who has fallen in love with Tommy, asks the others to clear the room. The scene begins with Tommy's response to his request.

TOMMY: Better not. I'll kill him! The "black people" this and the "Afro-American" ... that ... You ain't got no use for none-a us. Oldtimer, you their fool too. 'Til I got here they didn't even know your damn name. There's something inside-a me that says I ain' suppose to let nobody play me

43

cheap. Don't care how much they know! *(She sweeps some of the books to the floor.)*

BILL: Don't you have any forgiveness in you? Would I be beggin' you if I didn't care? Can't you be generous enough ...

TOMMY: Nigger, I been too damn generous with you already. All-a these people know I wasn't down here all night posin' for no pitcher, nigger!

BILL: Cut that out, Tommy, and you not going anywhere!

TOMMY: You wanna bet? Nigger!

BILL: Okay, you called it, baby, I did act like a low, degraded person ...

TOMMY: *(Combing out her wig with her fingers while holding it)* Didn't call you no low, degraded person. Nigger! *(To CYNTHIA who is handing her a comb)* "Do you have to wear a wig?" Yes! To soften the blow when y'all go up side-a my head with a baseball bat. *(Going back to taunting BILL and ignoring CYNTHIA'S comb)* Nigger!

BILL: That's enough-a that. You right and you're wrong too.

TOMMY: Ain't a-one-a us you like that's alive and walkin' by you on the street. You don't like flesh and blood niggers.

BILL: Call me that, baby, but don't call yourself. That what you think of yourself?

TOMMY: If a black somebody is in a history book, or printed on a pitcher, or drawed on a paintin'... or if they're a statue ... dead, and outta the way, and can't talk back, then you dig 'em and full-a so much-a damn admiration and talk 'bout "our" history. But when you run into us livin' and breathin' ones, with the life's blood still pumpin' through us ... then you comin' on 'bout we ain' never together. You hate us, that's what! You hate black me!

BILL: *(Stung to the heart, confused and saddened by the half truth which applies to himself.)* I never hated you, I never will, no matter what you or any of the rest of you do to make me hate you. I won't! Hell, woman, why do you say that! Why would I hate you?

TOMMY: Maybe I look too much like the mother that give birth to you. Like the Ma and Pa that worked in the post office to buy you a house and a screen door with a damn duck on it. And you so ungrateful you didn't even like it.

BILL: No, I didn't, baby. I don't like screen doors with

ducks on 'em.

TOMMY: You didn't like who was livin' behind them screen doors. Phoney Nigger!

BILL: That's all! Dammit! Don't go there no more!

TOMMY: Hit me, so I can tear this place down and scream bloody murder.

BILL: *(Somewhere between laughter and tears)* Looka here, baby, I'm willin' to say I'm wrong, even in fronta the room fulla people ...

TOMMY: *(Through clinched teeth)* Nigger.

SONNY-MAN: The sister is upset.

TOMMY: And you stop callin' me "the" sister ... if you feelin' so brotherly why don't you say "my" sister? Ain't no we-ness in your talk. "The" Afro-American, "the" black man, there's no we-ness in you. Who you think you are?

SONNY-MAN: I was talkin' in general er ... my sister, 'bout the masses.

TOMMY: There he go again. "The" masses. Tryin' to make out like we pitiful and you got it made. You the masses your damn self and don't even know it. *(Another angry look at BILL)* Nigger.

BILL: *(Pulls dictionary from shelf.)* Let's get this ignorant "nigger" talk squared away. You can stand some education.

TOMMY: You treat me like a nigger, that's what. I'd rather be called one than treated that way.

BILL: *(Questions TOMMY.)* What is a nigger? *(Talks as he is trying to find word.)* A nigger is a low, degraded person, any low degraded person. I learned that from my teacher in the fifth grade.

TOMMY: Fifth grade is a liar! Don't pull that dictionary crap on me.

BILL: *(Pointing to the book)* Webster's New World Dictionary of the American Language, College Edition.

TOMMY: I don't need to find out what no college white folks say nigger is.

BILL: I'm tellin' you it's a low, degraded person. Listen. *(Reads from the book.)* "Nigger, n-i-g-g-e-r ... A Negro ... A member of any dark-skinned people" ... Damn. *(Amazed by dictionary description.)*

In plays, as in life, people speak through implication and draw conclusions through inference. Most of the time, they don't come out and say exactly what they mean. The following scene is from Franz Werfel's *Goat Song*, which takes place at the close of the eighteenth century. The parents of Stanja, who is betrothed to Mirko, have just dropped her off so she will get used to his farm. In the following, what Mirko really is saying — in the subtext or by implication — is that he does not understand Stanja. This makes him so frustrated that he says he'll beat her after they're married.

MIRKO: Your parents are gone now. Are you sad?

STANJA: No, I am not sad.

MIRKO: Then you don't love your parents?

STANJA: I love them.

MIRKO: Then you must be sad. Doesn't it hurt you when something is over? The axle creaks, the horses draw up, the whip ... And then, something is ended.

STANJA: I never ache for what is past.

MIRKO: Oh, I often do. I can lie in the meadow hour after hour longing for the games I played there on the grass.

STANJA: That is because you are a man.

(Short pause)

MIRKO: Do the house and the farm please you?

STANJA: Why shouldn't they? House, rooms, chimneys, stables, pigsties, and hencoops and dovecotes, same as everywhere.

MIRKO: And do I please you?

STANJA: Why shouldn't you please me?

MIRKO: Do you know, Stanja, I would have liked it better if you had cried before, when they left you ... *(Suddenly turns on her.)* You! What if you've loved someone before! Tell me! Have you loved someone else?

STANJA: *(Hesitatingly)* No.

MIRKO: *(Slowly, his eyes closed)* I think, when we're married, I will beat you.

STANJA: That's what all husbands do.

A playwright rarely spells everything out. Elizabeth Wong's *Letters to a Student Revolutionary* is about an American girl, Bibi, and a Chinese girl who calls herself Karen. They meet and speak for only a few minutes when Bibi is vacationing in China, yet their correspondence continues for years. The audience never discovers for certain whether Karen, who participated in the Tiananmen Square revolt in which hundreds of students were massacred, dies or not. Wong never states in words that the situation was an atrocity, though that's what she means.

Other Types of Structure

Thematic Structure

Although the story play is the most common, there are other structures, as well. One is **thematic structure**, in which a variety of scenes deal with the same basic issues but are unrelated in continuity and/or characterization. An example is Bertolt Brecht's *Mother Courage and Her Children*, which shows Mother Courage's blind reliance on war to provide a living for her family. The play makes a strong statement for pacifism.

A play that relies on theme for unity often is episodic; it does not build toward a single turning point and climax. For example, Guillermo Reyes's *Men on the Verge of a His-Panic Breakdown*, presented Off-Broadway in the late 1990s, is a series of monologs all dealing with a gay Hispanic immigrant trying to fit in successfully in America.

Circular

A play using **circular structure** starts and ends with a similar set of circumstances. Such plays usually are thematic as well. An example is Eugène Ionesco's 1948 play, *The Bald Soprano*, typical of absurdist (theatre of the absurd) drama, which expresses the idea that life is neither good nor bad at face value. Only what we choose as moral or immoral makes life good or bad to us as individuals. The characters speak recognizable words and sentences, but overall they make no sense. Although there is the appearance of struggle and conflict, as this excerpt reveals, the play does not progress toward a resolution:

MR. SMITH: *(Still reading his paper)* Tsk, it says here that Bobby Watson died.

MRS. SMITH: My God, the poor man! When did he die?

MR. SMITH: Why do you pretend to be astonished? You

know very well that he's been dead these past two years. Surely you remember that we attended his funeral a year and a half ago.

MRS. SMITH: Oh yes, of course I do remember. I remembered it right away, but I don't understand why you yourself were so surprised to see it in the paper.

MR. SMITH: It wasn't in the paper. It's been three years since his death was announced. I remembered it through an association of ideas.

MRS. SMITH: What a pity! He was so well preserved.

MR. SMITH: He was the handsomest corpse in Great Britain. He didn't look his age. Poor Bobby, he's been dead for four years and he was still warm. A veritable living corpse. And how cheerful he was.

MRS. SMITH: Poor Bobby.

MR. SMITH: Which poor Bobby do you mean?

MRS. SMITH: It is his wife that I mean. She is called Bobby too. Bobby Watson. Since they both had the same name, you could never tell one from the other when you saw them together. It was only after his death that you could really tell which was which. And there are still people today who confuse her with the deceased and offer their condolences to him. Do you know her?

MR. SMITH: I only met her once, by chance, at Bobby's burial.

MRS. SMITH: I've never seen her. Is she pretty?

MR. SMITH: She has regular features and yet one cannot say that she is pretty. She is too big and stout. Her features are not regular but still one can say that she is very pretty. She is a little too small and too thin. She's a voice teacher.

Samuel Beckett's *Waiting for Godot* also is the same at the end as at the beginning. It opens with Estragon and Vladimir waiting for someone or something called Godot. They complain about life, pretend repentance, and fall asleep to have nightmares. They wake up and quarrel and wonder what to expect of Godot if Godot comes. Pozzo, a pompous taskmaster, comes down the road with Lucky, a near-idiot through being a slave and ever obedient. Now forced to think, Lucky pours out a mixture of theology and politics before he stumbles down the road with Pozzo. In Act II, Estragon and Vladimir trade hats, recite what they think is humorous poetry, play slave and master, and argue about the past. Pozzo and Lucky come back, the former blind and the latter dumb. Neither of them remembers who he is or was. Godot sends word that he won't come today but he certainly will tomorrow. Vladimir and Estragon know they should move on, but neither does, so they just go on waiting.

To an extent, Thornton Wilder's *Our Town* follows a circular pattern in showing that life is a continuing process, overall just about the same at one period of time as at another, though different people may be involved. The play begins with the Stage Manager acting as narrator, telling what is to come. The play ends with his relating what has transpired, showing that it is similar to what will continue to happen.

Ritualistic Structure

One of the first persons to advocate a return to ritual was Antonin Artaud of France. His book, *Theatre and Its Double*, published in 1938, discusses his ideas for using theatre more directly to bring about social change. Playwright Jean Genet (1910–1986) also believed in ritual. In his play, *The Maids*, two maids perform charades as the lady of the house and act out her symbolic murder. In Peter Weiss's *Marat/Sade*, the inmates of an asylum act out their crimes in a primitive, symbolic manner in the course of participating in a play on the French Revolution.

Ritual follows a certain pattern or structure over and over again. This gives comfort and a sense of continuity, a feeling that the world is ordered. David Storey emphasizes the idea of ritual for comfort in *The Changing Room*, where the members of the rugby team follow a pattern or ritual in the way they change in and out of uniform and so on.

Experimentalists such as Artaud and British director Peter Brook view ritual as a means of evoking strong emotions. They believe that ritualistic and primitive movements put people in touch with the dark places in their souls and the basic patterns of human nature. Ritual allows the actor, like the primitive priest, to lead the audience to participate in the performance and thus become a part of nature.

Episodic Structure

Episodic structure expands rather than condenses. Although this structure is by no means new, it has been used differently in recent years. Jean-Claude Van Itallie's *The Serpent: A Ceremony* switches constantly from recent or current times to biblical times, encompassing events from the Garden of Eden to the assassinations of John F. Kennedy and Martin Luther King, Jr., to the here and now of the individual performers, who state their names and tell about themselves. The play begins with a ritualized procession to the rhythm of the actors beating upon their bodies. The characters often are symbols much more than individuals. There is no continuity of action. Time and place switch abruptly, and the actors often improvise. A more recent example is Mary Zimmerman's *Metamorphoses* (2002), which presents various Greek myths mostly in and around a shallow pool of water.

Additional Structures

There are plays that don't seem to fit any category. An example is Paul Zindel's *The Effects of Gamma Rays on Man in the Moon Marigolds*, which has strong characterizations but no real cause-to-effect plot. It deals with the relationships among a mother and two daughters and is presented simply to portray a facet of life or a way of life. Another example, though it does have something of a plot, is *Torch Song Trilogy*. It comprises three one-act plays (tied together more closely in the film than the stage version) that explore gay experience in New York a few decades past.

Sometimes, plays without a plot show incidents following each other in chronological order, but not necessarily growing out of the preceding material. Historical or biographical plays often are like this, as well as plays that are tied to a specific action, such as a trial. When the trial ends, so does the play, which may or may not have a plot. An example is Carlos Morton's *The Many Lives of Danny Rosales*.

Summary

Throughout history the story play has been written and produced more than any other type. The story itself encompasses everything that has happened in the world of the play before, during, and after the events of the plot. This sort of play involves a clash of wills or forces between the protagonist and the antagonist. The former most often is an individual, while the latter can be a person, a group, or a non-individualized force.

A basic plot involves an inciting incident, rising action, a turning point, a climax, and falling action and can involve one of various types of central problems.

There are various other structures besides the story play. These include thematic structure, circular structure, ritualistic structure, and episodic structure.

Questions for Discussion

1. Why do you think the story play is the most popular structure?
2. What are the characteristics of a story play?
3. Describe thematic structure.
4. How can ritual be used as thematic structure?
5. What would be wrong with changing a story play's world or universe during the progression of the action?
6. Why do you suppose each character in a story play has a goal?
7. Think of a television series with which you are familiar. What types of central problems are most often presented? Give examples.
8. Go back to the excerpt from *Who's Afraid of Virginia Woolf?* Where do each of the beats occur? How do you know this?
9. What films or television shows have you seen that rely on a non-plot structure. Describe them.
10. Read *Death of a Salesman*. What sort of structure does it use? Explain.
11. Compare and contrast the dramatic structure of *Death of a Salesman* and Ionesco's *The Bald Soprano*.
12. What provides the universality in *Wine in the Wilderness*? In what way are Bill, Tommy, and Oldtimer symbols? Are they individuals as well? Explain.

Chapter 3
DRAMATIC STYLE AND GENRE

Theatrical Styles

Today's theatre encompasses a myriad of styles, many of them the legacy of bygone periods. **Romanticism**, for example, was a direct revolt against the rigid **neoclassicism** of the Renaissance. Then came the Industrial Revolution and a move toward presenting a more realistic view of life. Some of these styles try to present life as it is, while others are more allegorical and abstract.

Overall, style is related to the way the playwright views life. Thus it often is directly related to genre, the division of plays into categories like comedy or tragedy. As you might infer, certain plays require a particular style in production, but others can be done in a variety of ways, depending on the director's interpretation of the script. Indeed, in postmodernism, there even is a tendency to deny analysis and to mingle styles. Yet the majority of directors and designers still seem to believe that the writing and scenic styles must match.

Figure 3-1: Emily in Our Town

Representational and Presentational Styles

Theatrical styles fall into two overall categories, **representational** and **presentational**. The former leans toward the realistic, the latter toward the nonrealistic.

In representational theatre the dialog, setting, characters, and action are represented as true to life. The action on-stage shows the audience as clearly as possible the sort of world they can see outside the theatre. Yet, because the actions occur as part of a planned production, representational theatre cannot actually depict life as it is. Actors speak memorized dialog, the director plans the movement, and the play takes place in a space specifically set up for a production. Even naturalism — the most representational style — has to be selective. Audiences at a production of Jack Kirkland's *Tobacco Road* know that the action takes place on a stage that is covered with a few inches of sawdust or dirt that only represents poor southern land and is not the land itself.

It would be fair then to say that the representational style is a closer approximation of life than the presentational. The former is **stage-centered** and the latter **audience-centered**. Actors in a representational play do not openly acknowledge the audience; in a presentational play they do, sometimes speaking directly to them. Often the stage is bare, or elements of setting suggest location rather than portraying it. Any scenery is likely to be nonrealistic. The presentational style says that theatre may come from life but should not be depicted as life.

Yet no style is pure. Thornton Wilder's *Our Town* is presentational in that it calls for no scenery, and from time to time a character speaks directly to the audience. It is representational in that occasionally the actors move into specific scenes, such as one at a soda fountain. But even in these more realistic scenes, the Stage Manager assumes another role, whereas George and Emily keep the same roles that they have throughout the play.

Musical theatre is presentational in the use of singing and dancing but often representational in the dialog.

Of course, in representational drama, actors usually play to the audience. Performers on a proscenium stage don't turn their backs on the audience, except sometimes for effect. Furniture isn't placed across the front of the proscenium opening.

Specific Styles

The other styles of theatre are offshoots of the representational and presentational.

In pure **naturalism**, an attempt is made to include everything found in life. In writing, this means including all the details of conversation and physical movement. In setting, it means placing on-stage everything that we would find in an actual location.

Realism, which depends on the playwright's and the designer's perception of reality, attempts to present life as it is, but selectively. Not all details that are found in real life are presented, only those essential for the audience's understanding of the play and the establishment of mood are included.

Realism in writing means that the dialog sounds lifelike, but doesn't have the hesitations, the changes in direction, the false starts, or the inconsequentiality of everyday conversation. Although they do not acknowledge an audience, actors in a realistic play consider them in projecting their voices and remaining aware of **sightlines** (the line of vision for the audience).

A style that is more audience-centered, though still it has elements of the representational, is **expressionism**, meant to show the protagonist's inner self. An expressionistic script deals with the internal reality of the mind, and the setting shows how the character views life. This means attempting to let the audience see reality as the protagonist does, to present the protagonist's inner feelings externally.

Symbolism tries to present truth subjectively or allegorically. Symbolic settings may contain unidentified shapes and strong contrasts in light and darkness.

With **impressionism**, the director and designer determine what they want to stress or call attention to regarding the play's theme or message. For example, in the Broadway production of Tennessee Williams's *Cat on a Hot Tin Roof*, Brick and Maggie's bedroom was constructed to resemble a boxing ring because the two characters quarrel so much.

Theatricalism, formalism, and **constructivism** sometimes are called styles, although they really are only treatments of other styles. With theatricalism, the designer breaks down any suggestion of a fourth wall, and viewers are constantly reminded that they are in a theatre. Lighting instruments and backstage areas may be open to view; actors may enter and exit through the audience. Formalism, which overlaps theatricalism and impressionism, uses only what is necessary to the actor and only because it is there. Drapes rather than flats may conceal backstage areas or provide the means for exits and entrances. Constructivism uses only those elements necessary to the action. Only part of the interior of a room may be built, and a ceiling light may hang directly from an overhead railing.

Style in the Modern Theatre

Styles often overlap. Basically realistic plays such as Tennessee Williams's *The Glass Menagerie* contain elements of symbolism and expressionism. As you know, *Death of a Salesman* contains expressionistic scenes in showing the workings of Willy's mind, particularly in his scenes with the woman or with his brother Ben, now dead.

On the other hand, some plays use a single style throughout. The audience members viewing *The Universal Wolf* are constantly reminded that they are in a theatre. Besides Grandmother, the Wolf, and Little Red Riding Hood, there is a fourth character called Reader. The following stage directions open the play:

> The READER sits in the chair waiting to begin the play. PLAYWRIGHT'S NOTE: The READER will read all the stage directions that the actors can't, won't, or don't do (indicated by indented material). The READER will also create the voices of the structuralists, the bird, the post-structuralists, the audience, the stagehands, and LITTLE RED RIDING HOOD's mother. The READER is very lightly miked.[1]

Throughout the play, the Reader announces that various images or people are being projected, though actually they are not. At times the characters follow the directions that the Reader gives. Her script was influenced in great part, Joan Schenkar says, by the absurdist writers, particularly Samuel Beckett.

In contrast, David Mamet's *Glengarry Glen Ross*, which, like Schenkar's play, deals with human nature at its most base, is presented realistically, with the rough language a person might expect to hear in everyday life. *The Universal Wolf*, as Schenkar says, is about "appetite," in which the Grandmother "will not merely survive, but will devour all the other characters."[2] Mamet's play is

---

1. Joan M. Schenkar, the opening lines of *The Universal Wolf*, © 1990, 1991, by the author.

2. Rosette C. Lamont, ed. *Women on the Verge: Seven Avant Garde Plays*, (New York: Applause, 1993), Introduction, XXXIV–XXXV.

about men who lie, deceive, and cheat in their hungering after the quick deal, the fast buck. The play depicts five real estate salesmen who compete for "leads" — names of prospective buyers of the worthless land they are selling. The five are ruthless in their attempts at winning an office sales competition after which the loser will be fired. The setting is realistic, an attempt to convince the audience that they actually are viewing a real estate office. Despite the similarity in theme, the two plays are entirely different.

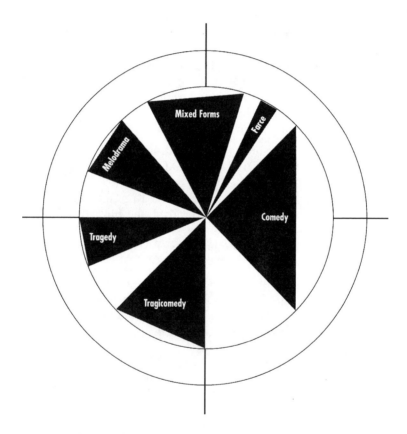

Figure 3-2: The various dramatic genres and their proportional relationships in the spectrum of theatre.

Dramatic Genres

Genre refers to the manner in which playwrights classify their subject matter. Usually the treatment is closely related to the writer's outlook on life. Is it optimistic or pessimistic? Comic or tragic? The outlook, at least in part, determines the purpose.

As illustrated in Figure 3-2, there is a relationship among various genres of drama. For instance, tragedy is the direct opposite of comedy, which is the most encompassing genre.

No one views all of life in the same manner. Each may regard some matters as ludicrous, others as sacred, and some unworthy of any kind of treatment. In contemporary theatre it's often difficult to categorize plays, which many times are a mixture of genres. Some comedies have tragic elements, some tragedies have comic elements. There are serious plays that do not end in the death or defeat of the protagonist, as does traditional tragedy. An example is *The Glass Menagerie*, in which the four characters are trapped by circumstances and their own limitations:

> Amanda is trapped in the present but longs to return to the past. Laura is trapped by extreme shyness and a physical handicap. Tom is trapped by his family and circumstances. He manages to escape physically but, like Amanda, is still held by the past. Even the gentleman caller, Jim, is trapped by his own inadequacies and his inability to get ahead, though he has dreams of doing so. The characters are all victims of things they cannot control.[3]

Abandoned by her husband, Amanda has reared her two children alone and seen Tom into his first job. Now her goal is to see that Laura marries. Yet the pressure from her mother to do so drives Laura mad. Still, Amanda urges Tom to bring home a co-worker, Jim, whom it turns out Laura knew in high school.

Williams called this a "memory play" for two reasons. Tom is looking back upon his youth, and the play is semiautobiographical in that Williams is talking about his own relations with his mother and sister. The audience feels compassion for them, but there is no point of defeat in the play. The defeat has started long before the play opens.

---

3. Marshall Cassady and Pat Cassady, *An Introduction to Theatre and Drama*, (Skokie, Ill.: National Textbook Company, 1975), 416.

As theatre critic Walter Kerr says: "The moment we succeed in consciously patterning our theater, in making it do precisely what we think it ought to be doing, we are apt to paralyze it."[4] All we need ask is that a play depict the truth of the human condition as the playwright sees it. Whether this takes the form of comedy, farce, tragedy, melodrama, or a mixture of genres doesn't matter.

Basically, there are two ways of treating subject matter — serious or comic. A serious treatment of theme contributes to empathy, while a comic treatment generally increases aesthetic distance. This means that comedies are more presentational or audience-centered than tragedies. A playwright can reach an audience by making it feel what the character is feeling or by appealing to the intellect. Comedy often is funny because of aesthetic distance. In many comedies, even though we identify with the characters, usually it is to a lesser degree than in a serious play. In real life, falling and breaking a leg would not be funny. In a comedy it might be. Yet all of this is a matter of degree. Protagonists in some tragedies seem fairly remote, while we sometimes identify closely with those in certain comedies.

As Eric Bentley explains, a good play transcends its framework:

> Plays are generally about the big people, though what they say applies to the little people. And there is a converse to this proposition: that when a great playwright, such as Chekhov, presents the littleness of everyday life, he manages to suggest — as indeed he must — the largeness of everyday life, the size of those fantasies which range from the secret life of Walter Mitty to the chivalric musings of Don Quixote.[5]

Tragedy

The purest form for the serious treatment of a theme is tragedy, which presents a protagonist who struggles against overwhelming odds and is defeated by them.

According to Aristotle, tragedy "is an imitation of an action that is serious, complete, and of a certain magnitude; in language embellished with each kind of artistic ornament, the several kinds being found in separate parts of the play; in the form of action, not

---

4. Walter Kerr, *The Theatre in Spite of Itself,* (New York: Simon and Schuster, 1963), 19. Originally appeared as "Cheers for the Uninhibited U.S. Theatre," in *Life* Magazine, Feb. 7, 1959.
5. Eric Bentley, *The Life of the Drama,* (New York: Atheneum, 1964), 7.

narrative; through pity and fear effecting the proper purgation of these emotions."

Many theatre scholars believe that the only true form of tragedy is that which conforms to Aristotle's definition. Thus, tragedy must deal with problems that are highly serious and profound. Tragic characters battle a flaw in themselves or evil in others. They struggle against forces greater than they.

Tragedy is serious in nature. Its purpose, through our responses to the characters and their struggles, is to teach us and to make us feel. We grieve at the protagonist's defeat, which is what Aristotle means by pity. Fear is the anxiety aroused in the play, an anxiety that should carry over to our concern for all human beings.

There should be a **catharsis**, or purging of emotion — a release of all emotional tension. We should be left with a sense of tranquility. When the tragic protagonist pursues a goal to the end, we feel that strength and persistence in ourselves. If the character's actions are affirmative, we too feel the capacity for affirmation. If the character endures great suffering, so can we. Yet we also can feel superior to the tragic hero because we don't have to face the same sort of conflicts. Above all, tragedy maintains our faith in ourselves as a part of the human race. Even when tragic characters die, their heroism continues to live. What the playwright says about life, not death, is important. The issues, the heroic adherence to the dictates of conscience, and the reaffirmation of our belief in humanity are the vital aspects of tragedy.

Truth in Tragedy

Even though we suffer with the protagonist, we find aesthetic beauty in the total conception of the drama. Tragedy is concerned with grandeur of ideas, theme, characters, and action, and grandeur is aesthetically pleasing. Through the tragic character we come to terms with our own deaths. We accept the beauty of trying actively to improve the lot of humanity, rather than passively accepting our doom.

Although the conflict concerns human welfare, universal themes, and general problems, the workings of the protagonist's mind are the most important aspect of a tragedy. It is how the character reacts deep within to exterior events that makes for tragedy. When we hear of the death of another person, we may feel pity. But the more we know about the person's character, the more compassion and sorrow we feel. We can read of a plane crash that kills a hundred people, but unless we know one of those killed, the news usually doesn't affect us strongly. A dramatist allows us to know and thus care about the tragic protagonist.

Even though they are morally good, tragic protagonists are imperfect. We see their weaknesses as well as their strengths. They appear to be human, and so we can relate to their problem.

Tragic protagonists must face the consequences of their actions. We know they will be defeated; no fate will intervene. In this respect the genre is true to life. As the characters discover new insights into themselves, we discover new insights into ourselves. We know that there cannot always be happy endings, but we can take satisfaction in our struggles.

Just as in life, the innocent in tragedies often suffer. Ophelia goes mad and commits suicide because Hamlet, the man she loves, kills her father. Society or individuals suffer many times because of the actions of others, even though the suffering seems unjust. Tragedy points out the injustice of life and the suffering of humanity. It shows cruelty and despair; but it also shows the heights to which the human being can rise.

Modern Tragedy

Few tragedies throughout history have reached the Aristotelian ideal; yet that doesn't necessarily make a play invalid. The definition of tragedy depends on a person's viewpoint. If we consider that tragedy occurs when a basically good person commits an irrevocable act because of a particular character flaw, the genre encompasses many more plays than those that follow the strict Aristotelian definition. We feel compassion for Blanche in *A Streetcar Named Desire* and for the foolish Don Quixote in *Man of La Mancha*.

Even though tragedy usually no longer deals with those of noble birth, characters like Tony in *West Side Story* fight for what they believe. They still are basically good. They still pursue the only course of action that is consistent with their own moralities. We can identify with people such as these; we can feel the grandeur of their efforts. They are noble in their motives, if not by birth.

Comedy

The opposite of tragedy is comedy, which usually makes us laugh at ourselves and our institutions, taking them less seriously.

Of all dramatic forms, comedy has the most variety. It can be the subtle **comedy of manners**, which relies on the intellect, or it can be the physical shenanigans of burlesque. Comedy even has been defined at times as any play that has a happy ending, such as the sentimental comedies of the eighteenth century. Today, however, this definition is not widely accepted. Most often, comedy shows a deviation from the norm of everyday life, although it often deals with mundane problems and the pettiness of day-to-day living.

Comedy makes us laugh, though the dramatist may have another purpose, as well, for writing the play. Some writers want to teach us not to take ourselves so seriously. If we see a fault or frailty as humorous, maybe we can begin to correct it. But similarly, the playwright may want to point out a social injustice by showing how ridiculous it is, thus setting us on the path toward eliminating it. Such was the case with *How the Vote Was Won* (1909) by Cicely Hamilton and Christopher St. John (both women). Intended both as a comedy and as propaganda to secure voting rights for women in England, the play opens with the following premise:

WINIFRED: Well, good-bye, Ethel. It's a pity you won't believe me. I wanted to let you and Horace down gently, or I shouldn't be here.

ETHEL: But you're always prophesying these dreadful things, Winnie, and nothing ever happens. Do you remember the day when you tried to invade the House of Commons from submarine boats? Oh, Horace did laugh when he saw in the papers that you had all been landed on the Hovis Wharf by mistake! "By accident, on purpose!" Horace said. He couldn't stop laughing all the evening. "What price your sister Winifred," he said. "She asked for a vote, and they gave her bread." He kept on — you can't think how funny he was about it!

WINIFRED: Oh, but I can! I know my dear brother-in-law's sense of humor is his strong point. Well, we must hope it will bear the strain that is going to be put on it today. Of course, when his female relations invade his house — all with the same story, "I've come to be supported" — he may think it excruciatingly funny. One never knows.

ETHEL: Winnie, you're only teasing me. They would never do such a thing. They must know we have only one spare bedroom, and that's to be for a paying guest when we can afford to furnish it.

WINIFRED: The servants' bedroom will be empty. Don't forget that all the domestic servants have joined the League and are going to strike, too.

ETHEL: Not ours, Winnie. Martha is simply devoted to me,

and poor little Lily couldn't leave. She has no home to go to. She would have to go to the workhouse.

WINIFRED: Exactly where she will go. All those women who have no male relatives, or are refused help by those they have, have instructions to go to the relieving officer. The number of female paupers who will pour through the workhouse gates tonight all over England will frighten the Guardians into blue fits.

ETHEL: Horace says you'll never frighten the Government into giving you the vote.

WINIFRED: It's your husband, your dear Horace, and a million other dear Horaces who are going to do the frightening this time. By tomorrow, perhaps before, Horace will be marching to Westminster shouting out "Votes for Women!"

In most comedies, traits, situations, and characters are exaggerated to show that what we think is important may not be. Particularly in period comedies, but even today, the ending shows a marriage, symbolizing a rebirth of a better set of circumstances. Shakespeare does this in many of his comedies, such as *As You Like It*.

Deviation from the Norm

The humor of comedy often comes from treatment of character or situation. Any subject matter can be used if it can be treated in a humorous light. It is only if the deviation becomes too painful that the comedy ceases to be funny. It would be cruel to treat physical deformities or handicaps as sources of comedy — even though this often has been done, for example, on television's *Saturday Night Live*. More often, the things over which we have control, or our views of uncontrollable forces, comprise the subject matter.

Comedy often deals with eccentricities — greed, hypocrisy, laziness, deception, overwhelming ambition, or pomposity. Comic protagonists may become involved in situations outside their knowledge or experience — an office worker posing as a diplomat, a janitor posing as a psychiatrist. Comedy mocks our desire to be what we are not, or to place too much importance on our goals.

Although comedy usually deals with deviation in a normal society, the theatre of the absurd shows "normal" individuals in an insane, abnormal world. Whether society or the individual is viewed as normal, comedy begins with an idea in which normalcy is somehow reversed.

Unlike tragedy, comedy ends happily; the protagonist wins. Otherwise, the audience would feel uncomfortable for having laughed. It's important that the writer establish a comic frame of reference, or the audience may not know how they are expected to respond. They should know from the beginning that what they are seeing is not to be taken seriously and that they aren't to identify too strongly with either the character or the situation ... unless it's a matter of laughing with instead of at the character.

Often, comedy does not hold up across the years as well as tragedy. Many comic devices depend on the present, with allusions to current society, trends, and individuals within the play's framework.

Comic Devices

Writers of comedy rely on certain devices or techniques in establishing a comic frame of reference. They are: **exaggeration, incongruity, automatism, character inconsistency, surprise,** and **derision.**

Exaggeration is intensification or enlargement through overstatement. Most people are not as miserly as Harpagon in Molière's play, nor as finicky as Felix in Simon's *The Odd Couple.* Then there's the musical *Hairspray,* which one critic, Jim Farber of the *Daily News* referred to as "campiness squared" in its exaggeration of nearly every element of the production.

Incongruity refers to conflicting elements that in some way deviate from the norm, such as a man's tuxedo worn with a tie-dye T-shirt.

Automatism is repetition, as in a person's acting without thought rather than rationally (like a mechanical person). It includes a visual or verbal gag repeated time after time, thus becoming funnier each time. Suppose for the first three entrances a character walks into a heavy floor lamp. On the fourth entrance she approaches the lamp carefully to see that she does not bump it. Someone calls her, and she turns her head to listen. She murmurs a reply and walks into the lamp.

Character inconsistency, similar to incongruity, exposes a trait that does not seem to fit in with the rest of a character's personality. In Kesselring's *Arsenic and Old Lace,* for example, the two elderly women seem to be almost a personification of goodness, except that they murder lonely old men.

Surprise includes many of the other comic devices. It is the unexpected. We know that each joke will have a punch line that we anticipate, but don't know ahead of time. The pun, the wisecrack, or the insult can surprise us. In *The Importance of Being Earnest*, the audience expects to hear a criticism when Jack admits to Lady Bracknell that he smokes. Instead, she responds that it is a good thing he does, because a man needs an occupation.

Derision is mocking people and institutions. Writers often deride hypocrisy, pomposity, or ineptitude. Yet if derision becomes too bitter, it defeats its purpose. Sarcasm can make the audience feel sorry for the intended victim.

Closely related to derision is **satire**, sometimes classified as a subgenre of comedy. Satire also ridicules, but for the purpose of reform. It is gentler than sarcasm.

Types of Comedy

Because there often is such a mingling of types, comedy frequently seems to defy any sort of categorizing. However, the two extremes are **high comedy** and **low comedy**. This doesn't mean that one is better than the other, but only that the appeal differs. High comedy uses verbal wit and so appeals more to intellect. Low comedy is largely physical or slapstick.

According to playwright S.N. Behrman: "The immediate concerns of the characters in a high comedy may sometimes be trivial; their point of view must never be. Indeed, one of the endless sources of high comedy is seriousness of temperament and intensity of purpose in contrast with the triviality of the occasion."[6]

High comedy includes **comedy of manners**, which pokes fun at the excesses and foibles of the upper class. At the other end of the spectrum is **burlesque**, which relies on beatings, accidents, and, often, vulgarity for humor. Picture the antics of The Three Stooges, for instance.

Romantic comedy usually is gentle in showing the complications the hero and heroine face in their quest for living "happily ever after." **Situation comedy** places the characters in unusual circumstances, whereas **character comedy** deals with the eccentricities of the individual.

All types of comedy have common ground. First, they establish a comic framework. Second, the humorous aspects are exaggerated, both in writing and performance. Third, comedy relies on timing. Fourth, the characters tend to be more stereotyped than in tragedy. Often, the writer is concerned with plot involvement rather than with characterization.

---

6. S. N. Behrman, "Query: What Makes Comedy High?" *The New York Times*, March 30, 1952.

Farce

A third genre is farce, somewhat similar to melodrama (see below) in that coincidence or fate can play a large part in the outcome. Farce is more similar to comedy than to tragedy. The primary purpose is entertainment. The appeal is broad, and it takes little imagination or intellectual effort to follow the plot. Like melodrama, farce has stock characters who are one-dimensional. The plots are highly contrived and rely on physical actions and devious twists to hold the audience's attention.

The play contains no message of significance, and the progression shows only how the major characters manage to release themselves from entanglements. Throughout the years the form has changed little.

William Butler Yeats describes farce this way:

A farce and a tragedy are alike in this, that they are a moment of intense life. An action is taken out of all other actions; it is reduced to its simplest form, or at any rate to as simple a form as it can be brought to without our losing the sense of its place in the world. The characters that are involved in it are free from everything that is not a part of that action; and whether it is, as in the less important kinds of drama, a mere bodily activity, a hairbreadth escape or the like, or as it is in the more important kinds, an activity of the souls of the characters, it is an energy, an eddy of life purified from everything but itself. The dramatist must picture life in action, with an unpreoccupied mind, as the musician pictures her in sound and the sculptor in form.[7]

Because many farces are concerned with illicit sexual relationships and infidelity, they have been criticized for their immorality. But they neither condemn nor condone illicit sex. They are amoral in their outlook. The aim is to provide laughs for the audience by presenting a pattern of humorous actions.

The success of a farce relies heavily on the actor and director. They must present ludicrous actions and deliver gags and absurdities of speech. A farce that is delivered well in one language probably could succeed before an audience that speaks only another, because much of the humor is visual. Farce uses many of

---

7. William Butler Yeats, "Language, Character and Construction," in Toby Cole, ed., *Playwrights on Playwriting*, (New York: Hill and Wang, 1960), 37. Reprinted from *Plays and Controversies*, (London: Macmillan & Co., Ltd., 1923).

the devices of comedy: automatism, incongruity, derision, and physical violence.

The plot often relies on misunderstanding, mistaken identity, deception, and unfamiliar surroundings. The characters are the victims of their vices, and when caught, they appear ridiculous. An example is Georges Feydeau's *The Happy Hunter*. The title has a double meaning: the protagonist wants his wife to think he is hunting game, when actually he is "hunting" illicit female companionship. The action is highly improbable and the entanglements along the way are completely divorced from reality.

Melodrama

Like comedy, melodrama ends happily, at least much of the time. Like tragedy, it treats a serious subject, and the audience identifies with the protagonist. Rather than exploring a character's inner being, however, pure melodrama presents one-dimensional characters — either all good or all bad. When it deals with the painful and the serious, the subject matter is exploited only for its theatrical value. Melodrama often appears to show three-dimensional characters in conflict, but the struggle usually is only on the surface, and the audience knows that good will triumph. Action generally is much more important than characterization.

With a simple and suspenseful plot and a strong emotional appeal, melodrama became highly popular during the nineteenth century. The name "melodrama" goes back to the time when musical accompaniments were used to heighten the changes in mood and pace, a device borrowed from opera and then modified.

Melodrama offers entertainment and escapism, but it can bring the plight of individuals and groups to the attention of the audience. Generally, rather than evoking the Aristotlean "pity and fear," it is much more likely to arouse feelings of excitement and horror. In other words, it deals most often with sensationalism and incredibility.

Melodrama deals with serious problems or actions which are presented or examined in light of conventional morality. For instance, most police or detective shows on television fall into the category of melodrama. Examples have been such series as *Law & Order* and *Cold Case*. Though there may be setbacks and occasionally a patrolman or detective is hurt or killed, the victory always belongs to the good guys, the defenders of what we view is "right."

Melodrama began as a separate form in the eighteenth century and reached its height of popularity in the United States with such shows as George Aiken's *Uncle Tom's Cabin*, based on the Harriet

Beecher Stowe novel of the same name. Here, for instance, audiences could witness Eliza's attempt to race across the ice floes to escape a life of slavery.

Within recent years, melodrama has become more realistic. The characters are less stereotyped, and sometimes the play does not end happily. There are still exaggeration and scenes of suspense and high excitement. An example is Shaffer's *Sleuth*. Though the genre has changed outwardly, it has the same basic appeals: a virtuous hero or heroine, a despicable villain, and sensationalism.

Tragicomedy

Throughout the history of Western theatre there has been a mingling of the comic and the tragic. There is some humor in Sophocles' *Antigone* and in several of Euripides' tragedies, all written during the fifth century BC in Greece. Many of Shakespeare's tragedies include scenes of comic relief. Probably one of the most familiar is the gravediggers' scene in *Hamlet*. There is even more mixing of comic and tragic elements in Shakespeare's *Troilus and Cressida* and in his romances.

Within the past few decades the term *tragicomedy* has been applied to various types of drama. The term is a paradox. A protagonist who is a truly noble figure cannot appear comic. Neither can a humorous character possess the scope of a tragic hero. Nevertheless, some plays do mix elements of tragedy and comedy. Often the term is applied to absurdist plays. There is a great deal of controversy over what the form really is and when it began to exist as a new form. Some theatre scholars suggest that we discard the term altogether and call such plays tragic comedies or comic tragedies.

It takes a skillful playwright to mingle the serious and the comic effectively. Tragicomedy is one of the most difficult genres. The playwright must advance the plot without totally confusing the audience. The play must reflect the way life itself intermingles the tragic and the comic. Often, the writer of tragicomedy will present a situation that appears to be comic and later let the audience realize that it is serious.

Harold Pinter's *The Birthday Party*, an excellent example of the form, is a total mingling of the comic and the serious, and some scenes can even be taken either way. The action occurs in a cheerless rooming house run by Meg and Petey. Stanley, a pianist who has sought refuge from the world, is the only boarder. Two men who seek lodging in the house suggest that a birthday party be held in Stanley's honor. During the party the two men destroy Stanley's personality and leave him speechless before they take him to their big black car waiting outside. It is never made clear why the two men are after him. Pinter called the play a "comedy of menace." The purpose is to point up the lack of contact among people. The situation appears funny, but its point is melancholy.

Theatre of the absurd playwright Eugène Ionesco said he wants his audience at times to view the tragic as comic and the comic as tragic. Although such plays as *The Lesson, The Killers,* and *Rhinoceros* present an unhappy outlook on life, they are written in such a way as to be amusing. One reason is that Ionesco often employs automatism. Examples are the repetition of nonsensical lines in *The Lesson* and the discussion about Bobby Watson in *The Bald Soprano.* To point up the comedy, Ionesco wants ludicrous situations to be played with deadly seriousness.

Often in tragicomedy the audience is jolted from comedy to horror. Whatever method the writer chooses to mingle the elements, the genre is well established.

Mixed Forms

Many modern plays defy classification in any genre. Some are serious plays that have more depth than melodrama but lack the scope of tragedy. An example is Lorraine Hansberry's *A Raisin in the Sun.* The protagonist, Walter Lee Younger, changes his outlook on life and thus succeeds in keeping his dignity.

In modern plays the characters frequently are three-dimensional, and we can empathize with them, but their actions are neither serious nor tragic. Often, too, modern characters are people with ordinary problems.

Summary

Theatrical styles fall into two overall categories, the representational and the presentational. The representational style is stage-centered while the presentational is audience-centered. Within these two categories are a number of specific styles such as naturalism, realism, expressionism, and symbolism.

Genre refers to the manner in which playwrights classify their subject matter. The purest form for serious treatment of a theme is tragedy. Comedy usually makes us laugh at ourselves and our institutions and has the most variety of the dramatic genres.

Most comedies exaggerate traits, situations, and characters. The primary purpose of farce is to entertain. The appeal is broad, and it takes little effort to follow the plot. Melodrama, like tragedy, treats a serious subject, though the characters are one-dimensional.

Tragicomedy is a mingling of the serious and the comic, making it one of the most difficult genres since the playwright must advance the plot without confusing the audience.

Questions for Discussion

1. What is the difference between realistic and nonrealistic styles, between representation and presentation?
2. Why is it impossible to have true naturalism on the stage?
3. What is the difference between naturalism and realism?
4. What is the difference between expressionism and impressionism?
5. How does symbolism differ from impressionism?
6. Explain the various ways of treating style.
7. How would you define genre?
8. Playwrights each present the truth of the human condition as they see it. Why is this consideration so important?
9. What are the characteristics of tragedy?
10. What devices might a playwright use to establish a comic frame of reference? Give your own examples of the different types.
11. What are the characteristics of melodrama? Of farce?
12. What is tragicomedy?

Chapter 4
ARCHITECTURE AND SPACE

Theatres can spring up almost anywhere — in barns, warehouses, banquet rooms, and churches. In big cities and in small communities, plays are presented in parks, vacant lots, cultural centers, and school auditoriums. In fact, theatre can exist in any space large enough for the performers and the spectators.

We tend to think that going to the theatre means entering a specific structure designed solely for the purpose of presenting live productions. Yet theatre began in much simpler environments. In the 1960s, there was a move to bring theatre to those who wouldn't otherwise have the means or inclination to attend a performance. In fact, this concept of bringing theatre to the people is nearly as old as theatre itself. Throughout history, performers have gone from community to community or house to house to present short plays. Actually, the only requirements for a theatre are that the audience be able to see and hear and that the performers have enough space in which to present the play.

To a great degree, the type of theatre structure affects audience expectations and even helps determine the type of audience. Many people who stop to watch a performance in a community park might don more formal clothing to attend a professional production at a nearby cultural center. Theatres draw different audiences because of their architectural features. As a general rule, the more ornate the theatre, the more exclusive the audience. In the past few decades, new theatres have leaned toward simplicity of design to attract more varied audiences and to focus on the performance itself instead of on the gold leaf designs bordering the walls. The architecture of the theatre has a bearing on what play is successful. Mountain Playhouse in Jennerstown, Pennsylvania, is a stock theatre in a converted barn. The setting is quite different from the Vivian Beaumont Theatre at Lincoln Center for the Performing Arts in New York City, and from the old opera houses of the nineteenth century with their intricate carvings and statues in recessed niches.

The physical arrangement of a theatre — in a word, its architecture — can either enhance or detract from the efforts to create a satisfactory live experience. At the very least, performers should be able to project to an audience without strain; for its part, the audience should be able to see, hear, and respond readily to the impulses being directed toward it.

A well-designed theatre should facilitate an unfettered flow of energy back and forth within whatever spatial arrangement has been devised to accommodate performers and audience. A well-designed theatre should also be able, at the proper moment, to unite those components into a totality that fulfills the ultimate potential of the live event. It should be capable of bestowing an aura of the extraordinary on the merely human. It should so focus attention on the event unfolding within its precincts that the audience, released from the concerns of the mundane, becomes, for the "two hours' traffick of the stage," completely involved in the unfolding theatrical reality.[1]

Areas of the Theatre Structure

The theatre can be divided into two distinct parts: the "player area" and the "audience area," or the private and the public areas.

This particular spatial relationship thus characterizes theatre even when it is not enclosed in a physical structure, and it sets theatre apart from spatial organizations employed in other cultural systems ... The church or temple has perhaps the closest systematic architectural relationship to the theatre, since it involves the meeting of a secular celebrant with a sacred celebrant, but the sacred may be only spiritually or symbolically present, not spatially, as a player must be. Certain religious structures, such as the traditional Quaker meeting house, are thus able to avoid the setting aside of a "sacred" space within their confines. Without a player's space, however, there would be no theatre.[2]

---

1. Martin Bloom, *Accommodating the Lively Arts: An Architect's View*, (Lyme, NH: Smith and Kraus, 1997), 7.

2. Marvin Carlson, *Places of Performance: The Semiotics of Theatre Architecture*, (Ithaca, N.Y.: Cornell University Press, 1989), 128–129.

Even in experimental theatre, where the actors attempt to make the audience a part of the production, the areas, though they overlap briefly, still are separate "where each performer may have only a private 'pocket' of performance space." But "even when no *specific* space is set aside for players ... the actor ... [inhabits] a world with its own rules, like a space traveler within a personal capsule, which the audience, however physically close, can never truly penetrate."[3]

Overall, the private area includes the acting space and other spaces that support it — dressing rooms, storage areas, and, in some theatres, scene shops. The public area comprises the seats, the lobby, the cloakroom, and so on.

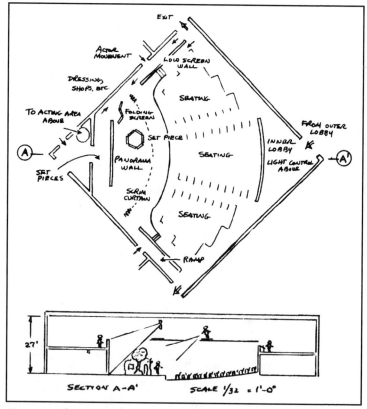

Figure 4-1: The areas of the theatre structure.

---

3. Carlson, 130.

Another way to classify the areas is to separate them into four categories: (1) the performance area, whatever its shape and/or dimensions; (2) the performance support areas, such as the costume room; (3) the audience areas (seating, concession stand, restrooms, lobby, etc.); and (4) the administrative areas (offices and, perhaps, the ticket booth, though the ticket booth could be classified either as part of the audience or the administrative areas).

Each section is dependent to some extent on each of the others. For instance, a theatre would not be likely to have a large stage area and a small seating area, nor vice versa.

Much of the building's design depends on the theatre's purpose and on the budget for erecting or adapting the building. Another factor is the relationship between actor and audience — separation, as in picture-frame staging, or intimacy, as in arena theatre, where the audience is close to the performer.

Although a theatrical production requires nothing more than an open space large enough to accommodate performers and spectators, there are four basic forms theatre takes structurally: proscenium- or picture-frame; arena stage; thrust stage; and found space, or environmental theatre. The first type has a ceiling space intersected by an arch. The other three, sometimes collectively called **open stages**, share a common and continuous ceiling or, in other words, a more unified space.

A stage is, ideally, a strategically created void capable of receiving and accommodating whatever modifications of space and light a particular production might require. Under appropriate circumstances, it allows the presentation of a heightened reality — more focused, more persuasive than anything that can be experienced outside a theatre. When filled with a creative presentation, this atmosphere bonds a collection of individual spectators into an assembly which can remain unified for the duration of a theatrical event.[4]

In the 1960s, along with the trend to attract wider theatre audiences, there was a reaction against the proscenium theatre, which does separate audience and actor to a greater degree than any of the other types. Thus, theatres were built in a variety of alternative forms, so that "with so many varieties of mainstream and alternative theatre coexisting, the second half of the twentieth

---

4. Bloom, 20.

century became the first era without a standard form of theatre building. In response to this situation, there has been a search for a multi-purpose theatre building which would adapt to meet the requirements of all sorts of performance scales and styles from opera to drama and from proscenium to thrust. Alas, such buildings have to include so much compromise that they are rarely satisfactory even in their main form."[5]

The Proscenium Theatre

The traditional type of theatre is the **proscenium theatre**. The proscenium or proscenium arch frames the stage in much the same way a painter frames a landscape. The audience members, seated facing the opening, are asked to believe that they are viewing the action of a play through an imaginary fourth wall.

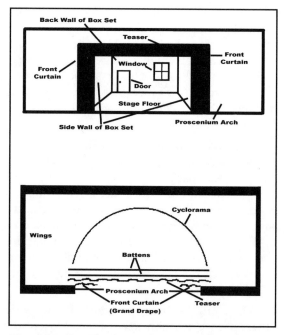

Figure 4-2: Top: The front view of a proscenium stage. Bottom: The stage area and wing space. The semicircle represents a cyclorama, which can frame the action for outdoor scenes.

5. Francis Reid, *Designing for the Theatre*, 2nd edition, (New York: Theatre Arts Books/Routledge, 1996), 16.

Since the proscenium stage allows for great flexibility and the presentation of most styles of production, many directors and designers feel that it is the most flexible. For instance, it can accommodate minimal or elaborate scenery. "The proscenium frame may also be best for the creation of illusion and magic. The frame hides the 'magician's strings' ..."[6] Actors and objects can appear and disappear above, below (through trapdoors), or to the sides. Almost anything can happen behind a curtain which then can open to an astounding or unexpected sight.

Scenery

Because there is a psychological as well as a physical separation of audience and actors, a setting can be portrayed more realistically in a proscenium theatre than in any other type of structure. With this type of stage the scenery that is used most often is a **box set**, or **flats**, lightweight frames on which fabric is stretched, fastened together to look like the interior walls of a room or several rooms. Flats, which are "free standing" and portable so that sets can be stored or changed between scenes, can be constructed to incorporate doors, windows, or fireplaces. More and more, theatre is adopting the television or film practice of building "hard" flats, those covered with luan (1/8-inch plywood) rather than unbleached, cotton muslin, the usual material.[7]

Often, the scenery for a proscenium stage looks as much as possible like an actual, specific location. The box set offers further realism by providing an environment in which the actors can perform with the setting surrounding them.

Sometimes other types of settings are used. The **backdrop** or, simply, **drop** is usually theatrical muslin, canvas, or occasionally luan, that stretches across the stage. The drop is weighted at the bottom and painted to represent scenes. With drops, top curtains and side curtains mask the backstage areas and the **fly space** — the performance support area behind the top of the arch, above the floor of the stage. At other times, **wings**, or flats that stand independently, are placed at intervals from the front of the stage to the back. Sometimes the latter type of scenery, called the **wing and drop** because the flats extend into the wing or side areas of the stage, is used for unspecified locations. It is painted in neutral

---

6. William Faricy Condee, *Theatrical Space: A Guide for Directors and Designers.* (Lanham, MD: Scarecrow Press, Inc., 1995), 47.

7. For an excellent discussion of scenery and flat construction, see Harvey Sweet, *Handbook of Scenery, Properties, and Lighting,* 2nd ed., (Boston: Allyn and Bacon, 1995).

shades for various changes of location indoors or outdoors, which the audience is asked to imagine.

Drops are useful because they can be flown, that is, raised into the fly space. Musicals, for instance, often require quick changes of scenery. It is simple to raise one drop and lower another. The drops attach to rods called **battens**, which can be raised and lowered in a matter of seconds using a system of ropes and pulleys called the **counterweight system**.

The disadvantage of using backdrops with side curtains is that the actors now must play in front of the scenery. They cannot be part of the scenic environment. Thus, this sort of scenery lends itself better to presentational productions. Wing and drop settings can be used as interiors, but they aren't as realistic as box sets. Sometimes they are used to represent interior scenes for period plays written before the box set was developed.

Scrims, or semitransparent cloths, sometimes are used for drops. When lighted from the front, they appear opaque and the audience sees a painted surface. Backlighting allows the audience to see through them, creating a dreamlike effect.

In addition to drops, two-dimensional set pieces such as walls or cutouts of trees or rocks (and even some three-dimensional pieces) can also be flown. For example, in the musical *Once Upon a Mattress*, based on the fairy tale "The Princess and the Pea," a large bird cage is used, and the "bird" is a person. The cage can be stored in the fly space until it is needed, then lowered into place.

Another type of setting used in the proscenium theatre is the **wagon stage**, a set constructed atop a platform that can be rolled on- and off-stage. It sometimes fits into grooves in the stage floor. Wagons can be effective for quick scenery changes when the theatre has a large enough wing space for storing them when not in use. Wagons aren't practical when space is limited or when many scene changes are required. They can be large enough to cover the width of the stage, or smaller for intimate scenes.

Other elements sometimes have been added to proscenium stages to provide further spectacle. Most, however, have not remained in use long. One is the **elevator stage**. The stage itself is an elevator that can raise and lower entire sets. Another type, still in use in some theatres, is the **revolving stage**. A circular portion of the stage floor is constructed on top of a shaft that is run by a motor and rotates the cutout portion of the stage floor. This allows two sets to be constructed back-to-back and changed quickly.

The revolving stage can also be used in other ways. For instance, when Ray Bradbury's play *Fahrenheit 451* had its world premiere at San Diego State University, William R. Reid designed a set that could be adapted, largely through rear-screen projection, to many locales. At several points in the play two of the characters strolled from one locale to another. To provide the illusion of covering distance, the stage revolved as the two actors "walked."

The designer in a proscenium theatre plans the setting and placement of furnishings so that the audience can have a clear view of the set from any seat in the house. Because of this, box sets are wider at the front of the stage than they are toward the back.

Stage Areas

During the Italian Renaissance, stages were **raked**, or sloped gradually upward toward the rear wall of the theatre. That's why we use **Upstage** to refer to the area furthest from the audience. The area closest to the audience is **Downstage**. **Stage Right** is the portion of the stage to the right of an actor facing the audience, and **Stage Left** is to the actor's left. The other portions of the stage draw on these terms. **Down Right** is closest to the audience and nearest the right side of the stage. **Up Center** is closest to the back wall and in the center of the stage.

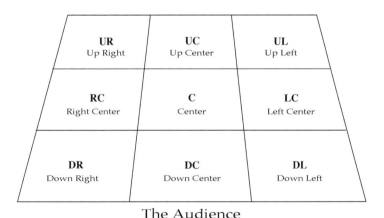

The Audience

Figure 4-3: Stage areas diagram.

In most proscenium stages there is an **apron**, or **forestage**, that projects out in front of the proscenium arch. It can be almost any size. The more it projects, the more playing space there is near the audience. Forestages are used particularly for presentational plays, and sometimes are constructed and added as part of the setting.

Advantages and Disadvantages

One of the greatest advantages of a proscenium stage is the variety of special effects that are possible. Since the stage and auditorium are separate, the front curtain, or **grand drape**, can be closed to mask changes and to indicate the end of an act. Any number of settings or set pieces can be flown in, wheeled in, or changed by hand. Properties can be stored backstage and carried on when needed. Because the backstage area is masked, the actors can wait immediately off-stage to make their entrances.

A disadvantage is the psychological and physical separation of the audience and actor. According to Richard Southern: "The cardinal problem about the proscenium-arch convention is that it creates a line. It is no more than ordinarily difficult to play *behind* that line; but it is very difficult indeed to discover in what tone to handle a passage where you propose to *cross* that line."[8]

However, some believe that the proscenium can be more adaptable simply by adding a forestage or apron. Others argue that an apron provides the worst of both proscenium and open staging.[9]

One of the major concerns with a proscenium theatre is **sightlines**, that is, constructing the theatre and the scenery so that any audience member in any area of the seating area can see all parts of the stage. For a proscenium theatre this generally means constructing the auditorium in a fan shape. Thus, the more seats, the wider the fan must spread, requiring a large seating area. In the 1970s, designers began to realize "that theatres with pure cinematic sightlines ceased to be effective above about four or five hundred seats." When the entire audience is placed centrally with a clear view of the stage, "the volume of auditorium required to accommodate a particular size of audience increases very quickly."[10]

---

8. Richard Southern. *The Seven Ages of the Theatre*, (New York: Hill and Wang, 1961), 275.

9. Condee, 48.

10. Reid, 9.

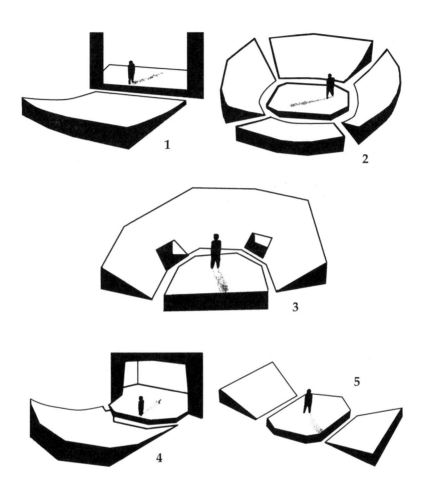

Figure 4-4: Theatre forms: 1. Proscenium stage 2. Theatre-in-the-round, or arena stage 3. Three-sided thrust stage 4. Semi-thrust stage 5. Two-sided, or transverse, stage. Illustrations by Ming Cho Lee. Reprinted from American Theatre Planning Board, *Theatre Check List* (1969), Wesleyan University Press, xii-xiii. Reproduced with permission of University Press of New England.

On the other hand, it can be argued that one of the major advantages of the proscenium is that it provides the means for a director to control the focus, much more than on any other type of stage. "On the proscenium stage, the viewing angles are greatly narrowed, so the director can compose a picture with the confidence that a greater portion of the audience will perceive it as intended."[11]

The Arena Theatre

In **arena staging** the audience surrounds the action. Although often referred to as theatre-in-the-round, the playing area usually is a square or an oval. It has historical precedent in the arena-style theatres of ancient Greece.

> Theatre in the round means three things; the first is obvious — it is a theatre where the audience completely surrounds the action on all sides. The second follows from this but is not so immediately obvious — it is a theatre where it is quite impossible to give the effect of a painted picture come to life. The third is that, speaking in general, it is a theatre which has no stage. Thus it can be properly called an *arena theatre*.[12]

As opposed to a picture-frame stage where the action is on a raised platform, the playing area for an arena theatre generally is lower than the seating area, which slopes downward. The seats closest to the playing area are at the lowest point.

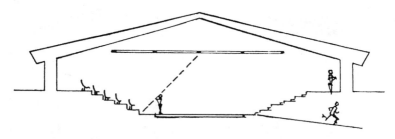

Figure 4-5: A cross-section drawing of an arena stage

---

11. Condee, 50.
12. Southern, 284.

Scenery

Because the audience surrounds the action, arena theatre has many requirements of setting not found in proscenium staging. There can be no realistic box sets, although scrims sometimes are used with backlights. Although the setting cannot be as realistic as that of the proscenium stage, the properties for representational shows have to be more realistic. The audience sits closer to the action and can spot substitutes.

Makeup in arena theatre must be more subtle and costumes more realistic. Properly dyed and lighted costumes on a proscenium stage can look rich and costly from the audience, even when constructed from a relatively inexpensive fabric. For example, monk's cloth can look like brocade. However, audiences in an arena theatre would immediately detect such fakes.

The designer in an arena setting has to be careful to include set pieces and furniture that are low enough that the audience member seated closest to the action can see over them.

Advantages and Disadvantages

In arena theatre there is a grid above the stage, and the lighting instruments are always in view of the audience, whereas in proscenium theatre the lighting instruments can be masked behind the **teasers** and **borders**[13] or focused on the stage from points in the ceiling of the auditorium.

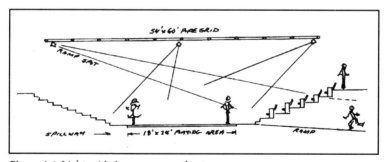

Figure 4-6: Light grid above an arena theatre.

---

13. The teaser is the front short or horizontal curtain, and the borders are those that hang behind it.

There are other problems of concealment. The actors are in view of the audience at all times or have to make long entrances and exits down the aisles. Changes in setting are limited and must occur in full view of the spectators.

Another disadvantage of arena staging is that the director cannot be so concerned with presenting an aesthetically pleasing picture. A bigger concern is to make sure that all of the audience will be able to see at least most of the action. Difficulties arise when bodies must fall from closets, when someone must appear to be dead for a long period in view of the audience, and when someone has to exit quickly. (Chapter 7 discusses the special demands arena staging makes on a director.)

Still, arena theatre has many advantages. Most important, the audience is close to the action; there is not the physical barrier of the proscenium theatre. There can be more intimacy between spectator and performer, and there can be more subtleties of facial expression and movement than in a theatre where the audience is seated a great distance from the playing area. Indeed, with arena staging, performers and audience members feel shared involvement.

A major advantage is that almost any room or space can be adapted for arena staging. The playing area itself can be much smaller because it is three-dimensional — unlike the two-dimensional effect of the picture-frame stage. Also, because the audience closely surrounds the action, the seating area covers a smaller space than in proscenium theatre, where the spectators view the action from only one side and generally sit farther from the stage.

The Thrust Stage

The third major type of theatre structure is the *thrust stage*, developed in the 1940s by British director Tyrone Guthrie, from his stage at the Edinburgh Festival. Guthrie continued his use of this sort of staging in the 1960s at what later was named the Guthrie Theatre located in Minneapolis.

Sometimes the playing area is raised above the level of the audience, but most often the audience looks down on the action, which is the usual practice in arena theatre.

Basically, a thrust stage consists of an open playing area similar to that of an arena theatre, with a stagehouse or wall in the background through which the performers enter and exit (and behind which scenery can be stored). The audience area is three-sided or occasionally two-sided. The arrangement probably resembles ancient Greek staging — after the appearance of the *skene* building in Greece's Golden Age — more closely than either of the other theatre structures do.

Because there is a stagehouse at the rear, more scenery can be used than is possible in arena theatre. At the least, there can be a background for the action if the director and designer want one. There also is a place for storing properties and set pieces, which can be changed more quickly than in arena theatre, although the changes still occur in full view of the audience. As in arena theatre, lighting instruments hang in view of the spectators, and there can be no curtains except sometimes for masking borders.

The audience can become more involved than is generally possible in a proscenium theatre, because they are closer to the action, but again realistic properties must be used for a representational production.

A variation of the thrust and arena theatre is **end stage** theatre, which is somewhere in between thrust and proscenium staging. "An end-stage is essentially a proscenium theatre with the arch removed: The audience sits in parallel rows facing a stage at one end of the space." Although the audience and the actor share a common ceiling, the audience views the action essentially from one direction.[14]

Variations of Stages

There are several other types of stages, but they are variations of the proscenium, arena, and thrust stages. A common type is a **modified thrust stage** or one with a proscenium opening, thus making it a combination of thrust and proscenium. The Downstage area has the intimacy of a thrust while the Upstage frame provides a place for scenery. A disadvantage is that the portal does divide the space architecturally. Thus any staging or action behind the frame denies the very reason for the existence of the thrust stage — the actor and audience sharing the same "architectural volume."

In addition, those members of the audience on the sides may not be able to see the scenery which from the front section of the stage can serve as the actors' background. For many of those "seated on the sides of a three quarter thrust, the scenery will be 'over there,' off to one side, and separate from the action of the play ... Too much scenic emphasis in the portal may also cause problems

---

14. Condee, x.

by pulling the focus and action Upstage, away from the Downstage thrust." A simple solution is to block off the portal or else to place in it a scenic structure that projects forward. This can help focus the action further Downstage where it is more effective.[15]

Platform stages are similar to proscenium stages, but without a framing device. Theatres occasionally have ramps reminiscent of beauty pageants, but most often the ramps are part of a setting for one play rather than a permanent part of the theatre structure. There have been experiments with **wraparound stages**, which form an arc around part of the audience, similar to the film industry's experiment several decades ago with Cinerama. Many theatres also have both a proscenium opening and **side stages**, or small playing areas, in front of and to the sides of the proscenium opening. Here, intimate scenes with simple settings or a few characters can be played.

There is a great deal of difference among structures of a single type. Some proscenium theatres seat only a hundred spectators and have a small stage, whereas others seat several thousand before a giant stage. The difference in size does have an effect. In a large theatre there is not the intimacy of a small one. The actors have to project their voices more and use broader gestures and movements to convey physical action. They forgo the subtleties of facial expression and the nuances of vocal tone that work in small theatres. On the other hand, a small theatre would not be able to handle elaborate productions such as *Hairspray*.

Many theatres — particularly those with several performance areas — contain a flexible staging area, or what sometimes is referred to as a **black box**. It allows for various staging and seating areas with temporary seats that can be moved according to the way a production is staged. "The premise behind flexible theatres is that the audience-performance relationship is determined by the production; that is, by the play and the style of performance. If one makes the assumption that every play has an ideal performance space, then, the theatre should be able to conform to that space ..."[16]

The staging area can be anything from a thrust stage to an arena stage to a modified proscenium stage. San Diego Repertory Theatre, for instance, which occupies the bottom level of Horton Plaza shopping center, usually runs two productions concurrently. One is performed in what is called simply The Space, which can be

---

15. Bloom, 92-98.
16. Condee, 154.

arranged to suit any number of seating and staging arrangements. Although it can seat several hundred spectators, the typical black box is smaller, often seating only fifty to a hundred spectators. Many colleges and universities have such experimental theatres, largely for productions that are directed, designed, or written by students.

Despite the theory behind the black box arrangement, "many soon settled down into a semi-permanent form, evolved from the proportions of the room and its access points, and rarely changed because of the labour costs in effecting a rearrangement. Consequently there has been a move to design studio theatres which are flexible yet have a definite form which favours certain arrangements."[17]

Environmental Theatre

Environmental theatre, or **found space**, adapts whatever space is available to a theatrical production. Antonin Artaud of France was an advocate of this type of theatre. He believed theatre should affect more people more directly than has been the case throughout much of theatre history.

The term **environmental theatre** was introduced by Richard Schechner. Jerry N. Rojo, who designed for Schechner's Performance Group, says: "The term *environmental theatre* defines an aesthetic approach to production. It provides highly controlled conditions so that transactions involving performer, space, and text may be developed organically."[18]

Schechner was also an advocate of drastic change in the audience-actor relationship. With his group, he presented plays in an abandoned garage in New York City. Hè experimented with seating audience members at various places, in various groupings, and even amidst the action. Sometimes the spectators sat on scaffolding and ledges.

The purpose of using found space is to break down all barriers between stage and auditorium so there can be more direct communication between actor and audience.

Rojo explains the experience this way:

---

17. Reid, 18.
18. Jerry Rojo, "Environmental Design," in *Contemporary Design U.S.A.*, Elizabeth B. Burdick et al., eds., (New York: International Theatre Institute of the United States, Inc., 1974), 20.

The environmentalist begins with the notion that the production will both develop from and totally inhabit a given space; and that, for the performer and audience, time, space, and materials exist as what they are and only for their intrinsic value. All aesthetic problems are solved in terms of actual time, space, and materials, with little consideration given to solutions that suggest illusion, pretense, or imitation. An environment, for example, never creates an illusion of, say, a forest, although actors and audience may discover danger literally in a precarious arrangement of platforms, or a sense of safety may be achieved where a high place is conquered. In the more traditional theatre experience, the production is appreciated from *outside*, in a world especially created for the relatively passive observer. In the environmental experience, on the other hand, appreciation generates from *within* by virtue of shared activity. Each environmental production creates a sense of total involvement.[19]

Found space includes street theatres. Actors may perform in the street to provide cultural experience, to entertain, or to express the concerns of the audience.

Off-stage Areas

Whatever the type of theatre, many behind-the-scenes areas directly affect the production. The "player" area alone is many times the size of the stage. Ideally, the area from the proscenium opening to the back wall should be about one-and-a-half times as deep as the proscenium opening is wide, both for actors to have adequate crossing space from one side of the stage to the other, and for storage of props or set pieces. The wings and fly space should allow for scenery to be shifted quickly and easily, and so must be large enough to give stagehands and technicians room to store and move scenery and set pieces.

In a proscenium theatre, generally a teaser keeps the audience from seeing the battens from which lights and scenery are flown. Again, ideally, the fly space should be at least two-and-one-half times the height of the proscenium arch, so that full-length drops or other set pieces cannot be seen by the audience.

---

19. Rojo, 20.

The wings on both sides of the proscenium opening (masked or hidden from the audience's view by **tormentors** — vertical curtains or flats) should at least equal the width of the proscenium opening. The wings are used for storing scenery and properties and for providing space for actors to wait prior to making entrances.

In non-proscenium theatres, the storage space, of necessity, is farther from the playing area. There should be storage space underneath the stage as well, accessible by trapdoors that accommodate both equipment and human beings. The stage floor itself should be of a soft wood, generally pine, so there is no problem either in using nails and screws to anchor scenery, or in ruining expensive wooden floors.

Lighting and Sound

A theatre uses three different sorts of lighting systems: **house lights**, **work lights**, and **stage lights**. House lights provide illumination for audience members to enter and exit. Work lights are used for rehearsals, for erecting sets, and for hanging the stage lights. Since the stage lights are hung differently for each show, it would be impractical to use them for general illumination, and they also are expensive to operate.

The main criterion for stage lighting is to provide good visibility. Like the two other systems of lights, they are separately controlled. During the course of a production, a lighting operator runs the lights from a control room at the rear of the theatre. Often it's a glass-enclosed room that affords a good view of the stage. (Stage lighting is discussed in detail in Chapter 8.)

Scene, Costume, and Property Shops

In academic theatre, some community theatres, and large opera houses, there are scene and costume shops. However, professional theatres usually are not much more than "shells" with little or no space for the construction of scenery and costumes. At best, they have small areas for repair. In theatres like these, the sets and costumes usually are built elsewhere and then shipped to the theatre.

In college and university theatres, however, scenery and set pieces are constructed and often painted in the scene shop, although some theatres have a separate paint shop. Ideally, the scene shop should be the same size as the combined wings and stage space.

It should be near the stage and, if possible, on the same level and close to both a loading dock and the playing area, so scenery or supplies can easily be transported from one area to the other. The doors to the shop should be large enough to accommodate wagons, flats, and other large set pieces.

Costumes are built, dyed, repaired, and generally maintained in the costume shop, so it must be equipped with sewing machines, ironing boards, dress forms, fabrics, storage space for finished work, and full-length mirrors. It should have fitting areas, counter space, sinks, and washing machines, and there should be an area for long-term costume storage.

Some theatres have property shops, but large props usually are built in scene shops. There also should be an area near the stage to store props for current productions. Another work and storage area is the electrical shop where lighting instruments are maintained and repaired. Dressing and makeup rooms ideally are located near the playing area. Many theatres also have large rehearsal rooms.

Just as the types of writing and performance in theatre are changing, so are the concepts and manners of production, which makes theatre much more exciting than ever before.

Summary

Theatrical productions can be presented in nearly any sort of space, yet the sort of structure affects audience expectations. No matter what the structure, a theatre building can be divided into two distinct parts: the "player area" and the "audience area."

There are four basic structures: proscenium, arena stage, thrust stage, and found space. Proscenium, the most traditional, has an arch that frames the action so that various types of settings can be used. In arena staging, the audience surrounds the action, which generally is lower than the seating area. Although scenery for an arena theatre cannot be as realistic as that for a proscenium stage, the properties, costumes, and makeup must be more realistic since the audience is closer to the actors. A thrust stage consists of an open playing area similar to that of an arena theatre, with a stagehouse or wall in the background through which performers enter and exit. Thus, more scenery can be used than in an arena theatre. A variation to the thrust stage is the end stage where the audience sits on two sides of the action.

Various other types of stages are variations of the proscenium, the arena, and the thrust stages. A black box is a theatre that contains a flexible staging area which allows for various staging and seating arrangements. Environmental theatre involves adapting whatever space is available to a theatrical production.

Questions for Discussion

1. How does the type of theatre structure affect the type of audience and its expectations?
2. What are the characteristics of the proscenium stage, the arena stage, the thrust stage, and found space?
3. What are the advantages of producing a play in a proscenium theatre? The disadvantages?
4. Would you rather see a play in a proscenium or open stage theatre? Why?
5. What are some problems you can see that are unique to an arena or thrust theatre?
6. What are the advantages of a "black box" theatre? What are the disadvantages?

Part 11
THE PRODUCTION

Chapter 5
THE PLAYWRIGHT

With the exception of a self-indulgent misanthrope, no one is quite so much alone as a writer, unless, of course, he owns a collaborator, in which case no two people are quite so much alone together.[1]

In most cases, the playwright, working in solitude, begins the creative process that results in a production before an audience. Due to background and experience, each playwright has a different perspective, a different starting point. Because a play most often begins as one person's work, playwrights have more freedom than other theatre artists — their observations, experience, background, sensitivity, and skill are the only limiting factors of their work.

Actor/playwright Sam Shepard says he writes plays because:

I love the form. You have the actor, dialog, lights, audience, sets. I can't think of another art form that combines so many elements and has so many possibilities. I've always had an affinity for it. I don't know why. It's like when a musician picks up a saxophone, he doesn't even look at a guitar or fiddle, it's all sax.[2]

It has been said that the actor and audience are the only essentials of theatre. Yet actors cannot exist as separate entities. Performers need a script, either created by the actors themselves or by someone else. This script is the spring from which the production flows.

Plays almost always deal with characters' passions, those things that they care about, maybe even too much. They deal with strong feelings, with standing up for beliefs, with achieving what Don

1. George Oppenheimer, ed., *The Passionate Playgoer: A Personal Scrapbook*, (New York: The Viking Press, 1958), 221.

2. Don Shewey, "Rock and Roll Jesus with a Cowboy Mouth (Revisited)," *American Theatre*, Vol. 21, Number 4, April, 2004, 26.

Quixote in the musical *Man of La Mancha* calls "The Impossible Dream."

Jeffrey Sweet, author of such plays as *Porch* and *The Value of Names*, feels that "the best theater has not been separate from the society of which it is a part." He says that "most of the glorious moments of the American stage can be traced to some degree of social awareness ... Most of the greatest achievements have been the product of artists who were deeply involved in the passions of their times."[3] Terrence McNally says that playwrights should:

> Write plays that matter. Raise the stakes. Shout, yell, holler, but make yourself heard. It's time for playwrights to reclaim the theatre. We do that by speaking in our own unique voices. We do that by speaking from the heart about the things that matter most to us. If a play isn't worth dying for — not to mention months, perhaps years, of rewrites and frustration — maybe it isn't worth writing ... Yes, theatre is fun. Yes, theatre is passion. But above all, theatre is the oldest way we have of trying to tell the truth about who we are.[4]

Jerome Lawrence puts it this way: "The greatest experience as a playwright is to have your words sandpaper other people's souls."[5]

The dramatist's job compares with the actor's in that both assimilate a diversity of material into a production. Both select, heighten, and expand. To do this, a playwright needs to know the theatre — the technical aspects, what sort of scenery is practical, and how actors approach their roles.

Getting and Developing Ideas

The idea for the musical *Urinetown*, winner of three Tony Awards, came from a simple idea. When Greg Kotis, who wrote the book and lyrics, was visiting Europe and had almost no money, he resented having to use the little that he had for pay toilets because that was the only type available. He started thinking of using this as a whimsical idea for a play, not thinking it would get anywhere. But he and a collaborator, Mark Hollmann, who composed the music

---

3. Jeffrey Sweet, *The Dramatist's Toolkit: The Craft of the Working Playwright*, (Portsmouth, N.H.: Heinemann, 1993), 161–162.

4. Terrence McNally, "What I Know About Being a Playwright," *American Theatre*, November, 1998, 26.

5. Jackson R. Bryer, "Jerome Lawrence," *The Playwright's Art*, principal questioner, Richard L. Coe, (New Brunswick, NJ: Rutgers University Press, 1995), 169.

and some of the lyrics, kept working on it, finally developing a plot that revolves around the government's outlawing the use of private toilets.

Even in improvisational theatre — that which is created on the spur of the moment — an idea has to come from somewhere. An audience may suggest a line or a situation that the actors immediately build into a brief play. In these circumstances the performers and the audience collaborate in developing ideas. Sometimes a theatre company or a group of individuals improvises a play. This was the case, for instance, with the musical *A Chorus Line*, based on conversations by dancers and then developed into a musical by director Michael Bennett, lyricist Edward Kleban and composer Marvin Hamlish, and writer James Kirkwood.

Jeffrey Sweet describes getting together with two friends to improvise from an outline he had written. "Stephen, Sandra, and I sat around a cassette recorder and improvised our way through this scene three times. I then transcribed the three versions. I edited what I thought were the most effective passages and wrote some new material until I had the final piece, a short play called *Cover*."[6]

Tony Kushner, author of *Angels in America, Parts 1* and *2*, and *Homebody/Kabul* wrote:

> ... as the work nears completion I find myself thinking a great deal about the people who have left their traces in these texts. The fiction that artistic labor happens in isolation, and that artistic accomplishment is exclusively the provenance of individual talents, is politically charged, and, in my case at least, repudiated by the facts.
>
> While the primary labor on "Angels" has been mine, more than two dozen people have contributed words, ideas, and structures to these plays, including actors, directors, audiences, one-night stands, my former lover, and many friends ... Had I written these plays without the participation of my collaborators, they would be entirely different — would, in fact, never have come to be.[7]

---

6. Sweet, 84.

7. Tony Kushner, "Is It Fiction That Playwrights Create Alone?" in Jeane Luere and Sidney Berger, eds., *The Theatre Team: Playwright, Producer, Director, Designers, and Actors*, (Westport, CT: Greenwood Press, 1998), 91-92.

Although most playwrights complete what they hope will be a finished copy of a producible play, there are often many hurdles to production. Playwright and film actor Jeff Daniels presents his work at a professional company he founded in his hometown of Chelsea, Michigan. There he works closely with the artistic director Guy Sanville. "[Sanville] knows the outline, the synopsis, and what I'm trying to do, before I've even turned in the first draft. So, [the company is] aware, but if the idea doesn't stimulate them or I can't explain it well, then I'll look for something else."[8]

Despite many instances of collaboration, most theatrical productions involve a script completed by one person but to which others add their interpretations and sometimes rewritings or suggestions for revision. Yet all this emending or change, according to the Dramatist Guild contract, cannot be done without the playwright's consent. Not a single word can be changed unless the writer agrees. Of course, most writers will agree if they recognize the need for the change, if they recognize that it in fact improves the script.

Yet "the notion that a playwright begets theatre alone slights the tie between text and staging. The moment a producer espies a script's potential, the playwright may become senior member and source of a production team. From that point on, a collaborative effort begins."[9]

Neil Simon, probably the most widely produced contemporary playwright, welcomes revision during rehearsal and beyond. In his book, *Rewrites: A Memoir*, he tells of an out-of-town tryout of his play *The Prisoner of Second Avenue* before its New York opening."As with *The Odd Couple*," he writes:

> I ran into third-act troubles. And as happened with *The Odd Couple*, neither [director Mike Nichols] nor I saw it coming in the months we prepared the play. Since I don't save or remember a single word of anything I've cut from a play, I have no idea now what was wrong then. Something about the kitchen bursting into flames and smoke, which seemed hilarious on paper and embarrassing in the rehearsal room. This time, however, Mike and I pounced on the trouble

8. T. E. Klunzinger, "Jeff Daniels: Nurturing a Rose in Chelsea," *The Dramatist*, November/December, 1998, 27-28.

9. Jeane Luere and Sidney Berger, *The Theatre Team: Playwright, Producer, Director, Designers, and Actors*, (Westport, CT: Greenwood Press, 1998), 88.

early enough, and we quickly doused the fire and got back on track with a large rewrite before we ever left for the tryout in New Haven.[10]

Then after the first performance of the New Haven tryout, Mike Nichols told Simon that the play's ending wasn't going to work. The two of them sat in a hotel lobby until early the following morning. Then Simon came up with the last in a string of ideas, one which Nichols liked.

> We both got into the elevator, Mike getting off before me. Neither one of us had the strength to say good night. The next night, the ending worked like a charm. We envied each other's abilities. He hated me for thinking of it, and I hated him for making me think of it. Such are the ways of a perfect collaboration.[11]

Tony Award and Pulitzer prize winner James Lapine feels much the same way: "What I want when I'm writing," he says, "is someone who can stimulate my thinking on whatever the subject is I'm dealing with, whether a collaborator, a director, or dramaturg."[12]

On the other hand, Edward Albee, winner of multiple Tony Awards and Pulitzer Prizes, is completely against theatre artists other than writers changing a script.

> Somewhere along the line, it's become the assumption that the playwright is there to be worked upon instead of letting the playwright work his magic upon the people. Let's put it this way: as a metaphor or a simile, whichever you like, for a play let us take a string quartet composed by a composer. Let's go back to Beethoven's time ... Nobody workshops a string quartet. The first violinist doesn't get together with the second violinist and say, "You know, the composer wrote a C-sharp there; we don't like that, do we? Let's make that into an F." Everybody — directors and actors and producers and dramaturgs and theatre owners and theatre managers — feels that a play is there to be collaborated upon. A play is a work of art ... [13]

---

10. Neil Simon, *Rewrites: A Memoir*, (New York: Simon & Schuster, 1996), 337.

11. Simon, 341-342.

12. Gregory Bossler, "Makes Lapine," *The Dramatist*, November/December 2003, 11.

13. Jackson R. Byer, "Edward Albee," The Playwright's Art, principal questioner, Laurence Maslon, (New Brunswick, NJ: Rutgers University Press, 1995),6.

There have been many instances of conflict between playwright and director and/or producer. One of the worst occurred in 1953 when director Joshua Logan insisted that William Inge drastically change his play *Picnic*. Logan objected to Inge's "focus and setting" and insisted on a complete rewrite, even adding a lot of his own dialog. Further, Logan reduced the original six settings to one, and changed the title of the play, which Inge originally had called *Front Porch*. It has been said that all of this greatly not only detracted from the usual "truth" of Inge's work but that it exacerbated his problems of "mood and temper."[14]

Yet there has to be a script before it can be changed. Where do these scripts come from? How do the ideas occur and germinate? There are as many answers as there are playwrights. Here's what a few of them say about getting and developing ideas:

> What I need to do is think about something often for a year or so and then set aside time to write the play. I don't tend to have ideas, try them out, and then get rid of them. I wrote the first scene of *The Heidi Chronicles* when *Isn't It Romantic?* was in rehearsal, and then it just sat there for two years. I don't get that many ideas for plays, and I don't write that many plays that often. My plays tend to come once every three years or so. Sometimes I'll think of something and say, gosh, that's a really good idea — not for me, for somebody else. And then I won't write it.[15]
>
> —Wendy Wasserstein

> What's this idea going to do that others I've seen don't do? How is this going to affect the way an audience thinks, feels, dreams about a particular subject, a particular feature of the perceptual world around us? What can this play do to make them deal with it in a way they haven't seen before? How can it make them see the values they have and make them question these values? Because affecting the audience is why one writes a play to begin with. You don't write it for yourself, the actors, or the director. You're there to do something to the audience.[16]
>
> —Lee Blessing

---

14. Jeane Luere, ed., *Playwright Versus Director: Authorial Intentions and Performance Interpretations*, (Newport, CT: Greenwood Press, 1994), 83-85.

15. Buzz McLaughlin, "Conversation with Wendy Wasserstein," *The Dramatists Guild Quarterly* , Winter 1994, 6.

16. Ramsey, 11.

I found the use of notebooks very helpful, because often I would get an idea that I would be very excited about (and I do a lot of thinking before I write), but then I'd get distracted and one day I'd wake up and the idea would have just evaporated, vanished. No matter how rudimentary or primitive or unlikely, if an idea comes to me I keep it in a notebook. Then I found that something mysterious happens, and I get more interested in one idea than another idea.[17]

—Horton Foote

I've never tried to plot out my plays through to the end, since I've found it as much an exercise in futility as trying to predict what would happen in my own life a month hence. They both invariably unfold and reveal themselves when the appropriate time comes.[18]

—Neil Simon

Ideas can come from anywhere, from reading a news item or feature story to overhearing a random snippet of conversation. They may start with a character, real or imagined, or with a theme. Once they have an initial idea, dramatists then add on to what they have read or heard, often in one of the following ways:

1. They examine something important or relevant in their lives. White South African Athol Fugard's 1990 drama *My Children! My Africa*, for instance, concerns the politics of his country in relation to apartheid. Many playwrights, such as Eugene O'Neill in *Long Day's Journey into Night* and Edward Albee in *Three Tall Women*, base some of their work on themselves or their families.

2. They begin by examining their feelings. In *FOB*, David Henry Hwang looks at the clash between Chinese and American cultures, examining what can happen to first- or second-generation Americans who live in one culture at home and are thrust into another at school or in the outside world.

This isn't to say that every play has to have an intense message. Neil Simon's earlier plays exist largely to entertain. Yet they do have something to say. *Barefoot in the Park* (1964), for instance, is about the

---

17. Buzz McLaughlin, "Conversation with Horton Foote," *The Dramatists Guild Quarterly*, Winter 1993, 17.

18. Neil Simon, "Introduction," *Rewrites: A Memoir*, (New York: Simon & Schuster, 1996), 10-11.

need to compromise in order to get along in life. A later play, *Broadway Bound* (1986), is entertaining, yet it is more serious in its examination of a family's problems, as shown in the following scene from Act I:

> JACK: There is no other woman.
> KATE: I don't care. Stop it anyway.
> JACK: Look, I know I've changed. I know I'm different.
> KATE: Yes, you are.
> JACK: I've stopped feeling for everything. Getting up in the morning, going to bed at night ... Why do I do it? Maybe it was the war. The war came along and after that, nothing was the same. I hated poverty, but I knew how to deal with it. I don't know my place anymore. When I was a boy in temple, I looked at the old men and thought, "They're so wise. They must know all the secrets of the world" ... I'm a middle-aged man and I don't know a damn thing. Wisdom doesn't come with age. It comes with wisdom ... I'm not wise, and I never will be ... I don't even lie very well ... There was a woman. *(KATE stares at him.)* About a year ago, I met her in a restaurant on Seventh Avenue. She worked in a bank, a widow. Not all that attractive, but a refined woman, spoke very well, better educated than I was ... It was a year ago, Kate. It didn't last long. I never thought it would ... and it's over now. If I've hurt you, and God knows you have every right to be, then I apologize. I'm sorry. But I'll be truthful with you. I didn't tell it to you just now out of a great sense of honesty. I told you because I couldn't carry the weight of all that guilt on my back anymore.
> *(JACK waits quietly for her reaction.)*

Antonio Skármeta chose to write his play *Burning Patience* about the Chilean poet Pablo Neruda, set against a background of the evils of a fascist government.

3. They choose to write about something that arouses their curiosity. *Rupert's Birthday*, by Ken Jenkins, examines how one incident in a woman's childhood, helping to birth a calf, affected her entire life.

A play such as this sets up a situation and then says "what if ..." What if a few high-school girls stop in at a restaurant and see an older man staring at them? What if they become uncomfortable, and one of them decides she has to know why he's staring? And what if she's wearing an old high-school letter jacket that she picked up at a thrift store? And what if this jacket had belonged to the man's son? And what if the son is dead? The forgoing is what happens in Mark O'Donnell's *Fables for Friends*.

4. They choose a subject or a situation that is haunting. Tennessee Williams based much of his writing on his sister, who had had a lobotomy. Arthur Miller was haunted by the McCarthy hearings, and so used the analogy of a witch hunt in his play *The Crucible*.

5. They begin with a real person, current or historical. Molière is said to have used himself as a model for the hypochondriac in *The Imaginary Invalid*. Examples of other plays based on real people are Peter Shaffer's *Amadeus* (admittedly loosely based on Mozart's life) and Moisés Kaufman's *Gross Indecency: The Three Trials of Oscar Wilde*. To a degree, events will influence the content, but the playwright is free to interpret events and express feeling about them. In fact, Kaufman says:

I was interested in questions of how one reconstructs history and historical characters, and how you deal with many versions of the same story ... In a sense I was just asking — and answering — all my own questions ...

Someone gave me a book called *The Wit and Wisdom of Oscar Wilde* ... [T]he last ten pages ... contained part of the trial transcript, and the events of those ten pages shocked me. Here was an artist in a court of law being asked to defend his art, and it seemed so appropriate for our time. Right now we tend to look at art from a political or social or religious standpoint, and that's all very valid. But Wilde is a purist — he's talking about art as art and trying to isolate what only art can do that nothing else can do. For me, that's a very valid question, because in my work I've always tried to understand what is the thing that only theatre and no other medium can do ... [19]

---

19. Jesse McKinley, "As Far As He Could Go," *American Theatre*, November 1997,

6. They begin with a set of circumstances. Charles Kray did this with *A Thing of Beauty*, which is set in Nazi Germany and tells the story — based on fact — of Edith Stein, a Jewish woman who has become a Carmelite nun, Sister Benedicta. Tina Howe used both the circumstances and her memories ("hauntings") in *Painting Churches*, which takes place as the mother and father are leaving a house in which they've lived for years.

7. They begin with a setting. Louis Phillips must have done this with his comedy *Carwash*, in which vehicles driven through the Charm School Car Wash fail to come out the other side.

8. They adapt a play from another medium. Playwrights have adapted plays from novels, biographies, nonfiction books, or collections of stories. Some stay faithful to the original, while others interpret broadly. Examples are Stephen Sondheim and James Lapine's *Into the Woods* (fairy tales), Wendy Kesselman's *My Sister in This House* (an article about a crime), and *The Laramie Project* (interviews done by a number of people).

According to Sam Shepard, the theatre should deal with important problems.

There are predicaments and there are predicaments. There's *King Lear*, and there's Mickey Mouse and Donald Duck ... [There are] some predicaments that resonate and there are predicaments that don't mean anything.[20]

Choosing the Audience

Most playwrights, whether consciously or instinctively, choose a certain type of audience for a play. As William Archer says, "The drama has no meaning except in relation to an audience. It is a portrait of life by means of a mechanism so devised as to bring it home to a considerable number of people assembled in a given place."[21]

The way a play is written — the characters, the setting, the dialog, and the situations — determines the sort of audience. A. R. Gurney says he tends "to see myself writing for a kind of ideal, educated middle class, but not necessarily a white middle class. I sort of have an ideally democratic audience in my mind."[22] On the

20. Don Shewey, "Rock-and-Roll Jesus with a Cowboy Mouth (Revisited)," *American Theatre*, April, 2004, 23.

21. William Archer, *Play-Making: A Manual of Craftsmanship*, (New York: Dover Publications, Inc., 1960), 9. Reprinted with permission.

22. Bryer, "A. R. Gurney," 88.

other hand, playwright and performance artist Danny Hock envisions a different sort of audience.

> With *Jails, Hospitals & Hip-Hop*, these Off-Broadway producers came to see my workshop and said, "We're going to spend $300,000 on your show." Then they got back to me with a budget that had $35 tickets. I said, "Listen, $35 tickets tell my entire audience they can't come to the show." They said, "We know how you feel about young people, so we'll have some special matinees where you let young people come." I said, "No, young people are not gonna come to any special matinees. Young people deserve to be there every night with everybody else. They deserve to dominate my audience."[23]

There has to be common ground where the playwright and the audience meet. Audiences relate the action on-stage to their own backgrounds and personalities. Here is what David Ives, writer of *All in the Timing* and *Lives and Deaths of the Great Harry Houdini*, says about the subject:

> I think of theatre as an arena for communal empathy. To write for the theatre, you have to have a kind of imaginative empathy for people in order to understand how and what they feel. You then bring that to an audience. The audience has to empathize with what you're saying, and the actors have to empathize with what you've written, and all the people who put a production together have to empathize with each other for the space of four or eight weeks. I think of theatre as this great civilizing arena where people find a common ground. It's where, in one way or another, we realize that we're in the same leaky boat, and we realize it in person.[24]

---

23. Wendy Weiner, "Bricks, Asphalt and Language," *American Theatre*, July / August 1998, 30.

24. Stephanie Cohen, "No Comparisons," *American Theatre*, July / August, 1994, 26.

Beginning the Play

There is no particular way to begin writing a play. Almost anything can become the starting point. Many playwrights feel as Albee does:

> I'm not a didactic writer. I don't start with thesis, and then create characters, and then create a situation to illuminate the predicament ... Writing, for me, is something of an act of discovery, of discovering what I'm thinking about.[25]

A writer needs a balance between what is common to all of us and what is unique to the individual. To achieve this balance, it helps playwrights to be aware of the world around them, to be attuned to what they see and hear, and to recognize prevailing attitudes and concerns so they have more specific information to draw upon in creating a set of circumstances or a character. Not only does this provide the source and substance for a play, it lends veracity to the writing.

Characterization

The most memorable element of most plays is the characters. Chances are that if you are asked about a play you saw, you will begin, "Well, it was about this woman who ..." Most often, we identify with people first and ideas or subject matter second.

Tennessee Williams says:

> My characters make my play. I always start with them; they take spirit and body in my mind. Nothing that they say or do is arbitrary or invented. They build the play about them like spiders weaving their webs, sea creatures making their shells. I live with them for a year and a half or two years and I know them far better than I know myself ...[26]

Just as in life it is impossible to learn everything about another person at first meeting, a playwright's relationship with the characters is a changing and growing process. Yet Williams says that although he knows his characters better than himself, "they must have that quality of life that is shadowy."[27]

25. Roy Newquist, *Showcase*, (New York: William Morrow & Co., Inc., 1966), 19.
26. Tennessee Williams, "Critic Says 'Evasion,' Writer Says 'Mystery,'" *New York Herald Tribune*, April 17, 1975. Reprinted in Tennessee Williams, ed., *Where I Live: Selected Essays*, (New York: New Directions Books, 1978), 72.
27. Williams, 72.

After developing the characters, a playwright needs to decide what parts of them — which of their traits — an audience should see. Novelists can write pages about personality, background, motives, or actions. Playwrights describe character only through appearance or dialog. A playwright has to be more selective than a novelist, since a play takes only a limited amount of time on the stage. Joyce Carol Oates, a novelist who later began writing plays, compares the two forms to swimming and jogging.

> Both are exercises and can be very rewarding, but they use completely different muscles. The challenge of the theatre is to make the characters vivid enough to be alive on-stage and carry the weight of the action. The prose narrative voice doesn't require this; you're telling a story ...

Oates explains that writing a play is unlike writing fiction because "I can't tell the story — they [the characters] have to tell their own stories."[28]

A character has to want something, which he or she then tries to obtain. Often the reaction, rather than the problem, is more important because it shows a different side to the person, giving the play life and making it more enjoyable. Most plays deal with something that touches directly on the central character's past — that brings about reactions based on important personality traits.

In *Death of a Salesman*, Willy Loman's wife, Linda, cannot understand why he found suicide necessary. All the bills are paid, and she and Willy wouldn't have needed much to live on. She says that he had the wrong dreams. Because of the kind of person he is, Willy reacts differently from anyone else in similar circumstances. It would not be logical, for instance, for Regina, the protagonist in *The Little Foxes*, to commit suicide because she has failed financially. Nor would Willy ruthlessly trample anyone in his path to achieve success, as Regina does.

In addition to their uniqueness, characters should possess universal qualities — traits and feelings with which we all can identify. These draw us to the characters, help us to sympathize with their plight, and generally make us care about their lot.

One way playwrights have of revealing a character is by having other characters talk about him or her. But we don't learn much this way. We have to meet someone to discover what that person is really like.

---

28. Laurence Shyer, "The Sunny Side of Joyce Carol Oates," *American Theatre*, February 1994, 25-26.

In Tina Howe's *Painting Churches*, it's much more effective to see firsthand that the three characters, though tied by blood and feelings, nevertheless exist in their own worlds than it would be to have a narrator tell us these things. We learn firsthand that Gardner, the father, a well-known and highly respected poet, seems to be experiencing the beginning stages of senility. His wife Fanny creates her own world in which she amuses herself by buying hats in thrift shops and ignoring or pushing away the seriousness of her husband's mental state. The daughter, Mags, appears to be concerned with her parents, yet is more interested in painting their portrait and having them accept it as good.

Dialog

Dialog has three main functions: to reveal character, to create atmosphere, and to advance the plot. To accomplish these, the dialog has to have clarity; it has to be appropriate to the character, the situation, and the setting; and it has to be natural.

No matter how uneducated the characters, no matter how strong an accent or dialect, the audience should not have to strain to understand what they say. It not only has to fit personality, but it has to depict character. Some people are more hesitant than others. Some are shy, others outgoing. Dialog has to be appropriate to the mood. It needs a rhythm and flow that fits the emotions of the scene and the characters. Since most plays present the actors as real people in real situations, the dialog has to sound like everyday speech.

Sometimes physical activity can be more effective than dialog in revealing character or advancing the plot. The following occurs near the end of Eugene O'Neill's *Long Day's Journey into Night*. Mary, addicted to morphine given to her by a "quack" doctor, has lost touch with reality.

TYRONE: *(Heavily)* I wish to God she'd go to bed so that I could too. *(Drowsily)* I'm dog tired. I can't stay up all night like I used to. Getting old — old and finished. *(With a bone-cracking yawn)* Can't keep my eyes open. I think I'll catch a few winks. Why don't you do the same, Edmund? It'll pass the time until she —

(His voice trails off. His eyes close, his chin sags, and he begins to breathe heavily through his mouth. EDMUND sits tensely. He hears something and jerks nervously forward in his chair, staring through the front parlor into the hall. He jumps up with a hunted,

distracted expression. It seems for a second he is going to hide in the back parlor. Then he sits down again and waits, his eyes averted, his hands gripping the arms of his chair. Suddenly all five bulbs of the chandelier in the front parlor are turned on from a wall switch, and a moment later someone starts playing the piano in there — the opening of one of Chopin's simpler waltzes, done with a forgetful, stiff-fingered groping, as if an awkward schoolgirl were practicing it for the first time. TYRONE starts to wide-awakeness and sober dread, and JAMIE's head jerks back and his eyes open. For a moment they listen frozenly. The playing stops as abruptly as it began, and MARY appears in the doorway. She wears a sky-blue dressing gown over her nightdress, dainty slippers with pompons on her bare feet. Her face is paler than ever. Her eyes look enormous. They glisten like polished black jewels. The uncanny thing is that her face now appears so youthful. Experience seems ironed out of it. It is a marble mask of girlish innocence, the mouth caught in a shy smile. Her white hair is braided in two pigtails which hang over her breast. Over one arm, carried neglectfully, trailing on the floor, as if she had forgotten she held it, is an old-fashioned white satin wedding gown, trimmed with duchesse lace. She hesitates in the doorway, glancing round the room, her forehead puckered puzzledly, like someone who has come to a room to get something but has become absent-minded on the way and forgotten what it was. They stare at her. She seems aware of them merely as she is aware of other objects in the room, the furniture, the windows, familiar things she accepts automatically as naturally belonging there but which she is too preoccupied to notice.)

JAMIE: *(Breaks the cracking silence — bitterly, self-defensively sardonic.)* The Mad Scene. Enter Ophelia! *(His father and brother both turn on him fiercely. EDMUND is quicker. He slaps JAMIE across the mouth with the back of his hand.)*

TYRONE: *(His voice trembling with suppressed fury)* Good boy, Edmund. The dirty blackguard! His own mother!

JAMIE: *(Mumbles guiltily, without resentment.)* All right, Kid. Had it coming. *(He puts his hands over his face and begins to sob.)*

Writing and Rewriting

Some writers say that they record whatever comes to mind. Yet most writers have some sort of an idea about the progression of events, the theme, or even the resolution before they put words on paper. Some work out an intricate synopsis before starting to write. A. R. Gurney (author of plays like *The Cocktail Hour* and *Later Life*) says: "I do believe that drama is about what happens next, and if I don't know what's going to happen next, or have some instinct of what I want to have happen next, then I don't think the play will have the necessary momentum."[29] Others use only a minimal outline.

A writer often begins planning a play by choosing and analyzing the characters and their relationships and then goes on to determine the type of setting.

Marc Connelly describes his collaboration with George S. Kaufman on the play *Dulcy* like this:

All our free hours were spent on building the outline of the play. George and I established working methods then that we have followed through all the years we worked together. Having decided that our play should be in the mood of a warm but satiric comedy, we first fumbled about trying to visualize characters and plot progression. As Dulcinea — immediately shortened to Dulcy — was to be a girl of eccentric impulses, we saw possibilities in her engaging as a butler a convict thief, out of jail on probation. She also was the kind of girl who would invite, among ill-assorted weekend guests, an egomaniac movie producer, so we invented one she had met at a dinner party. Quickly, the characters, their development, and the narrative progression were sketched in great detail. Within a few days we had a completely articulated synopsis of about twenty-five pages. We then individually chose scenes for which we had predilections, wrote drafts, and then went over them together for improvement.[30]

29. Bryer, "A. R. Gurney," interviewed by Arvid E. Sponberg, 95.
30. Marc Connelly, *Voices Offstage: A Book of Memoirs*, (New York: Holt, Rinehart and Winston, 1968), 59-60.

The Opening Scene

Each play needs a "hook" that captures the audience's attention immediately, as in the following scene, which opens *Pails by Comparison: The Continuing Story of Jack and Jill.*

(JACK and JILL stand Center Stage facing each other. JILL carries an umbrella; JACK carries a pail.)

JILL: What are you doing, Jack?

JACK: I'm getting a pail of water.

JILL: A pail of water? What on earth for?

JACK: Nothing on earth. Rather for the spirit.

JILL: The spirit.

JACK: I stick with the old values, Jill. A little of all this new-fangled stuff goes a long way.

JILL: New-fangled stuff?

JACK: Faucets. Running water.

JILL: For heaven's sake, Jack. The ancient Romans had running water. The Aztecs of Mexico had running water.

JACK: Perhaps that's true. But some of us weren't so lucky.

JILL: That was long ago, Jack.

JACK: The old values are the ones that last.

JILL: I suppose you think women should marry at twelve or fourteen and by the time they're thirty, look sixty from caring for a brood of useless brats.

JACK: Jill!

JILL: Come into the present, man!

JACK: Man? I'm just a boy.

JILL: Boy, schmoy. It's not how we mark our years that counts. It's how we live them.

JACK: I see we have some fundamental differences here. I suppose you haven't carried a pail of water in —

JILL: No, Jack, I haven't. I have better things to occupy my time.

JACK: What things?

JILL: Women received the right to vote decades back, true?

JACK: Is this a history lesson?

JILL: But no woman has ever been president of the United States. Nor even vice president.

Planning the Exposition

A writer can also plan the exposition ahead of time. **Background exposition** deals with the opening situation of the play; the **progressive exposition** continues throughout and is related to the unraveling of the plot and the revelation of character.

There are many techniques for presenting exposition:

1. Using a narrator, such as the Stage Manager in Thornton Wilder's *Our Town*, who becomes the "bridge" between scenes.

2. Using flashbacks, a means of "showing" past events that have a direct bearing on the play. This can be effective since the action of a play, unlike a novel, occurs in a continuing present time. This means that even when we travel backward in time to pick up a scene of this sort, we restart the clock, so to speak, so that the audience "sees" the scene as it is occurring.

3. Through characters talking about another person.

4. Through such devices as meetings, partings, reunions, or other special occasions where people are likely to reminisce.

5. Through situations in which people are introduced to each other and try to find common ground for conversation.

6. Through touches of anger or irritation in dialog: "Damnit, Charlie, this is the second time today I've had to clean up your dishes. Half the time you don't put your clothes in the hamper or hang up your jacket."

7. Through scenery, lighting, costuming, props, and makeup. The setting, unless it's abstract, shows the location and often the circumstances of the characters. The lighting and costuming can give clues to the season and the time of day, for instance.

8. Through conflict, which not only is more interesting but also moves the plot forward, since the conflict usually has its basis in the central problem.

It may take many drafts before a dramatist is satisfied with the result. The revisions may include rearranging the scenes, cutting sections or speeches, adding new scenes and dialog for clarity, or trimming and sharpening the dialog.

Some plays are written, others are rewritten. The works of Tony Kushner belong firmly in the second category. Sitting in his office in Union Square, a tiny, book-lined room that is taller than it is wide ... he talked in specific detail about how he nurtures a work through its creative process. After seeing a play performed, he goes on "tinkering and tightening and tweaking and trying to get it right." This was the case with his first great success, *Angels in America*, and it is equally true with *Homebody/Kabul* ...[31]

Even when the playwright is satisfied, the producer, the director, the actors, and the designers may suggest or insist upon additional alterations.

Presenting the Play

You know you're a writer when your ultimate reward is not the money that comes with it, but the precious opportunity to write again. And again. To let the hearts and minds and souls of your characters live inside you again and again as you head to work or do chores around the house. What greater feeling is there than that? Playwrights know what I mean.[32]

It isn't an easy task to have a play produced. Often writers have a better chance of having their work presented in theatres with which they are affiliated, or at least where they know someone on the staff.

Before a show is even close to production, many writers present their plays at workshops, either independent of or connected to a theatre. For instance, in San Diego a group called Script Teasers gives readings of new plays with members reading the various roles. This is followed by critiques by the members.

Such groups can be helpful in allowing a playwright to hear the lines — which often sound different than they appear on the page. What reads well silently may come across orally as stilted or contrived, as inappropriate to a character or as wordy, or the dialog may seem to make the action drag.

There are many testing labs for plays across the country, and many colleges and universities have laboratory or experimental

---

31. Mel Gussow, "Tony Kushner Continues to Tinker with "Homebody/Kabul," *New York Times*, September 9, 2003, http://www.nytimes.com/.

32. Philip Vassallo, "The Reasons to Write," *The Dramatists Guild Quarterly*, Autumn, 1994, 35.

theatres that are willing to present untried plays.

Lanford Wilson, author of such plays as *Burn This* and *Redwood Curtain*, says, "Hearing [my play] read to me or hearing it read to a small lab audience ... is very important. I don't consider it finished until a couple of drafts after that."[33]

Many theatres have play development programs, offering staged readings to plays they feel have the potential to be successful. That is, actors rehearse the play a few times but read from the books. They perform physical actions and use props, which (despite there being no specific set) gives a better idea of how the play will move. New plays are developed at such places as the Yale Repertory Theatre, the National Playwrights Conference at the Eugene O'Neill Center in Waterford, Connecticut, and the Humana New Plays Festival at the Actors Theatre of Louisville. Playwrights Horizons in New York has developed such plays as Wendy Wasserstein's *The Heidi Chronicles* and Alfred Uhry's *Driving Miss Daisy*. Unlike some groups that give only readings or staged readings, Playwrights Horizons is much more involved with the script from revision and rehearsal through different productions of the same play with revision and rewriting in between times.

According to playwright Buzz McLaughlin (*Sister Calling My Name*, 1996), the development process with its "seemingly endless readings, workshops, and feedback sessions" can have its drawbacks. Before becoming a dramatist, McLaughlin, as founder and artistic director of Playwrights Theatre of New Jersey, functioned as a "developer." He says:

> [L]ittle by little as I worked with writers over longer periods of time, I began realizing that play development has its drawbacks. That perhaps my "partnering" with a writer and the rewriting process was taking away more than it was putting in. That maybe I was actually trying — subtle though it was — to mold these new works to focus more clearly on the themes I thought were important, instead of letting the playwright's voice ring out loud and clear ...

Yet McLaughlin admits that "like it or not, the development process has become a permanent fixture in this country and, while it runs the gamut from being extremely beneficial to totally disastrous, most of us simply have to learn to live with it."[34]

---

33. Bryer, "Lanford Wilson," interviewed by Jackson R. Bryer, p. 287.
34. Buzz McLaughlin, "Playing the Development Game," *The Dramatist*, November/December, 1998, 15.

At any rate, many playwrights revise and rewrite on up through rehearsals and New York previews, which are open to the public but from which critics are excluded.

Playwrights have the choice of submitting their work to producers, contests, professional theatre companies, educational theatres, community theatres, various summer theatres, agents, and drama publishers.

Producers and publishers are listed in such books as *Dramatists Sourcebook*, published each August by the Theatre Communications Group in New York, and *The Playwright's Companion*, published yearly by Feedback Theatrebooks of New York. Each has a fairly comprehensive list of producers, publishers, and agents as well as listing various playwriting prizes, festivals, conferences, and workshops for playwrights.

Many playwrights join the Dramatists Guild, which publishes both newsletters and quarterly journals giving listings of theatres looking for scripts. There are a variety of organizations, including arts councils in many states, that provide grants or aid to playwrights. Some offer an opportunity for production.

Summary

In most cases, the playwright, working alone, begins the creative process that results in a production before an audience. In order to assimilate a diversity of material, a writer needs to be acquainted with the various areas of theatre.

Most theatrical productions involve one person's script to which others add their interpretations. Ideas for the script can come from anywhere. Often playwrights choose a certain type of audience for their plays, one with whom they have common ground.

The most memorable element of most plays is the characters. There are various ways of revealing character, but the most important way is to show them in action. Dialog is important in revealing character, in creating atmosphere, and in advancing the plot. Physical activity can sometimes be more effective than dialog in revealing character or advancing the plot.

There are various ways of presenting exposition such as using a narrator, using flashbacks, having characters talk about another character, and through scenery, costuming, and lighting.

It is difficult to have a play produced, but there are workshops, various types of theatres, and organizations that help a playwright develop a script before submitting it to such places as producers;

contests; professional, educational, community, and summer theatres; agents; and drama publishers.

Questions for Discussion

1. Why is the playwright one of the artists without whom theatre cannot exist?
2. What are some of the ways writers can begin working on plays?
3. Why is it necessary for playwrights to know their characters thoroughly? What kinds of things should they know about the characters?
4. Why is character usually important to the development of a play?
5. What are the characteristics and functions of good dialog?
6. How do playwrights begin developing their ideas? How would you proceed if you were going to write a play?
7. Why do you think it is desirable for playwrights to have a particular type of audience in mind for their plays?
8. Why is it important to be knowledgeable about the various aspects of a production in order to write a play?
9. What does it mean to say that there needs to be common ground where a playwright and an audience can meet? Why is this important?
10. Why do you think it is difficult to have most plays produced?

Chapter 6
THE ACTOR

Theatre cannot exist without an actor, the person with whom the audience most closely identifies, the one who provides the glamour, who personifies theatre in the eyes of the spectator. Yet, according to British psychologist Brian Bates, the general attitude toward actors is confused.

We admire them and detest them. We deify them and sneer at them. We watch in our millions when they appear on television interview shows, but then we require them to talk about the most trivial aspects of their lives. And while a few actors are rewarded with knighthoods, others are served up for breakfast as titbits of notoriety beneath the cheap headlines of the popular press.[1]

Despite the admiration, the sneering, the constancy of performers in the public eye, actor John Gielgud says, "Of all the arts, I think acting must be the least concrete, the most solitary."[2]

Why, in light of the prominence of the actor among theatre artists, is he or she the most solitary? Perhaps because in some ways an actor's work is similar to a playwright's examination of self, of delving inside for answers to questions, of focusing inwardly before or in addition to working with the rest of the cast, the director, and the other theatre artists.

The actor takes what comes from inside and makes it real for an audience in an attempt to persuade them that what they are seeing is much like life itself. "If somebody asked me to put in one sentence what acting was, I should say that acting was the art of persuasion. The actor persuades himself, first and through himself, the audience ..."[3]

---

1. Brian Bates, *The Way of the Actor: A New Path to Personal Knowledge and Power*, (London: Century, 1986), 15-16.
2. John Gielgud, *Early Stages*, (New York: Macmillan, 1939), 311.
3. Hal Burton, ed., *Great Acting*, (New York: Bonanza Books, 1967), 23.

Where other artists use canvas and paint, or fabric and light to birth their work, actors rely on little else but themselves. They have setting, lights, makeup, and costumes, but these are accessories, accouterments. The actor alone is on display.

Painters frame and hang their work at exhibits; authors publish novels. But actors exhibit themselves; their art is themselves, not divorced and apart. The art they exhibit is the most direct and intimate of all, and because of this one of the most demanding.

According to Tony Award winner Mary Alice:

What an actor has is himself or herself: the body, the mind, the imagination, the psyche, the voice — whatever makes up me. This is the instrument and learning how to use this is very important. It's related to knowing oneself — who I really am, how I really think, how I really feel, being very honest in my life so that I can be very honest in my work. How can I bring truth to a character that is written by someone else? How can I tell that person's story if I don't know my own?[4]

A ballerina dances; a vocalist sings; a reader interprets a poem or a piece of prose. Actors often use all these arts in a given performance.

Painters can change a landscape or even discard it if it fails to meet their standards. Actors have only one given moment to convey their message, and then the moment is past. According to early American actor Lawrence Barrett, "Acting is like sculpting in snow."

Noel Coward summed up the demands an actor faces on-stage:

You've got first of all to remember the character you've learned and studied and know about; you've got to remember your voice pitch, which has got to reach the back of the gallery, without shouting; you've got to remember your other actors — vitally important to get their eye, speak to them, not to the audience, to them. Then you've got to listen to the audience's reaction ... I believe that all acting is a question of control, the control of the actor of himself, and through himself of the audience.[5]

---

4. Joan Jeffri, ed., "Mary Alice," *The Actor Speaks: Actors Discuss Their Experiences and Careers*, (Westport, Conn.: Greenwood Press, 1994), 23.

5. William C. Young, "Noel Coward," *Famous Actors and Actresses on the American Stage*, (New York: R. R. Bowker Co., 1975), 226, from an interview on the BBC by Michael MacOwan, (1952).

On-stage and Off-stage Acting

Because each person possesses the rudiments necessary to becoming a professional actor, it often is difficult to distinguish acting from role playing in everyday life. In realistic productions the actor who most successfully conveys the impression of life or of being natural is the most successful. Therefore, it may seem that there is little difference between "acting" in life and acting on the stage. However, live theatre is not and can never be life.

There is an old saying: "Everyone thinks he can be a writer." The same is true of acting. Because we each use the mimetic instinct and because stage acting appears to be like life, many people think there is nothing difficult about appearing in a play. All you have to learn is to project your voice a little more than normal, and you can do just as well on the stage as the next person can.

Even if acting is instinctive, the person who successfully plays the role of history student in real life may have difficulty playing the role of a serious history student in a stage production. On the other hand, the stage actor who never seriously studied history may successfully portray such a role, relying on other experiences to "feel" the part.

When we see actors in a performance, we can be fairly certain that they always are aware that they are acting, that they are playing to a particular audience. Yet everyday role playing often is an unconscious act. A student returning home after class does not consciously think, "Now I am going to assume the role of a roommate, friend, or relative." Actors on a stage are conscious of their surroundings. They remember to move in a certain manner, to use properties in a particular way at a certain time, and always to project their voices to fill a theatre. They are aware of body placement, of the arrangement of the other actors, and what is expected of each as a part of the total production. Role playing is more spontaneous. In trying to reach a goal, people in everyday life may have several alternatives. For the actor (unless the situation calls for improvisation), a playwright has written the script, the director has planned out action, and the scene occurs within a certain framework and setting, still, of course, with room for the actor's own creativity.

An actor is more aware of fitting into an overall scheme than is a ruthless business tycoon who tramples everyone to reach the top. The actor must consider (except in one-character plays or performance pieces) that to constantly dominate the scene means failure for both the performer and the production.

Helen Hayes once said of acting, "What you're doing ... is projecting yourself into someone else entirely, into the mind of the author, into the being of the character. You are trying to settle down to be comfortable in that character and speak the author's words. You are merely an instrument for what he is saying."[6]

To become an actor requires a strong drive to succeed — a drive that most often is a prerequisite to endless training and years of hard work. Geraldine Page explains:

> I read everything I could about people in the theatre. The ones who stayed in the business for a long time and established themselves, strangely, took an average of about ten years to get a foothold ... So I said, "Oh well, it'll take about ten years, and the broader a base I can build, the firmer I'll be." But then the tenth year began to go by. And I had always had this conviction that "I've got it and I'll get it. I'll get well-paid and I'll get recognition someday because I'm terrific." I'm still my best fan. So, the ten years were almost up, and I was talking to some of my acting friends and I heard this same firm tone of conviction from them. I thought, now wait a minute. Evidently this subjective feeling that you are it, that you are anointed and that you're going to live happily ever after is not a full guarantee.[7]

Even performers who have acted professionally for years often continue their studies. Just as a dancer spends years on elementary exercises and a singer repeats scales endlessly, the actor keeps practicing.

Tools of the Actor

Any art that belabors its medium or draws attention to technique is not good art. We appreciate acting that involves us in a total production and that fails to call attention to itself. If we stop to think that actors are performing well, they probably are not. They most likely have not worked long enough or hard enough at honing their tools — their minds, bodies, voices, and selves.

---

6. Roy Newquist, *Showcase*, (New York: William Morrow & Co., Inc., 1966), 204-05.
7. Joan Kalter, ed., "Geraldine Page," *Actors on Acting*, (New York: Sterling Publishing, 1979), 14-15.

It is wrong to suppose, as many actors do, that a true inner feeling will inevitably express itself in a true outward form. This will only happen when the voice, the speech, and the body have acquired by rigorous training and discipline a flexibility instinctively at the command of the inner truth, and no physical technique is of any use to an actor until it is so much an organic part of him that he is not really conscious of its employment.[8]

The Mind

As important as any of the other aspects of an actor's mind is the willingness to learn. Stage and film actor Paul Muni once said:

If I were to use a principle at all in acting ... it would be that if the mind — the basic generator — functions alertly and sums up its impulse and conclusions to a correct result, it is possible for the actor to achieve something creative. Technique, which comes with practice, gives you a firm foundation on which to build your structure. But unless the mind sends out the sparks, the forces that stimulate the body to perform a series of actions that generate a spontaneous emotion, nothing creative can happen.[9]

Actors, of course, need to understand the techniques of acting — the various styles in which a production can be presented, and how to execute these styles. This is an intellectual process. Then they analyze; they try to discover the most effective way to project characters, emotions, and reactions. This is technique.

The Body

Much more is involved, however, than mental processes alone. Actors' bodies must be in shape to sustain high levels of performance.

Hugh Jackman starred on Broadway in *The Boy From Oz*, a musical in which he sang all of the twenty songs and which was presented eight times a week. He was on-stage for all but a few minutes of each show and never missed any of the nearly 400 performances. He said director Trevor Nunn told him "This is *[King] Lear*. You can't do this eight times a week." He admitted that, of course, doing the show was extremely difficult. To be able to

8. Phillip Burton, *Early Doors: My Life and the Theatre*, (New York: The Dial Press, Inc., 1969), 165.
9. Young, "Paul Muni," 841.

continue day after day, he had painful massages twice a week, went to someone for body alignment every week, did yoga twice a week, trained in the gym once or twice a week, and did tai chi once a week.[10]

Even after years of performing, Sir Laurence Olivier refused to rest on his accomplishments:

> I keep myself very fit now; I have to. I go to a gym twice or three times a week, not merely to look tremendously muscular, but I have to keep fit for my job. I'm determined to hold on to my job. I love it. But it is no use pretending it doesn't involve a certain amount of overwork, because it does. I've seen a lot of contemporaries get a bit under the weather with such work, and I'm determined not to.[11]

Not only does the actor try to stay fit for good health, the demands of a role may require an athletic body. Actors often are called upon to perform exhausting feats, such as sword fighting or dancing.

The Voice

To be most effective, actors should develop their voices to the fullest potential. They should understand how the voice works and learn proper exercises to improve its use.

This means learning to portray emotions through various vocal qualities, to make pitch and volume fit the situation and character, to project, and to articulate clearly without calling undue attention to the words.

The voice has to have strength and endurance. It should be flexible to fit a variety of circumstances. The actor needs to have complete control over it. By doing proper exercises, much like a singer, actors learn to use their voices without strain.

The Self

It has often been said that actors should never look upon any experience in life as wasted. Years later, a certain incident or feeling may suggest an approach to a character or a scene. Anything a person sees or hears can be useful in assuming a role.

In this regard, Hume Cronyn says that an actor "must become so facile in the use of your physical equipment that it will respond

---

10. Jesse Green, "Exhausted But Proud, Hugh Jackman Retires His Sequins," *The New York Times*, Sept. 5, 2004, http://www.nytimes.com/.
11. Hal Burton, 16.

instantly and do what you want it to do." Yet even so, a person could still be "a bloody awful actor."

> Without the inner things — without being able to call on qualities of emotion or spirit — you're stuck with only a husk, a frame, a case. How do you go about developing what should be inside? How can you exercise that inner person, enrich it, make it immediately responsive? This is much more difficult because it's infinitely more subtle ...

> How one charges the batteries, how one learns and grows in the sense of total artistic appreciation and an understanding of the world we live in and our particular society, is a much more subtle and complex thing. One can't awake in the morning and say, "From now on I'm going to be aware, aware, aware. I'm going to be like a sponge and soak it up." You can't do it mechanically, yet without one's emotional antennae constantly aware of how people behave, respond, and react, without some degree of analysis of your own surging emotions — particularly in the moments when they're ungoverned — you're not growing. You have to find out these things because that's the grist of your mill ... All this must be, in turn, lent to the author by being brought to bear on the given emotional conflicts of a play.[12]

Much of an actor's training, in other words, should be self-training. Many people go through life paying little attention to the things or people around them, even to their own feelings. Yet the person who is able to feel both physically and emotionally, who has reservoirs to draw upon, has the better chance of success on the stage.

Actors have to be able to get outside themselves and see the world from different points of view. Only by using their imaginations and by being sensitive can actors project themselves into characters and situations.

---

12. Newquist, 66-67.

Freeing the Imagination

Youngsters have no problem using the imagination. They play "house" or "space travelers." They pretend/believe their stuffed animals are real, as Hobbes was real to Calvin in the comic strip *Calvin and Hobbes*. But Hobbes — a stuffed toy — came to life only when he and Calvin were alone. Unfortunately, this is how life is for many people, able only to pretend when they are alone. This is because most of our lives we've been told to pay attention and stop daydreaming.

An actor or director or designer needs to let the imagination soar, to imagine what it is like to live in fear of being ousted as a ruler (Henry in Goldman's *Lion in Winter*) or to have been treated merely as a toy (Nora in Ibsen's *A Doll's House*).

Observation

Actors imagine how they would react in certain circumstances so that they can play their roles effectively. They observe how other people stand, move, and sit, and how they react to pressure, happiness, anger, and all the other emotions. Performers get into the habit of observing and recording in their memories or journals the way individuals talk and any idiosyncrasies of character that might be transferred to a role.

Mercedes Ruehl describes an exercise involving a character sketch assigned in a workshop she attended:

You would study somebody on a subway, or a bus, or walking down the street; and the first thing you would do is, you would take them in. Like, I would notice that you're sitting with your leg crossed; and you're not looking at me straight on, but slightly at an angle. And that there is a smile, and that you wear lip gloss and that you have a very bright, keen, scrubbed healthy face and the long hair. And I would notice how your clothes make you sit. And then you have to get close enough to see what they smelled like. Every sense had to be involved in this character sketch. And if you didn't hear them talking, you would have to engage them in a conversation. Then you would have to watch how they gesture when they talk, and you would try to get just the timbre and the rhythm of their speech, and the accent. And as you were describing this person to the class, you would be incorporating every characteristic as you described it. What you were going for was a transformation — that thing that hooked you finally into the life of this other character.[13]

Becoming Creative

Creativity is often intuitive, based on prior knowledge. A good actor is not afraid to experiment — to see what works with a characterization and what doesn't. The actor maintains an openness of feelings and perceptions and is able to draw upon and mold them to fit a characterization.

Through characterization, actors present an illusion of life. Just as a child pretends that a stick of wood is a polished sword, so the actor creates an illusion that suggests reality to an audience. Actors take what previously has been internalized and externalize it.

Formal Training

Actor training involves both the body and the voice. According to vocal consultant and dialect coach Elizabeth Smith:

Body and voice are closely related. Posture has a great deal to do with the efficiency with which you can breathe. Ideally you're trying to rid the body of unnecessary tension, and you're trying to make it easier for someone to use their breathing mechanism. Breath is to voice what gas is to a car. It's the fundamental energy that makes it work.[14]

Actor training often begins with classes in oral interpretation, singing, dancing, and fencing — the last not only as an end in itself, but as a means of body control. There are some schools that have actors participate in team or individual sports to improve reflexes and to build stamina. Sometimes the games move into pantomime — playing ball games with imaginary equipment. Through these exercises actors learn to concentrate on how people actually respond in various situations. Actors often develop scenes from **given circumstances** (background information), and they may participate in exercises in **sense memory**, that is, remembering and portraying anything sensory such as walking in a light rain or eating an apple.

13. Joan Jeffri, ed., "Mercedes Ruehl," *The Actor Speaks*, 165.
14. Candi Adams, "Elizabeth Smith: Articulating the Actor," *American Theatre*, January 1994, 29.

Less traditional forms of training include psychological and emotional exercises to stimulate the senses. In addition to developing sensitivity to self, others, and the environment, such training builds confidence and breaks down inhibitions. Often, the training is closer to role playing than to acting.

Newer forms of actor training look back to ritual and tradition. The new movements often are reactions against some parts of the old, at the same time embracing some of their aspects. For example, at the Polish Laboratory Theatre in Wroclaw, founded by Jerzy Grotowski in the late 1960s, rigorous training exercises are based in such diverse areas as gymnastic movements, Chinese classical ballet, and yoga.

Technical Requirements

Actors must know the stage areas and the implications of various types of movement. They know that curved movement under many circumstances can indicate indecision, whereas one of the strongest movements in projecting determination is from Upstage Center (the central area near the back wall) to Downstage Center (the area closest to the audience). They understand what body positions can suggest and know how to balance the stage picture.

Actors may be called upon to do almost anything on the stage. Often they must handle unusual properties or move naturally in cumbersome costumes. They may need to work with all of these elements just to get their feel. They often may have to experiment with makeup to gain the right effects and to become used to moving about on a set built on different levels. An actor may have to sing or dance in addition to portraying a character.

Actors need to become acquainted with and be able to perform in a variety of styles — the unadorned movement of classicism, the gracefulness of romanticism, the earthy delivery of naturalism. They know that the audience and they themselves generally should be more involved in a tragedy or serious play, whereas both usually should stand somewhat apart from the roles in comedy. They should give the impression that they are sharing the joke with the audience in a comedy, and that they are playing for laugh lines while still maintaining balance between involvement and technique. Too much exaggeration, if it is inappropriate to a character, can destroy a role. So can too much naturalness, where the actor fails to project voice and actions.

Actors are responsible for communicating a variety of feelings with only a few words or gestures. They are oral interpreters who add their own interpretations to a written work while remaining true to the original purpose. Unlike writers or sculptors, they rely on many other artists, who in turn rely on them to present a successful play. They have a duty to the designers, the director, the other actors, the playwright, and most important, the audience. They must understand their roles and the whole play to fulfill this duty.

Approaches to Acting

Psychologist Bates says, "For most of us, the sensation of being taken over by an alien being, having our body possessed by an outside 'personality,' would be terrifying. We would fear we were going mad. But for some actors possession is not only what they experience, it is what they *seek* to experience."[15]

> For the actor there are many ways of achieving transformation; making the physical, emotional, even spiritual journey from one's being to that of a character, a role: another person. Quite often it is ... a combination of disguise and performance. But to concentrate on the physical appearance only is to miss a fundamental aspect of the actor's art of transformation. An actor can look different from his usual self because he is different "inside." Entering into the psychological, mental, emotional world of a character can result in quite startling physical changes. Sometimes a physical transformation can be literally "coloured" by inner concentration.[16]

This experience of "possession" accounts for many different actors being able to transform themselves physically, without unusual makeup or costumes, into the grotesquely deformed John Merrick in *The Elephant Man* by Bernard Pomerance, or to age fifty years over the course of a play and to do it convincingly. In effect, this involves, as least on one level, becoming the character.

The Internal Approach

In 1906 director Konstantin Stanislavsky of the Moscow Art Theatre first brought together all the elements that make up the internal approach, later referred to as the Stanislavsky System. The approach was a reaction against declamatory and extravagant

---

15. Bates, 69.
16. Bates, 94-95.

acting styles, which relied on memorized gestures and posturing to portray emotion. Stanislavsky sought to present dramatic truth through an observation of life or nature, and to make acting more naturalistic. He taught that actors should seek truth of feeling and experience in the characters they play, finding the psychological depth of each role. To do so, the actors needed highly trained bodies and voices.

Stanislavsky wanted to find the true nature of creativity in the human being and subsequently discover the means for its development. He became increasingly interested in the operation of the subconscious and emotions. He formed the concept of **emotional memory** — remembering how one felt in a particular situation and relating that memory to similar circumstances of a character in a play. Yet he felt that most often emotional memory isn't necessary, but can be used if an actor is having difficulty feeling the emotion in a scene. He felt actors need to move, perceive, concentrate, and feel while on the stage — not merely pretend to do so. In fact, he advocated a balance between experiencing the role internally and paying attention to precise vocal and physical expressions, or, in other words, to the external. The System also includes the "magic if" — actors determining what they would feel if they were a specific character in a specific situation. In addition, it encourages the actor's focusing concentration on the moment to moment unfolding of the action. Thus the System offered a precise plan for portraying a character.

In the U.S., the System led to the Method or Method acting, with its emphasis on examining one's psychological and emotional depths to extract the raw material for playing a role. The Method evolved largely through applying only certain portions of Stanislavsky's teachings, the result of both Stanislavsky's many changes in the System over the years, and the fact that it was published only piece by piece in the U.S.

Yet actress Judi Dench's "method of bushwhacking through her unconscious to find the emotional core of a character is, she says, completely instinctive." She feels that "'The subconscious is what works on the part ...'" She "describes herself as 'an enormous console with hundreds of buttons, each of which I must press at exactly the right time.'"[17]

---

17. John Lahr, "The Player Queen: Why Judi Dench Rules the Stage and Screen," *The New Yorker*, January 21, 2002, 58.

The External Approach

Those who follow the external approach are largely concerned with technique. They think it is unnecessary to undertake the study of a role by trying to understand emotionally what a character does and says. It is necessary only to determine what the emotion is and then modify outward, observed signs of this emotion to fit the role. Sir Laurence Olivier felt that:

> Method actors are entirely preoccupied with feeling real to *themselves* instead of creating the illusion of reality. They want the absolute kernel of a character before starting to express anything. I decided, perhaps rather hurriedly, that this was wonderful training for film acting, where the camera and microphone can come right in and get your reality — the tiniest shade of your tone of voice, every little twitch of expression. But our problem on-stage is to convey an illusion fifty or more yards away. That's where the big stretch comes — that's where imagination, where know-how above and beyond inner reality comes in. But I don't see that it matters where you start, inside or out, as long as the illusion ends up the same.[18]

Critics of the external approach say that the actors are using "tricks," because they are concerned with effect rather than feeling. They are, of course; but to some degree all portrayal of character involves "tricks" because the actors are aware of the audience and playing to them.

Often, the external can become internal. For instance, if we frown for a long enough time, we are going to be in a negative mood. If we smile, we begin to feel joy or happiness.

Those actors who play for effect are using the external method; those who seek the truth of the character are using the internal approach. Yet no matter which approach they use, actors have to be concerned with projection, the delivery of memorized lines, their spatial placement in relation to the other actors, and other technical aspects. Therefore, they perform on two levels — one concerned with analysis and technique, the other concerned with feelings and veracity and the appearance of life.

Acting is a combination of technique and "being" or feeling. It's been said that the best time for an actor to feel strong emotion is in

---

18. Young, "Laurence Olivier," 885, from Richard Merryman, "The Great Sir Laurence," *Life*, May 1, 1964, 81.

the early stages of rehearsal. After that, he or she has to be in complete control, or else risk not being convincing.

Other Approaches

Within the past few decades, methods of acting have begun to change. Part of the new experimentation in theatre can be credited to the Living Theatre of Julian Beck and Judith Malina, who sought to make drama fluid and poetic. They believed that new methods of acting should be discovered for new plays that were being written.

As Grotowski of the Polish Laboratory Theatre stated, "I believe there can be no true creative process within the actor if he lacks discipline or spontaneity."[19] Grotowski believed that the best approach to theatre and acting was to strip them of all nonessentials. That meant there should be no sets, makeup, lighting, or costuming. The actor, through discipline and control, creates these things in the minds of the audience. By controlled movement the actors create whatever they wish the audience to perceive. Impulse and reaction are simultaneous. The actor does not merely desire to perform a certain action but is incapable of not performing it. The skills become involuntary. The goal is to eliminate mental, physical, and psychological blocks. The result is the totally disciplined formation of a role in which all inhibitions are nonexistent and every phase of self is revealed.

Developing a Character

Denis O'Hare, who won a 2003 Tony award for *Take Me Out*, says, "My job as an actor is to be an advocate for my characters. I fight for their expression, and I want to get them everything they deserve. It's the director's job to then edit me ..."[20]

In reading a script, the actors see that the exposition or the development of the plot divulges certain character traits and uses these traits as a starting point, adding characteristics and features that are consistent with the character's personality.

Often, directors will have actors improvise a scene with the character. The scene is based either on the play itself or on an incident entirely divorced from the play. The actor learns how the character is likely to react in a variety of circumstances and becomes more comfortable with the role. The actors also project how the character reacts emotionally, psychologically, and physically to each situation and to the other characters within the play.

---

19. Jerzy Grotowski, *Towards a Poor Theatre*, (New York: Simon and Schuster, 1968), 209.
20. Bruce Weber, "Sing Out, Mason: Making an Accountant Bloom," *The New York Times*, June 1, 2003.

Figure 6-1: Three styles of acting: *Tobacco Road* (Top; outer, naturalistic approach) was directed by Louis Erdmann, Photo by James Gleason and used by permission of Kent State University. *HMS Pinafore* (Middle; outer, stylized approach) was directed by Jim Bob Stephenson. Used by permission of Kent State University. *The Lion in Winter* (Bottom; inner, realistic approach) was directed by Mary Sesak at Heidelberg College. Photo by Jeff McIntosh.

Analyzing a Role

Actors generally analyze a role in much the same way that the playwright (and the director) analyze the play as a whole. First, particularly if they rely on the inner approach, actors often seek the **spine** or **superobjective** — the goal the character wants to reach. The actor determines the overall goal first, and then breaks the play into short scenes or units to determine the reason for the actions and reactions in each section. In this way, he or she understands how a character builds, how a personality unfolds or gradually is revealed, and where the focus should be in each section.

Defining the spine works best with realistic or naturalistic plays in which the characters approximate real people. One actor conceivably could discover a different spine for a role than would another actor. Often the director helps the actor interpret, but, except sometimes in premiere productions, the actor has no chance to ask the playwright what the goal of that character should be.

After determining the superobjective, the actor analyzes each individual scene to figure out its specific objective and how it contributes to the overall goal.

Determining the Character's Makeup

Actors go on to determine as much as they can about their characters by asking themselves certain questions. For instance, what is the character's physical makeup? Actors, of course, cannot drastically alter their basic physique, but they can change things such as apparent age, hair color, and posture.

Although playwrights indicate what a character is like or even describe him or her, rarely can the actor find complete information within the given circumstances, which really serve only as a starting point.

Next the actors determine as much as possible the characters' backgrounds, much as a playwright does. Where were they born? Where did they grow up? What are their educational, sociological, ethnic, and financial backgrounds? What are their present circumstances? The more an actor "knows" about a character the easier it is to make him or her believable on the stage.

The actors also determine how their characters view the world. What are their basic beliefs about life in general and the circumstances in the play in particular? How are they most likely to react in certain situations? What are their most important personality traits?

Because of time limitations the actors can present only a few of a character's traits. Working with the director, they decide which are most important to the audience and why. They determine which facets of the character's personality should be emphasized and which de-emphasized.

As you learned, characters often are a combination of a type and an individual. For example, a universal trait is Oedipus's pride, whereas an individual trait is his limp. To individualize a character the actor often emphasizes a distinctive trait that may not be suggested in the script, but that immediately identifies the character in the minds of the audience. For instance, an actor portraying Tyrone in *Long Day's Journey into Night* could play with a silver dollar as a symbol that he has money, or pick up pieces of string and put them into drawers to indicate miserliness.

Figure 6-2: Hamlet's dagger shows his obsession with suicide.

Determining Relationships

Another consideration is how a character feels about the other characters. Why? What is the character's self-image? How do these feelings relate to the theme or action of the play? As Katharine Cornell says, "To understand one's own character thoroughly one must see it in relation not only to itself but to the other characters in the play."[21]

Figure 6-3: How do these characters relate to each other? Photo by James Gleason, used by permission of Kent State University.

Although the character analysis occurs before, or at least near the start of, the rehearsal period, the actor enters the role with the understanding that the character will continue to build until the play is presented. If this were not so, much of the rehearsal period could be eliminated. Rehearsal involves exploring relationships and projecting the actors more completely into their characters. Building and growth often develop naturally once actors appear on-stage together. It is much easier to act well when fellow actors are doing a good job; it is easier to establish the mood and to determine rhythm and pace.

---

21. Young, "Katharine Cornell," p. 222, reprinted from an interview in *Theatre Arts Monthly*, January 1977.

Memorizing Lines and Business

The rehearsal period begins with the memorization of lines, blocking, and **business** (physical actions necessary to the advancement of the story or to delineating character). Once the actors have learned the sense of the scene, the lines become easier to learn and to remember. Directors sometimes have actors who have not yet learned their lines ad-lib a scene, using the ideas but not the exact dialog. This exercise can help both in characterization and in giving the actors confidence that they do know the direction the action is taking.

Along with their own lines, the actors memorize their **cues**, the lines or actions preceding their own. They learn the sequence of ideas in order to convey the playwright's message or theme.

Most acting involves the **ensemble concept**, the willingness to yield to other actors when the script indicates they are the center of focus. Actors must understand each other's actions and speeches as well. Even when actors are not speaking, they listen to what the other characters are saying and react to what they hear. If not, the audience members will sense a false note in the performance.

Interpreting Ideas

Success in interpreting a role depends on the appearance of spontaneity. Unfortunately, it is common to see actors who have played their roles for a long time become automatic in their acting and responses.

Laurence Olivier once remarked, "I have a horror of a performance becoming mechanical, automatic, and I watch like a hawk for signs of it. Then we try to find fresh lines, fresh ideas and emotions — new deliveries to make them spontaneous again."[22]

While immersing themselves in their roles, actors also remain aware of technique. They are ready to meet unexpected audience response, and they watch for the occasional fluffs of lines or mistakes of technicians. Also, despite the fact that in real-life situations people sometimes become so angry that they scream and lose their voices, actors cannot afford to do so. They have to be aware of vocal technique and the technique of building a scene. If they wholly immerse themselves in the role, oblivious to outside changes or interference, they are setting themselves up for disaster.

---

22. Young, "Laurence Olivier," p. 886.

There has to be a balance between the purely artistic and the purely technical; between credibility and projection. Actors, through training and experience, learn to trust their own intuition. If they begin to doubt themselves, they will fail in their roles. They have to be confident that what they are doing is the right thing. They must be able to free themselves of doubts and inhibitions.

The actor's job, then, is to create, to interpret, to illustrate, to heighten, and to expand. The work bears the mark of the actor's own personality, because like all artists, actors give of themselves. Yet actors usually are interpreting the work of others, including the playwright, who provides clues to the building of a character, and the director, who works with the actors in the blocking and overall interpretation.

The Business of Acting

Tony Award winner Brian Stokes Mitchell, the star of several Broadway musicals, says, "Theatre gave me a chance to make a good living, and now I can pick and choose what I want to do ... It's been given to me on a plate, and when life gives it to you on a plate, you eat."[23]

However true this may be, making a living as an actor, unfortunately, is almost next to impossible. Little more than ten percent of those in **Actors' Equity Association** (the union for actors in legitimate theatre) are employed at any given time. And in all the actor's unions combined, only three thousand or so are working steadily. A much smaller percentage make a living as actors over their working lifetimes. Even those fortunate enough to land jobs in original New York productions may work only a few nights before the show closes due to poor reviews and lack of attendance.

Yet thousands try; thousands believe that they can make it. Some of them can, at least for a time. There are opportunities in nearly every medium-sized to large city to act for pay, and there are theatres off in small towns or even out in the country. There are non-Equity (non-union) jobs, but most of them will barely support a performer — if they support him or her at all. The picture is bleak. Of course, there are many other jobs connected with theatre and many opportunities for acting in community theatres on a nonprofessional basis.

---

23. Bruce Weber, "Broadway's Last Leading Man?," *The New York Times*, November 24, 2002.

Everybody loves a good story, and this season on Broadway, Sutton Foster has the best. It's a familiar one ... an unknown is plucked from the chorus, takes over the lead and becomes a star. In real life, though, hardly anyone experiences what Ms. Foster went through with *Thoroughly Modern Millie.*

When the [show] went into rehearsals for its pre-Broadway tryout at the La Jolla Playhouse in California ... Ms. Foster was in the ensemble. She had a tiny part and was the understudy for Erin Dilly, who had been cast as Millie ...

After the run-through, [Dilly was found to be unsuitable for the role], and the producers asked Ms. Foster to take over. She played Millie for the entire California engagement ... And against the recommendations of many advisers, [it] was decided to give the starring role of a $9.5 million production to a twenty-seven-year-old actress [Foster] whose peak moment on Broadway had been singing the role of Eponine in *Les Misérables* for one weekend.

Those who do make it as stars, or at least who work much of the time, nearly always wait for years for their break.[24]

* * * * * * * * * *

[S]ometimes I just want to get up in front of some bunch of kids and just say, "You know, you have to stay with something past despair." Because that point where all of my anger and pain and hurt and tired of wearing coats that were too cheap and not warm enough for these New York City winters and blah-blah-blah. That was a point of a certain kind of despair. And I just finally thought, "It's not going to happen. I could have sworn it was going to happen, but it's not going to happen." And in my life, at least, that was the point that I had to bust through and get on the other side. I had to stay with it past despair. And I think sometimes, you know, in relationships, just when you want to despair of the person ever coming through, you stick with them. You don't close them out of your life. You don't close this theatre out of your life entirely. Don't close

---

24. Don Shewey, "Plucked from the Chorus: It's Corny But True," *The New York Times,* May 19, 2002, http://www.nytimes.com/.

this dream out entirely. And sometimes that's when it happens. I guess you have to *want* to do it. As Tad, my great teacher, said, you have to be able to look somebody in the eye and unflinchingly say, "I would die if I couldn't do it ..."[25]

It is difficult to succeed as a professional actor. Yet when actors do succeed, they know beyond a doubt that their job is one of the most fulfilling undertakings in any form of art.

Summary

The actor is the person with whom theatre audiences most closely identify. Unlike painters or writers who can revise what they do, actors have only a given moment to present their art to the spectator. The actors' major tools are the mind, the body, and the voice. Actor training involves many areas such as oral interpretation, singing, dancing, fencing, and often team sports. Actors learn to collaborate with others, and so have a duty to the designers, the director, the other actors, the playwright, and the audience.

There are two major approaches to acting, the internal and the external. The internal — as first put together by Stanislavsky — involves approaching a role from the viewpoint of emotions, the subconscious, and the natural, along with paying attention to precise vocal and physical expressions. The external approach is largely concerned with technique. Other approaches were developed by the Living Theatre of Julian Beck and Judith Malina, who sought to make drama fluid and poetic, and Jerzy Grotowski, who proclaimed the need for discipline and spontaneity.

Involved in developing a character is the need to analyze a role by finding the superobjective (in realistic plays) and the specific objective for each scene. Actors also try to determine as much as possible about each character they are to portray. The process continues throughout the rehearsal period so that good acting has the appearance of spontaneity.

---

25. Joan Jeffri, ed., "Mercedes Ruehl," *The Actor Speaks*, 171.

Questions For Discussion

1. Discuss the differences between role playing in life and acting in a theatre.
2. In what way do you suppose actors train themselves?
3. Why do you think it's so difficult for actors to make a living as an actor?
4. In what way is acting solitary? Collaborative?
5. If you were to perform in a play at your school, which approach do you think you would favor in developing your character, the internal or external? Why?
6. What do you believe is Willy's superobjective in *Death of a Salesman*? Linda's? Biff's? Do these differ from anyone else's in the class?
7. Why do you think it's necessary for actors to know much more about their characters than they will ever portray onstage?
8. Other than earning a living, what do you think is the most difficult thing about being an actor? Explain.
9. What actors on television do you admire? Why? To your way of thinking, what makes them outstanding? Why is this important?
10. If you were an actor, would you rather appear in a comedy or a tragedy? Why?

Chapter 7
THE DIRECTOR

The director usually is the first theatre artist involved in bringing a script to life before an audience. Myriad responsibilities make the job one of the most exciting and satisfying. According to Harold Clurman:

> Direction is a job, a craft, a profession, and at best, an art. The director must be an organizer, a teacher, a politician, a psychic detective, a lay analyst, a technician, a creative ᵢ being. Ideally, he would know literature (drama), acting, the psychology of the actor, the visual arts, music, history, and above all, he must understand people. He must inspire confidence.[1]

The occupation of director as we know it today stems in large part from the practices instituted by Georg II, the Duke of Saxe-Meiningen (1826-1914), who developed the concepts of ensemble acting and directorial control over every aspect of production. (See Chapter 14).

To be a director requires training and/or experience in various phases of theatre. Directors need a working knowledge of the principles of acting, scene and lighting design, costuming and makeup, as well as an understanding of how to prepare and balance a budget. Sidney Berger says: "A director ... is not a 'stage-er,' not someone who makes pictures; a director is someone who takes the play ... to another stage of its evolution. He takes the print off the page and helps translate it into living terms."[2]

According to Jacques Copeau, "Directing is the sum-total of artistic and technical operations which enables the play as conceived by the author to pass from the abstract, latent state, that

---

1. Harold Clurman, *On Directing*, (New York: The MacMillan Company, 1972), 14.
2. "Sidney Berger, Director" in Jeane Luere, ed., *Playwright Versus Director: Authorial Intentions and Performance Interpretations*, (Westport, CT: Greenwood Press, 1994), 41.

of the written script, to concrete and actual life on the stage."[3]

David Alberts believes that "more than anything else, directing today is about leadership — artistic leadership, certainly, but managerial, motivational, and instructional leadership as well." He feels that "the modern director's overriding concern is to mold all the elements of a production into a unified artistic experience. To that end she must undertake a wide range of responsibilities that encompass not only purely artistic matters, but also matters having to do with human resources, budget control, and community relations."[4]

> The difference between directing a play and directing traffic is that as a theatre director your job is to influence all the drivers to go in the same direction, toward your destination — your vision for the production — rather than letting them go their separate ways to their own destinations. A director maintains traffic on a one-way street. Your job is to bring everyone in from the side streets and get them all going in the same direction.[5]

Selecting the Script

A theatre's success depends, in large part, on the scripts it produces. In many types of theatre, directors have at least some say in choosing a script, so they need to be able to judge what will be acceptable to potential audiences and what sort of people are likely to attend their productions. Of course, they also need to consider their own likes and dislikes.

If they are working with an established organization, directors choose plays that fit into the total season. If a college presents four productions a year, a director wouldn't want to do a melodrama when another is planned for the same season. Directors also have to consider plays done in recent seasons. If Alfred Uhry's *Driving Miss Daisy* was produced at a particular community theatre two or three years ago, it probably won't draw well in the current season, at least from the local citizenry. Directors also need to consider what has been done or is planned at nearby theatres.

3. Jacques Copeau, "La Mise en Scéne," *Encyclopédie Francaise*, December 1955, from *Directors on Directing*, 214.

4. David Alberts, *Rehearsal Management for Directors*, (Portsmouth, NH: Heinemann, 1995) ix-x.

5. Alberts, 2.

How do directors know what will be successful? They don't; they can only make educated guesses. Even the type of play that was a success in one season is not a guaranteed success in another. The socioeconomic and political climates change; tastes and styles differ from one year to the next. However, by studying trends and box office receipts, directors can make fairly accurate choices. This requires familiarity with a broad range of plays.

Directors also need to consider the type of theatre structure and the available talent. A small theatre group, or a theatre that has few seats and a small stage, would have a difficult time presenting a large-cast show.

Overall, directors fill a number of different roles or jobs depending on whether the theatre with which they are associated is commercial, educational, or nonprofit.

Analyzing the Script

Scheduling a play is just the beginning of a director's work. The next task is to analyze the script to determine what the writer means to say and how he or she wants to say it. This, in part, determines the style of the production — both in the acting and design.

Alberts cautions directors to:

> Learn all you can about the play, the playwright, the period in which the play was written, the period in which it is set, and any forces that may have exerted an influence on the play's genesis and development. Research the costumes of the period, the social attitudes of the time, and carefully review those aspects of the play with which you are not completely familiar. Read reviews of past productions for subtle and not-so-subtle hints on potential problem areas and for audience reaction. Read promotional materials from other productions for some idea of what others considered important to emphasize.

> Ideally, you need a minimum of eight weeks before rehearsals begin to become familiar with the script and assimilate all relevant information ... It's an absolute necessity that you know all there is to know about this play.[6]

---

6. Alberts, 36-37.

When the play is to be given its initial production, the director may have a chance to work directly with the playwright in asking questions of clarification or requesting rewrites.[7]

Finding an Overall Concept

As they work with the script and later with the actors and designers, directors may change some of their concepts. Most, however, do work out the largest portion of their analysis ahead of time, first reading the script through a few times simply to get a feel for it. Then they may research the period in which the play either was written or is set, and they may investigate the playwright's life to learn what influenced him or her.

Director José Quintero feels "that the main function of the director is to translate something from the literary form into an active dramatic life."[8] Directors who believe, as does Quintero, that directors are translators, often look for a theme or a metaphor that is carried out in the design and acting. The purpose is to say that a particular play is "like" this facet of life or this particular set of circumstances. For instance, Archibald Macleish's *J.B.*, which uses the book of Job from the Bible as its starting point, often has been done with a circus metaphor. The highest platform in the circus tent represents heaven and the lower levels earth and hell. The idea is to provide a focus for the entire design and, subsequently, for the audience.

Interpreting More Closely

After deciding upon the overall concept, directors become more specific in their analysis, which is somewhat similar to that of the actor. Yet it is much more inclusive in that the director deals with the overall play, while actors are more concerned with how their characters fit into it.

Directors determine which elements are the most important for the audience's understanding of the play and which are less so. Often, they add elements that are not in the script. An example is adding further "hokey" business to a farce to accentuate the silliness of the character or situation. Additions such as these may continue through the first few weeks of rehearsal.

---

7. "Robert Anderson, Playwright," in Jeane Luere, ed., *Playwright Versus Director: Authorial Intentions and Performance Interpretations*, 35.

8. José Quintero, interviewed by Jean-Claude Van Itallie, in Joseph F. McCrindle, ed., *Behind the Scenes: Theatre and Film Reviews from the Transatlantic Review*, (New York: Holt, Rinehart and Winston, 1971), 256.

The director next determines the basic action or the areas of conflict in the play as a whole and in each scene. Where does the major climax occur, and how can it be pointed up? Where are the minor climaxes in each scene, and how should they be presented? What is the prevailing mood or atmosphere? Is it nostalgic, comic, tragic, or sentimental? There often are subtle or abrupt changes in mood throughout a play; however, there is a prevailing atmosphere or feeling that is most important to the script's message. John Millington Synge's *Riders to the Sea*, for instance, has a heavy and somber mood throughout.

Directors determine how each character relates to the play as a whole and how the characters relate to each other, much as an actor does. Alan Schneider states: "To me a play is a series of relationships. A dramatic action ... means a change in relationship."[9] Directors determine why each character is included and how each advances the theme. What struggle is the most important in providing the play's dramatic movement? What needs or desires do the characters symbolize? How is each unique? According to Director Jerry Zaks, "One of the hardest things about directing is knowing when you have started to tell your own story at the expense of the author's story."[10] Elia Kazan says, "no matter whose play you direct or how sympathetic you are to the playwright, what you finally are trying to do is interpret his view of life."[11]

In the same vein, Director Sidney Berger is against any distortion of the playwright's attempt. Once, he writes, he was asked to be a guest critic at a play festival where another director "did a production of Williams' *Glass Menagerie*."

> [I]f you remember the last stage direction of the published play, when Tom says, "Blow out your candles, Laura," she does and the stage goes dark. But in this production, Tom said, "Blow out your candles, Laura" and she didn't. She walked off-stage and the candles were lit ... And afterwards I said to the director, "Why did you deliberately change a direction that the playwright gave you, one which had to do with the end of the play?" And he said, "Because I didn't

9. Alan Schneider, interviewed by Van Itallie, in McCrindle, 279.

10. Myrna Katz Frommer and Harvey Frommer, eds., *It Happened on Broadway: An Oral History of the Great White Way*, (New York: Harcourt, Brace & Company, 1998), 256.

11. Chaka Ferguson, Associated Press Writer, "Director-Writer Elia Kazan, Winner of Two Oscars, Dies at 94," *Los Angeles Times*, September 28, 2003, http://www.latimes.com/.

feel that the play was about what he wanted it to be about."
In that case he totally changed the play as it is written. This
is not "Laura goes to the sink and takes a glass of water"!
We're talking about a substantive direction that the
playwright is giving the actors and the director, one that has
to do with what the end of the play is. In changing it, he
completely destroyed the playwright's intent ...

[T]here is a principle involved, and that is, if you want to
direct a playwright's play, then you are accepting the work
that has been given to you. If you want to adapt the
playwright's play, then you had best deal with the
playwright first ...[12]

Directors, unfortunately, often are not true to the writer's intent.

Edward Albee had ... problems with William Ball's
direction of *Tiny Alice* at San Francisco's American
Conservatory Theater in 1969. Ball had directed the play
twice previously, but when ACT's production was to
transfer to New York, [the trade newspaper] *Variety*
reported that Albee asked to see a run-through as a result of
reports he'd heard about ACT's previous presentations,
which included "transpositions of scenes, alterations in
text, and offbeat interpretations of several characters."

After seeing the rehearsal, he allowed the play to go on, but
"Albee, unknown to the actors, viewed the final preview
performance [and said that Ball] 'had taken it upon himself
to destroy my play by cutting, juxtaposing, and actually
rewriting a good deal of the third act.'" Albee
understandably was upset, calling the changes
"inexcusable," and would not permit the show to go on,
unless the original text was restored.[13]

On the other hand, "playwrights laud" director Wendy C.
Goldberg of Arena Stage in Washington, D.C.

12. "Sidney Berger, Director," in Jeane Luere, 40.
13. Joe Stockdale, "Toward Mental Health," *The Dramatist,* March/April 2001, 20.

"It was a joy to work with a director who was so thoughtful and precise about the work," says Beth Henley, whose new play, *Exposed*, appeared downstairs last year in a reading directed by Goldberg. Stephen Belber, whose *Tape* Goldberg directed at the Contemporary American Theater Festival in 2001, agrees. "She's blessed with this ability to disarm large egos, to nullify overacting," Belber says, "to politely but firmly point out the overwritten aspects in a new script and to deliver a stage picture that never looks staged — all the while handling the press, the designers, the artistic audience, and (in my case) a meddling, neurotic, balding playwright."

Designers and actors are equally enthusiastic about Goldberg's collaborative gifts. After working with her on five productions, costume designer Anne Kennedy says, "The togetherness that Wendy promotes as a director with a designer makes for a very complete artistic experience." Set designer Mike Brown says that Goldberg "empowers designers to underscore the theatrical storytelling, through interpretation, with evocative abstracted metaphors." Actor Jack Willis ... describes the young director as "a gentle, great soul."[14]

The following are reconstructed "director's notes," showing part of the analytic process director Harold Clurman used in preparing for a production of O'Neill's *Long Day's Journey into Night*.

14. Terry Hong, "Wendy C. Goldberg, The Connector," *American Theatre*, January, 2004, 54.

Director's Notes for
Long Day's Journey into Night
Eugene O'Neill [15]

(Directed with an American company for the Kumo Theatre, Tokyo, 1965.)

FIRST IMPRESSIONS
Guilt — a keynote

↓

Apprehension-suspense

↓

More guilt

↓

Self-accusation

The characters are sustained by no faith.

The eyes of each character are on the other.

Foghorn — a desolate sound of aloneness.

Loneliness — everyone is alone with his or her own secret and guilt.

The play is a self-examination, a search into oneself and into others. Through understanding to find forgiveness, relief, the connection of love which may overcome loneliness.

Long Day's Journey (self-examination) into Night (the darkness of the self). The journey to self-discovery. The search for the true self which has somehow been lost.

15. Reprinted with the permission of Scribner, an imprint of Simon & Schuster Adult Publishing Group, from ON DIRECTING by Harold Clurman. Copyright © 1972 by Harold Clurman. All rights reserved.

MARY: "If I could only find the faith I lost so I could pray again!"

Later, "What is it I'm looking for? I know it's something I've lost."

The spine of the play: to probe within oneself for the lost "something."

TYRONE

SPINE: to maintain his "fatherhood" — the tradition (the crumbling grandeur).

He is a *positive* character: he wants to sustain the structure of his home and family, above all, his wife whom he still loves. If she were well, he thinks, all would be normal. There would be no suffering, no crises. He hopes and hopes — so that he may not see the failure of his whole life, his part in that failure, his guilt.

He still clings to his religion: his faith in the theatre, his world. (He takes pride at never having missed a performance.) His gods are Shakespeare and Edwin Booth ...

But the tradition has been shattered in the struggle for existence in the dark days of America's Gilded Age ... Tyrone is "redeemed" by the discovery of the past in his son.

Tyrone's heartiness is something more than a sign of physical health. It is part of the fortitude in his *struggle* with poverty, his *struggle* to educate himself, to lose his brogue, to learn Shakespeare, to become a stage star. (The theatre is his religion.) But he has betrayed his religion through his fear of poverty. He wants land, which means security to him ("the farm"). He seeks roots, lost in the departure from Ireland and in the effort to grow new roots in the new and different American "soil."

It is hard for him to admit the least fault or guilt in himself. He can't even admit that he snores, that he drinks too much, that he is greedy. He does not, at first, understand his faults as a consequence of his background and situation. He must maintain his self-respect to be a father, a god, a leader, a man.

(American children of immigrants rarely understand their fathers. They are always disappointed in them. They do not appreciate the hardships of their fathers' struggle as immigrants or as "pioneers": *Desire Under the Elms, A Touch of the Poet.*)

"Socialism," for Tyrone, means destruction of the tradition. His sons blaspheme against the theatre, Shakespeare, etc.

He shuns "Wall Street" — the forces, which without his realizing it, have conspired to ruin him. He doesn't understand his life — or his country. Hence, his constant self-contradiction, his absurdity.

He's a good man, a soft man. He always yields to his better nature, to sentiment and affection. Like most actors, he is susceptible to compliments. He's an "old-time" actor: life was composed of work on the stage, stage lore, companionable drinking, dreams of glory, celebration of success.

Clurman goes on to analyze each character in depth and to find the spine for each. Yet many directors feel that not everything should be spelled out for an audience, rather that they should be forced to connect some of the dots. Orson Welles once said:

"I want to give the audience a hint of a scene. No more than that. Give them too much and they won't contribute anything themselves. Give them just a suggestion and you get them talking with you. That's what gives the theater meaning: when it becomes a social act."[16]

16. "Theatrical Quotes," *American Association of Community Theatre*, http://www.aact.org/cgi-bin/webdata_quotes.p1.

Anticipating Design and Blocking

During analysis a director also thinks in terms of setting and technical elements. What type of environment will best portray the atmosphere, mood, actions, and circumstances? What should the lighting suggest? What sorts of costumes should the characters wear? Should the makeup be realistic or exaggerated? At some point in the planning the director meets with the designer to present or discuss ideas. Often, directors have their own ideas about the design concept; then it is necessary for the director "to reconcile the designer's ideas and preliminary designs with [his or her] concept of the production." Or else the director should "allow the designer as much freedom as possible to explore his own ideas," since the goal "is to come to some agreement regarding the direction that the designs will take."[17]

> Theatre is an interpretive art that relies on a close collaboration between and among many artists. [A director's] concept, [his or her] vision for the play, is the artistic and organizational force behind the production. Realizing [that] personal vision depends, however, to a greater or lesser degree on realizing the visions of all the other artists with whom [the director is] working. It is virtually impossible for any one person — designer, director, or actor — to impose his own interpretation, concept, or vision on the production to the exclusion of all others ...
>
> Unity of production is, or should be, the primary goal of every theatre artist ...
>
> There will be many, many compromises made throughout the production process. It should appear to the audience, however, that the production is the work of one single (notably single-minded) theatrical artist. It falls to the director to ensure that his overall vision for artistic unity is maintained in every aspect of the production. For this reason, it is imperative that the director have a well-defined concept of the production, and that he be able to express that vision clearly and unambiguously to every member of his production team.[18]

---

17. Alberts, 87.
18. Alberts, 83-84.

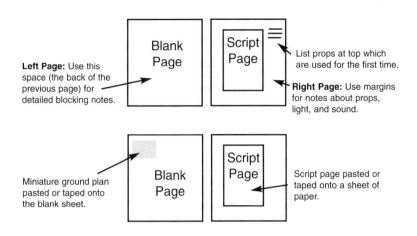

Left Page: Use this space (the back of the previous page) for detailed blocking notes.

Blank Page

Script Page

List props at top which are used for the first time.

Right Page: Use margins for notes about props, light, and sound.

Miniature ground plan pasted or taped onto the blank sheet.

Blank Page

Script Page

Script page pasted or taped onto a sheet of paper.

A sample "miniature" used for a production of *On the Verge*

Useful Blocking Abreviations

Λ = rise   V = sit

DRC = Down Right Center
(Plus all the other stage areas – DR, DC, DLC, L, LC, C, RC, R, UR, URC, UC, ULC, UL)

X = cross   I = pause

3/4 (R) = Three Quarter Right
(plus all the other body positions – 3/4 L, 1/2 L, 3/4 L, 1/4 R, 1/4 L, etc.)

Recording the Blocking

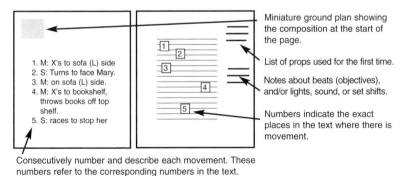

Miniature ground plan showing the composition at the start of the page.

1. M: X's to sofa (L) side
2. S: Turns to face Mary.
3. M: on sofa (L) side.
4. M: X's to bookshelf, throws books off top shelf.
5. S: races to stop her

List of props used for the first time.

Notes about beats (objectives), and/or lights, sound, or set shifts.

Numbers indicate the exact places in the text where there is movement.

Consecutively number and describe each movement. These numbers refer to the corresponding numbers in the text.

Figure 7-1: Sample layout for a prompt book.

149

After approving the set design, the director considers how much blocking to plan before the show is cast and rehearsals begin. As a general rule, directors plan the broad movements and leave the subtleties of gesture and characterization to the actor. Experienced actors are likely to have a sense of what is right for any situation, and directors may prefer to give them more freedom than they give beginning actors.

If the blocking has been planned in detail, rehearsals probably will proceed more smoothly, but there is a chance the physical action will appear too rigid and controlled. If there is too little planning, the director risks wasting time.

Casting the Play

The director has to be a good judge of human behavior, particularly in educational and community theatre. Because actors in these situations receive no financial compensation for their work, they must have other incentives for auditioning. The director tries to judge the actors' sincerity and reliability, as well as their talent. Another consideration is how well the actors and the director can work together, and whether a good rapport can be established among the cast members.

Although they have in mind the physical type they want for each role, directors usually do not precast shows, except perhaps for central characters in some professional theatres. Broadway shows, for example, often have been written with particular actors in mind.

Auditions

"Choose a good script," I sometimes advise students, "cast good actors — and you'll all be good directors!" There is more than a little truth in the jest. Casting constitutes the first step in the practical interpretation of a play.[19]

Most common is the **open audition**. The actors all appear at a certain time and audition in front of everyone there. Often the director makes scripts available a day or more ahead of time and takes a few minutes at the beginning to summarize the plot of the play and to explain the circumstances. Sometimes directors allow the actors to audition for specific parts; at other times directors ask them to read certain sections or roles. Some directors prefer that the actors present a pantomime or an impromptu or improvised scene.

19. Clurman, 64.

The open audition has several advantages. The director is able to judge how the actors will appear with one another, so there is little danger, for instance, of casting a father who is shorter than his thirteen-year-old son. The director also can see how well the actors relate to one another and how well their voices blend. An advantage for the actors is that they are able to judge the competition.

There are several disadvantages. One is that certain actors may have adverse reactions to the auditions of other actors, which can affect the way they read. Auditioning first, last, or in the middle may also affect how well an actor does. Further, if the auditions last a long time, the director may tire and lose concentration.

A second type of audition is the **closed audition**, also referred to as the **interview** since sometimes the director just talks with the actor. However, interviews often are conducted after the initial meeting. At any rate, the actor and the director meet without having anyone else present. Sometimes directors simply talk with the actors. Sometimes they have the actors read from the script or perform an impromptu scene. Advantages of this audition format are that the director can concentrate on one actor at a time and that the actors needn't experience the pressure of having to compete openly with others.

A disadvantage is that the director cannot see the way the actors look together nor how well they work with one another. Sometimes, too, the director has to read a part to cue the actor and loses concentration. In addition, because this type of audition often is held in an office or small room, the director is unable to consider vocal projection.

There are various other methods of auditioning. At times, for example, actors are asked to prepare a short scene or monolog of their choice to present either at open auditions or at interviews. Sometimes a director will interview actors and then have them come to open auditions. In professional theatre, directors often interview experienced actors, while most of the other actors go to open auditions, referred to as "cattle calls," where they may be eliminated on the basis of physical appearance even before seeing the director.

At any type of audition, the director has many aspects to consider: how easily the actors move; their emotional depth and range; the quality, range, and projection of their voices; and their overall potential for a role. Some actors do not read well, but have the potential for growth and development in a role. Others read well at first, but fail to develop their characters much during rehearsals.

Often actors need special abilities. For a musical, they may be asked to come to auditions with a prepared song to sing. They may perform their own dance steps, or be shown several steps to learn and execute.

Rehearsing the Play

After the cast is chosen and the technical elements are planned, directors devote most of their time to the actors. The rehearsal period can vary from a usual four weeks in professional theatre to six weeks in educational and community theatre. A shorter period is needed in professional theatre because the actors can spend an entire workday rehearsing, whereas in other theatres they have school and/or a job.

There are six stages of preparation: **reading rehearsals**, with the purpose of coming to a clear understanding and interpretation of the play; **blocking rehearsals**, where the action, movement, and business are worked out; **character and line rehearsals**, where the performers develop and build their characters and try to discover the most effective method of delivering their speeches; **finishing rehearsals**, in which all the elements of acting are developed and unified; **technical rehearsals**, devoted to coordinating the visual and sound elements with the total production; and **dress rehearsals**, in which the play ideally is given just as it will be in performance.

The length of the rehearsal period depends upon several factors. One is the background and experience of the actors. In educational theatre, the director often has to serve as a teacher. Also, some plays are easier to perform than others. It probably will take less time to ready a simple comedy for production than a musical in which the actors must memorize songs and dances as well as learn lines and build characters. The theatre schedule affects the rehearsal period. Often, summer stock theatres change the bill each week. In college or university theatres, plays sometimes are presented every two or three weeks during the summer.

The period of time needed for each type of rehearsal varies. When the business and blocking are intricate, blocking rehearsals have to be longer. This happens in stylized productions, for instance, where every movement is planned. Character and line rehearsals take longer if the speeches are difficult and the characterizations unusually involved. Often, if there are many special effects, additional technical rehearsals will be needed.

In nonprofessional theatre, the director usually schedules rehearsals of no longer than two or three hours. There is little advantage in holding rehearsals of less than an hour, except, perhaps, to work with individuals.

Sunday	Monday	Tuesday	Wednesday	Thursday	Friday	Saturday
Sep 22	Sep 23 Order Scenery Supplies	Sep 24	Sep 25	Sep 26	Sep 27 3:00 PM Production Meeting	Sep 28
			Announcements Auditions			
Sep 29	Sep 30 7:00 PM Auditions	Oct 1 3:30 PM Auditions	Oct 2 7:00 PM Callbacks	Oct 3 7:00 PM First Cast Meeting	Oct 4 3:00 PM Production Meeting Final Designs	Oct 5
Oct 6	Oct 7	Oct 8	Oct 9	Oct 10	Oct 11 3:00 PM Production Meeting	Oct 12
		7:00 PM - 10:00 PM Rehearsals				
Oct 13	Oct 14	Oct 15	Oct 16	Oct 17	Oct 18 3:00 PM Production Meeting	Oct 19
		7:00 PM - 10:00 PM Rehearsals				
Oct 20	Oct 21	Oct 22	Oct 23	Oct 24	Oct 25 3:00 PM Production Meeting	Oct 26
		7:00 PM - 10:00 PM Rehearsals				
Oct 27	Oct 28	Oct 29	Oct 30 Photos	Oct 31	Nov 1 3:00 PM Production Meeting	Nov 2
		7:00 PM - 10:00 PM Rehearsals				
Nov 3	Nov 4 Publicity Mailed	Nov 5	Nov 6	Nov 7	Nov 8 3:00 PM Production Meeting	Nov 9 Scenery On-stage
		7:00 PM - 10:00 PM Rehearsals				
Nov 10	Nov 11 Add Props	Nov 12	Nov 13	Nov 14 Program to Office	Nov 15 3:00 PM Production Meeting	Nov 16 10:00 AM Light/Sound Set
		7:00 PM - 10:00 PM Rehearsals				
Nov 17	Nov 18 7:30 PM Dress Rehearsals	Nov 19 7:30 PM Dress Rehearsals	Nov 20 7:30 PM Dress Rehearsals	Nov 21 7:30 PM Opening Night	Nov 22 7:30 PM Performance	Nov 23 7:30 PM Performance 10:30 PM Strike & Party
Nov 24	Nov 25	Nov 26	Nov 27	Nov 28	Nov 29	Nov 30
Dec 1	Dec 2	Dec 3	Dec 4	Dec 5	Dec 6	Dec 7
Dec 8	Dec 9	Dec 10	Dec 11	Dec 12	Dec 13	Dec 14

Figure 7-2: A typical production / rehearsal schedule.

Reading Rehearsals

For the first few rehearsals, directors often prefer to have a relaxed atmosphere in which the actors feel free to discuss the script. Reading rehearsals are somewhat misnamed, in that the major purpose is to agree on a script's interpretation. During reading rehearsals, directors explain what they see as the play's theme and the effects they hope to achieve.

The idea for both the actors and the director is to come to an understanding of the basic action and motivation. At the first rehearsal, a director may have the actors read through the play to grasp the overall concept, without attempting to develop character.

The director may listen to the actors' ideas, often telling them to go ahead and experiment if the suggestions are appropriate or consistent with the overall concept or interpretation and add something of value.

At some point the director may show sketches and floor plans to the actors so they can better visualize the action. After this, the cast is ready to move to a rehearsal hall or stage.

Blocking Rehearsals

One purpose of movement and business is to keep the play from appearing static, to give it life and activity. Another purpose is to present an aesthetically pleasing picture in both the placement and movement of the actors. The director has to keep in mind that the stage picture is constantly changing and is perceived differently from each section of the audience. He or she needs to consider sightlines and which stage areas are the strongest for emphasis. Body position, focus, and levels all are used to emphasize specific characters, speeches, and scenes.

Movement has to be motivated by the script, or at least appear to be. The blocking has to fit the situation and the type of play. In a funeral scene, for instance, the movement would be slower and more stately than in a party scene. Different types of characters also move differently.

There are two categories of movement and business: **inherent** and **supplementary**. The first is any action that advances the story or is an integral part of the plot. It includes exits, entrances, and phone calls. Supplementary business is added for effect, either to enhance the message of the play or to establish character. It includes how the actor stands, sits, or walks and is important in establishing personality traits and attitudes, as well as the mood of each scene and the characters' emotions.

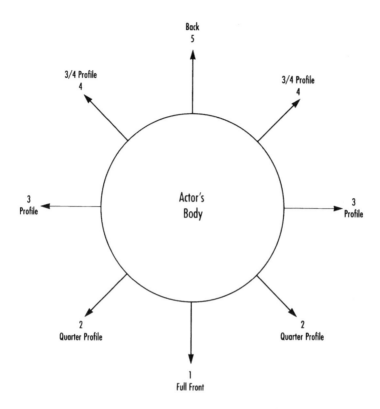

Figure 7-3: On-stage positions for the actor include the full-front body position, strongest for an actor on-stage. The quarter profile often is used when actors talk with each other. The further Upstage an actor turns, the weaker the positioning usually becomes. The back position is rarely used.

Both inherent and supplementary business are used for focus. A moving actor, whether walking from one spot to another or fiddling with a prop, attracts more attention than one who is stationary. Focus also applies to the characters' use and placement of furniture, and it can provide psychological groupings, as when a family is united around a table.

Figure 7-4 (see page 156) explains varying strengths of stage areas and some of the circumstances a director has to consider when planning movement and blocking.

In the top drawing (A) showing the numbered sections of the stage, the #1 area is the strongest. The areas decrease in strength the higher the number — if all else is equal. Of course, other factors affect

An Introduction to: The Art of Theatre

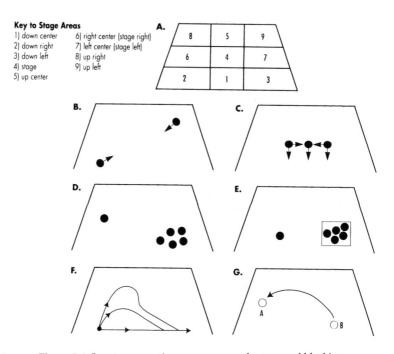

Figure 7-4: Stage areas, various movements of actors, and blocking.

relative strengths or weaknesses of any area. In the second drawing (B), the person in the #2 stage area actually is weaker than the one in #9 because of facing Upstage and away from the audience. In drawing (C), all three actors can be of equal strength when facing front. However, if the two on the ends face inward, the middle actor then becomes a strong focal point. (Yet, if one of these wears a more colorful or unusual costume, this person will be the center of attention.)

Drawing (D) shows that the isolated individual receives emphasis, while drawing (E) shows that the emphasis is equal when the group stands on a platform. Drawings (F) and (G) have to do with movement. The strongest movement, shown in drawing (F), is straight across the stage. The other moves show decreasing strength or uncertainty. Drawing (G), however, shows that it often is stronger to move in a curved line than a straight one because of final positioning. If the actor were to walk straight Upstage from the #3 stage position, he or she would be facing away from the audience, which is a weak position.

156

Physical closeness sometimes implies emotional closeness, whereas distance often implies disagreement. A tendency to stay in certain areas of the stage can reveal much about the psychological aspects of a character. One who stays Upstage can appear timid, whereas another who is Downstage may come across as extroverted or confident. A scene appears weak if the characters constantly move behind the furniture rather than in front of it. Unless it's done deliberately to provide humor, a dominant character usually wouldn't stand looking up at a platform while browbeating a weaker character.

A director needs to be aware of providing unity and variety in picturization, as well as showing conflict, focus, emphasis, and characterization. Movement can complement or even replace lines. Finally, although movement is planned just after the reading rehearsals, it continues to build and change throughout the rehearsal period.

Character and Line Rehearsals

Beginning with the reading rehearsals, the actors have been working on interpreting their characters and lines. However, it is only after the blocking is finished that this becomes the focus of rehearsal. During this period a director usually encourages the actors to experiment in building their roles. This is the stage of rehearsal in which a character really begins to come to life.

During this phase, the director makes certain that the actor understands the significance of each line, since the method of delivery is just as important as the content in conveying the mood and message. This also helps the audience to understand a scene's significance. Ultimately, it is the director's responsibility to see that the lines are delivered in character and in accordance with the play's mood and style.

> [I]f the director is looking at a play, sees what the actor is doing even in accordance with his direction, and discovers that the road taken by the actor and the director is the wrong road, then I think it's necessary to go back to the beginning and start over. We do it all the time — because you are choosing roadways and sometimes you get lost and sometimes you reach dead ends. Actors certainly do it all the time, as I do. An actor will come to me and say, "Let me try something," and it doesn't go anywhere. Or he'll try it and I as a director make a discovery because of the actor's success. So it is collaboration. The collaboration of the

playwright must be with the director, must be with the actors, and must be, ultimately, with the audience.[20]

The director is also concerned with how the actors are projecting lines and character. For instance, a good rendering of character for television would not be suitable for a proscenium stage. Many of the subtleties of movement and facial expression would be lost, and the lines probably would not be loud enough for the audience to distinguish the words.

Finishing Rehearsals

Action, interaction, delivery, and interpretation are refined and polished during the last few weeks of rehearsal. Up to this point the director has stopped scenes when necessary and corrected blocking or line delivery. Now, unless something major needs correcting, the rehearsals proceed without stopping. Often it is not until the finishing rehearsals that an actor can fully appreciate the impact of a role. The director usually takes notes and discusses inconsistencies between the running of the acts.

Until the finishing rehearsals, it has been difficult to concentrate on the show's overall movement because there have been so many stops and starts. Now the director concentrates on the three broad aspects of movement: pace, timing, and rhythm.

Pace refers to the fastness or slowness in handling business and speaking lines. The pace will be faster in scenes of excitement or tension and slower in a relaxed atmosphere.

Timing refers to the use of pauses within or between speeches. It is important both in pointing up specific lines and actions and in emphasizing reactions. In a comedy, an actor needs to pause just the right length of time before delivering a punch line or a humorous action. In a serious play, for instance, when a character hears of the death of a relative or friend, it takes time to absorb the shock before responding. Pauses also are effective in drawing attention to a character or in showing that something momentous is about to be said.

Rhythm refers both to the flow of the language and to the matter of picking up cues and changing scenes. Every piece of literature, largely through the author's style, has a certain inherent rhythm which can be ruined by actors who pick up cues either too slowly or too quickly, although the former is much more likely.

---

20. "Sidney Berger, Director," in Jeane Luere, 39.

Pace, timing, and rhythm are all tied closely to mood and emotional pitch.

Technical Rehearsals

By the time the finishing rehearsals end, the production should look as it will during the show's run. Out of necessity, during the usual two or three technical rehearsals the director will devote attention to the technical aspects of the production to the neglect of the actors. If the director has planned well and worked closely with the designers, there shouldn't be much to do, except to help the designers, or, more likely, the various stage technicians, to correct minor details.

Dress Rehearsals

There's an old saying: A bad dress rehearsal means a good opening. This simply is not so. Sometimes there can be a successful opening night despite a poor dress rehearsal, but never because of it. The dress rehearsal is a tryout of the production, much as a Broadway-destined production tries out either at the theatre where it will be presented (in what is termed previews) or out of town.

Usually there are two rehearsals in full costume with all the technical elements. Directors sometimes invite guests so that the actors can become accustomed to playing to an audience. From now on, the director's job technically is finished, unless the play has a long run, as may be the case in professional theatre. Then the director may call rehearsals to correct inconsistencies that have crept into the performance. During long runs, additional rehearsals may be necessary when one actor replaces another. Sometimes the entire cast rehearses with the new actors. At other times, the director, an assistant, or a production stage manager may rehearse the replacements with only certain members of the cast.

Occasionally, directors like to watch and take notes at early performances, then give them to the actors sometime before each succeeding night of the play's run. This is particularly true in community and educational theatre.

Directing in Arena Theatre

Many of the principles of directing are the same for arena theatre as for proscenium, but there are some differences. The director has to pay more attention to small details and subtleties of characterization, because the audience is closer to the action.

Although furniture can be placed in closer approximation of real life on an arena stage than on a proscenium stage, it is both ineffective and monotonous to line the edges of the stage as in a real living room. Some of the furniture, at least, can be centrally placed, and then the actor can play toward the audience rather than toward the center of the stage. Some directors place the furniture at the corners of the arena so that each section of the audience will have a good view of each actor at least part of the time.

The arena stage director also does not have the same control over picturization as in proscenium theatre, since the groupings of characters will be viewed from all sides. Focus is similar in arena theatre to that in proscenium theatre. The actor who is standing is more dominant than the one who is sitting, and the audience pays more attention to the moving actor than to the one who is still. There is an advantage in that there are no weak areas — except, possibly, Center Stage — because only half the audience can see the face of an actor who stands there. The actor who plays off center but faces center is facing more than half the audience. An actor in an aisleway or corner can, just by a turn of the head, face all of the audience.

Body position is of little value in arena staging, since an actor who is open to one part of the audience is closed to another. Similarly, Upstage for some viewers is Downstage for others. Often, the director will designate areas of the stage to correspond to the face of a clock. One area is the twelve o'clock position, one the three o'clock, and so on. The positions remain constant and are referred to in terms of the clock rather than as Down Right or Down Left. Another method is to designate positions according to geographic directions, such as Northeast or South. Both are shown in Figure 7-5 (see page 161).

Spacing is unimportant; an actor separated from the group at one angle appears to be part of it at another. Body positions relate to the other actors and not to the audience, but the actor can move away from or come closer to the other actors and give a sense of psychological closeness or separation.

If the actors keep a few feet of space between each other, the scenes will be opened for all parts of the audience. Most positions are not bad if they are held only briefly. Even subtle changes in movement give the audience the impression of having a better view.

It is easier to block three characters than two because there can be a triangular arrangement. Now most of the viewers will be able to see one actor full front and another in profile. Large groups can be divided into several triangles.

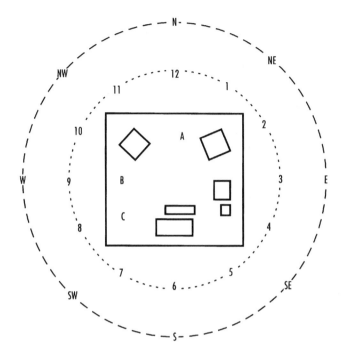

Figure 7-5: An arena stage theatre director establishes stage areas using a clock method or compass directions.

Movement can be less restrained and more natural in an arena, but it should have meaning. Levels, as much as anything, make the placement and composition interesting.

Although most plays can be adapted for arena staging, it may be difficult to present extravagant musicals. Plays with many changes of locale also will be difficult to stage with any appearance of realism.

Directing for the Thrust Stage

The third major type of stage is a thrust stage, which has some of the advantages and disadvantages of the proscenium and of the arena stages.

When working in a thrust stage theatre, a director would have to consider many of the same things in blocking and rehearsing a play as is the case for arena staging. Although a third of the audience faces the wall behind the stage, the other two-thirds face the action from the two sides. Thus, picturization must be handled much as it is in arena theatre.

There can be more background scenery than in arena theatre, although the director and designers must consider that the portion of the audience on either side of the stage would not have a clear view of two-dimensional scenery, such as painted backdrops or flats. On the other hand, there is at least some storage space through the doors behind the stage, and there is not the problem of timing entrances down long aisleways.

Backstage and Behind the Scenes

There are many other people who work backstage in a variety of capacities, some associated directly with the work of the director.

The Dramaturg

Increasingly in the United States, theatres are hiring **dramaturgs**, whose duties vary, depending on the theatre. (Dramaturgs have been used in German theatre since the 1700s.) In some cases, they solicit, read, and even select scripts for production.

In effect, dramaturgs are literary managers of a sort, knowledgeable about the history, genres, and structure of drama. As such, they are available for answering directors' and actors' questions about the period in which a play was written or about its interpretation. Sometimes their duties include educating audiences through lectures, discussions, or articles in the play program.

A dramaturg usually works closely with the director in researching a play's background and in analyzing and interpreting the script.

Being a dramaturg is a very complicated job. I didn't always think so. At first it seemed that a dramaturg was someone who did research for the director or playwright, wrote program notes, ran educational outreach programs, read new scripts, and helped with season planning. These are tasks that define a job description, but they tell us very little about what dramaturgs are. Fundamentally, dramaturgs are facilitators. "To facilitate" means, according to the Oxford English Dictionary, "To render easier the performance of [an action], the attainment of [a result]; ... to promote, help forward [an action or process]." I like this definition of the function of a dramaturg for several reasons. It does not limit the activities a dramaturg can undertake to a few tasks; rather it opens up a field of action ripe with possibilities. It suggests movement toward an end rather than a static state of affairs. It implies a service to an action or process that takes us outside of our self-interests, and that resists self-indulgence. But it also carries with it a strong sense of responsibility and an implied ethic.[21]

According to Dramaturg Winston D. Neutel, dramaturgy involves:

- Reading and assessment of new plays.

- In production, works primarily with director but may also be a resource for actors, designers and technicians.

- Consultation with artistic director on the development of artistic policy and repertoire.

- The supervision of the public pronouncements of the theatre insofar as they reflect its repertoire and aesthetics.

- Preparation of texts for performance. This is the main work of a dramaturg; can include:

  - revising/editing scripts
  - adapting non-theatrical text into a script
  - translation of scripts from other languages
  - advisor for playwrights writing or workshopping a new script
  - liaison between playwright and director

- "Official representative" of audience to the theatre company.

- Writing program notes.

- Writing of mission statements about artistic goals.

- Dramatic editor.

- Distinction is often made between a production dramaturg and literary manager.

  - production dramaturg's duties relate to a specific show

21. John Lutterbie, *Outside Looking In* , http://web.archive.org/web/20030421230336/ http://ws.cc.sunysb.edu/theatrearts/faculty/Outside_Looking_In.htm.

> - a literary manager (or company/resident dramaturg) has ongoing duties within the theatre company, including review and selection of scripts, etc. (as described above).

• Some distinguish, within what I'm calling the work of the production dramaturg, between production dramaturgy and audience dramaturgy.

> - i.e. distinguishing between the work a dramaturg does:
>
> 1. with cast, management and crew of the production — as described above
>
> 2. and in "meeting" the audience, e.g. lobby displays, program notes, study guides, post-show discussions, seminars.

• Dramaturgs, through their written work, leave a detailed documentation of the productions they work on, which can prove quite valuable to those attempting to do research of the production in the future. Otherwise newspaper reviews are often the only lasting documentation.[22]

The Stage Manager

The stage manager usually is considered second in command after the director. The job actually begins two weeks before the rehearsal period begins. Although the stage manager serves as a liaison between the cast/crew and the management, he or she also acts as the director's representative in meetings with the actors and other theatre artists. If necessary, the stage manager takes over rehearsals. Aware of all technical aspects of the production, the stage manager also helps solve any technical problems that come up. In effect, the job involves minor details that otherwise would confront the director.

During the final week of rehearsal, stage managers keep and correlate schedules while informing all those connected to the production of changes and upcoming meetings.

Stage managing is a big responsibility, particularly after opening, when the stage manager "calls the show" — that is, announces cues for scenery shifts, lights, and sound. A stage manager is responsible

---

22. Winston D. Neutel, "A Dramaturg's Tasks," *The Dramaturgy Pages*, http://www.dramaturgy.net/dramaturgy/, 1995-97.

for seeing that the entire production goes as rehearsed and according to schedule, and that the director's wishes are carried out from opening night until the production closes. In other words, stage managing involves seeing that everyone associated with the performance does the job according to plan and on time.

The Production Stage Manager, Assistants, and Other Crew

Some theatres differentiate between the stage manager and the production stage manager. Often the production stage manager arranges rehearsal times, recording sessions, and so on, at regional theatres where several shows are in rehearsal at the same time. For long running productions, he or she sits in the audience to check that the show is going according to plan, both technically and artistically. Although qualified to do so, the production stage manager usually calls a show only in an emergency.

In various theatres, there are other jobs such as production assistant, who works with the director, and casting agent (particularly in Broadway theatre), who chooses several of the most likely people for particular roles so that the director (or sometimes the producer) can make a final selection.

Various theatres have technical directors who supervise building and erecting sets, and, of course, there are various crews who help build scenery and costumes, handle lights, prepare the sound effects, and run the show in production.

The Choreographer

In musical theatre, the choreographer designs and stages the dance numbers and is responsible for rehearsing the dancers. He or she sometimes oversees the movement of the central characters during musical numbers.

The choreographer's job is similar to the director's in that it involves analysis and planning, although individual choreographers approach the job differently.

As part of the planning, a choreographer, particularly for an original show, often has to decide where to include dance numbers. Lee Theodore says that he works "from the literary end of it" absorbing the material and the "dances begin coming from that and the characters."[23]

---

23. Svetlana McLee Grody and Dorothy Daniels Lister, *Conversations with Choreographers*, (Portsmouth, NH: Heinemann, 1996), 15.

According to Tommy Tune:

It's very hard for a director who's not into dance to understand what the elements of dance can do for a show. Directors usually think of it as decorative, crowd-pleasing stuff. But dance can carry forth the story in all sorts of subtle ways. So you look for where the dance might belong, and it's usually not where you think. It's almost always not where the writer thinks it belongs.[24]

Summary

The director, who usually is the first theatre artist involved in bringing a production to life before an audience, has a myriad of duties. In selecting scripts for production, directors need to be able to judge what will be acceptable to potential audiences and what sort of people are likely to attend the productions. A director needs to analyze the script to determine what the writer means and how he or she meant to say it.

There are various types of auditions. The most common are the open audition, where the actors all appear at the same time, and the interview, which is conducted one-on-one between actor and director. Rehearsal periods generally last from four weeks in professional theatre to six weeks in educational and community theatre. There are six stages: reading rehearsals, blocking rehearsals, character and line rehearsals, finishing rehearsals, technical rehearsals, and dress rehearsals.

Many of the principles of directing are the same for arena theatre as proscenium, but there are differences, many involved with the need for detail since the audience generally is closer to the action in an arena theatre.

Dramaturgs serve as literary managers and work closely with the director in researching a play's background and in analyzing and interpreting the script, while the stage manager is second in command to the director and serves as liaison between cast/crew and management. It is this person's duty to see that the entire production continues as rehearsed. A choreographer plans and rehearses dance numbers for musicals. The preparation includes an analysis of the script similar to that done by the actor or director.

---

24. Grody and Dorothy Daniels Lister, 15.

Questions for Discussion

1. If you were in charge of a search committee to find a salaried director for your community theatre, what sort of background would you prefer the person have? Why?
2. In trying to judge what play will draw a good audience, what should a director take into consideration?
3. Besides the audience, what else should the director take into consideration when selecting a play?
4. What is involved in the director's analysis of a script? Why is such an analysis important?
5. What does it mean to determine an overall concept for a production?
6. What are the advantages and disadvantages of the two common types of auditions. If you were a director, which do you think you would prefer? Why?
7. What are the goals of each of the six types of rehearsal?
8. What are the major differences between directing in a proscenium theatre and an open stage theatre?

Chapter 8
THE DESIGNERS AND SUPPORTING ARTISTS

The designers are as responsible as the director for making a dramatic presentation appropriate and pleasing. Even when the director has definite ideas about how setting or lights should be handled, or how costumes or makeup should appear, the designers add their own personalities, their way of viewing the world, to the production.

Because of this, it's important to establish a good working relationship beginning with a free exchange where director and designers should be open to one another's thoughts and ideas. Although designers sometimes prepare rough sketches or images ahead of time to illustrate their ideas and generate discussion, they introduce more concrete concepts at later meetings, often as a result of these discussions.

Set designer Kevin Rigdon feels that "it is vital not to let the director come to early discussions and say, 'This is what I want to do.' That is treating the designer as a draftsman." A better approach would be for a director to discuss the play and allow the designer to be creative.

Rigdon tells of a time "a director brought his own design materials to a meeting and presented them; but after Rigdon explained his own concepts, the director swept all his own materials off onto the floor and accepted the designer's plans instead."[1]

Scene designer Michael Olich says he believes "absolutely" in collaboration. "It's the drug, the hook that has made me an addict of the theatre ... As frustrating as communication can be at times, it's also ecstatically energizing when ideas that come from outside of you draw you outside of yourself as well."[2]

1. Notes from Lecture by Set Designer Kevin Rigdon in Luere, Jeane and Sidney Berger, *The Theatre Team: Playwright, Producer, Director, Designers and Actors,* (Westport, CT: Greenwood Press, 1998), 120-122.
2. Michael Olich, "A Strong Conceptual Hit," from "And Another Thing: Interviews with Four Designers Who Also ", *American Theatre,* October 1993, 40.

Professor and designer Geoffrey M. Eroe says:

As a professional designer ... here and abroad, I would state the designer is almost singularly responsible for bringing visual substance to the words and dreams of the playwright. The most effective collaborations are those in which the director indeed wants the designer(s) to bring their own original ideas and sketches to the first production meeting. From this point the collaborative process begins with the director's response to the proposed designs.[3]

The Scene Designer

One of the collaborators is the scene designer, whose work must be as aesthetic as that of a painter and as practical as that of an architect. At the same time, the scene designer's work is different from either of these fine arts because it is not complete in itself. After the setting is constructed, it requires the actors, the costumes, the lights, the makeup, and the properties to complete the picture. Throughout the production, this picture changes continuously as the actors move and the lights come up or fade.

The Scene Designer's Background

To design a practical and aesthetically pleasing set to match a variety of styles and historical periods, a designer needs training, experience, and talent in many different areas. For instance, there is a big difference between constructing an apartment on-stage and constructing an apartment building. Scene designers know how to adapt architectural design to a theatre production. They know enough about stage carpentry to design a set that can be built without major difficulty. They plan so that scenery can shift quickly and quietly. This means that they build both illusion and practicality into their designs so that the settings elicit certain emotional responses from the audience at the same time that they are easily functional.

Scene designers need to be acquainted with the principles of lighting and know how light will affect their sets. They should know the emotional impact of various colors, textures, and masses. They must be familiar with the materials used in set construction and recognize which of these are best for particular effects.

Of course, they also should be acquainted with interior decorating in order to adapt various decors to the requirements of

---

3. Geoffrey M. Eroe, Phoenix College, November 6, 1998.

the stage. Then they must be able to visualize suitable furniture, and how this furniture will modify the stage picture. Designers must be familiar with current styles and also know where to research period furniture and architecture.

Designers should be familiar with various theatrical styles from expressionism to realism and know how each of these can reinforce the director's concept or vision. According to Francis Reed, "Choice of an appropriate style is the key decision facing any production team."[4] Once the style is discovered, it must be followed by all the designers working on the production.

Designer Donald Oenslager says, "Wherever he works, the designer is an artist and craftsman who translates the world around him into the theatrical terms of the stage."[5]

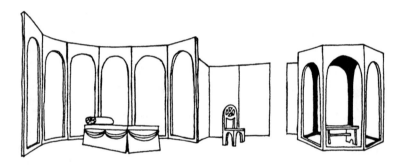

Figure 8-1: Drawing of stage set for Henry's Chamber from *Lion in Winter.*

4. Francis Reid, *Designing for the Theatre*, 2nd ed., (New York: Theatre Arts Books/Routledge, 1996), 29.

5. Donald Oenslager, *Scenery Then and Now*, (New York: W. W. Norton & Company, 1936), 11.

Functions of Scene Design

Beyond providing a channel for the playwright's message, the setting helps convey the theme and provides information essential to the understanding of the play. It fulfills the director's interpretation; provides an environment, mood, and playable area for the actor; remains faithful to the playwright's style; and complements the work of all the other designers.

The design provides a framework for the action and a **focal point**, where the audience's attention is directed. Even though the focal point may change from scene to scene, every member of the audience must have an undistorted view of each. For example, one scene may take place in a bedroom and another in the kitchen. The focus may be provided in part by lighting, but the designer makes each location — bedroom or kitchen — interesting and easily seen from any part of the audience.

A setting must be designed for easy use by the actors. For instance, treads on steps in a set usually are wider than those in a house so the actor can concentrate on action and character rather than on where to step.

The setting presents an aesthetically pleasing image, which, however, should not be so elaborate that it calls undue attention to itself. It should provide exposition for the audience. As Designer Kyle Chepulis says, "You've got to make the audience, and how they interact with the space, as important as what is on-stage."[6] The set can also locate time and place. The style of architecture and the furnishings can indicate the historical period and whether the play takes place in an upper class home or in an office. For instance, Tony Cucuzzella's design for Victor Herbert's *The Red Mill*, produced in the mid-1990s by the San Diego Comic Opera Company, immediately showed the audience that both the hotel and the mill were in advanced disrepair. The arms of the windmill were tattered; pieces of the hotel kept falling off throughout the performance. The architecture told the audience that they were in another country, probably Holland, and that the time was the past — as seen in the styles of the buildings. At the same time, in the background, a white cloud was projected onto a blue cyclorama, suggesting that although the buildings were falling apart, the mood was still lighthearted.

6. Kyle Chepulis, Interviewed by Jonathan Shandell, "On Site," *Theater* (Volume 29, Number 2, 1999), 131.

Figure 8-2: Symmetrical (top) and asymmetrical (bottom) stage sets.

Of course, providing exposition does not mean that the setting has to appear as if it is an actual environment. Depending on the type and style of the play, it can be more a suggestion of environment than a representation.

Balance and Harmony

The set should be balanced, either symmetrically or asymmetrically. **Symmetrical balance** means that the left half contains exactly the same elements as the right half. Scene designers often use symmetry for staging Greek plays.

Asymmetrical balance is achieved through mass, color, and shape that differ from one side of the stage to the other. If, for instance, a huge gray brick wall were facing front at Stage Left, another object or combination of objects should go at Stage Right to counterbalance the feeling of heaviness. The designer might use dark colors, a grouping of heavy furniture, or platforms to achieve the counterbalance.

A well-designed setting should have harmony and balance. Each element should appear to belong, to be consistent. In Kaufman and Hart's *You Can't Take It with You*, each member of the household has a separate interest, such as writing, dancing, or making firecrackers, and these interests show up in a diversity of elements in the set. Although diverse, the mixture contributes to the theme of nonconformity, which provides harmony to the production as a whole. On the other hand, if a person were to design a setting for

Wilder's *Our Town* using the bare stage with only a ladder to represent the second story of the Gibbses' house and sawhorses and a plank to represent a soda fountain, but then constructed a box set and placed actual furniture in the Webb household, the set would not have harmony.

Colors and shapes help convey the style and genre. Curved lines and shapes, for instance, can convey lightness or gracefulness, whereas straight, angular shapes can convey austerity or somberness.

A designer often may exaggerate an element of the setting to point up an aspect of the play. For instance, set pieces for a farce may be two-dimensional like the characters. In showing the characters' tastes, interests, hobbies, and financial status, the set becomes almost a character in itself.

Planning a Setting

The scene designer's work begins with a study and analysis of the script, first to determine the mood and theme. Then come the practical questions: How many doorways are needed? Where do they lead? Are windows, fireplaces, or levels needed? How can the set accommodate or add to the effectiveness of the action? A designer may even have to consider special needs, as when a character in a wheelchair is played by a handicapped actor. Such a situation occurred with the play *Pyretown* presented in Rochester.

> We brainstormed a variety of options and ultimately settled on one that was startlingly simple: We removed the front three feet of the stage and built a ramp that ran transverse to the proscenium, painted and textured to match the rest of the set. The ramp was not just a practical means of egress; it became an aesthetic emblematic aspect of the design.[7]

Designer David Jenkins likes to read a script "as early as possible — and then let the ideas wash over [him]."

> You can read the script and then, say, a week later you really start to work on it. That week that you waited, somewhere you're walking down the street, or you're lying in bed, trying to go to bed at night, your thoughts start, and you are actively beginning to work then.[8]

7. Marge Betley, "How Geva Got Harry On-stage," *American Theatre*, (April 2004), 60.

8. Arvid F. Sponberg, "David Jenkins, Scene Designer," *Broadway Talks: What Professionals Think About Commercial Theater in America*, (New York: Greenwood Press, 1991), 119.

Next, the designer often researches building architecture, both historically and geographically, since a type of structure seen in one country or even one part of a country may never have been erected in another.

Once they have ideas in mind, designers prepare sketches for the director. Sometimes directors have definite ideas about the setting; at other times they give the designer a freehand. In either case the director sees to it that the proposed design meshes with the work of the other theatre artists.

After the director approves the preliminary sketches, the designer prepares more exact plans for the construction of the set. A **floor plan** (also called a *ground plan*) of the setting as viewed from above shows how the set fits the stage. Sometimes the designer draws several floor plans, showing a shifting of furniture, so that the director can visualize where to place the actors. Some designers use storyboards that show the set lighted from different angles, for instance, or with furniture arranged differently for different scenes. Although the designer may make a variety of drawings for different purposes, the director usually needs to see only the floor plan, sketches, or sometimes a model of the finished set.

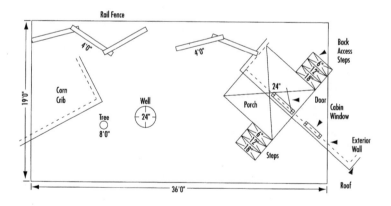

Figure 8-3: This floor plan shows a scale drawing of the exterior setting for a production of Jack Kirkland's *Tobacco Road* (1/4 inch equals 1 foot).

Both the floor plans and model are on a scale of one-fourth inch (or occasionally one-half inch) to the foot. Then the designer may draft elevations, showing the height of platforms, steps, other three-dimensional shapes, and flats. Often the designer prepares a sectional view of objects to show the method of construction, or isometric views that show an object from the corner and slightly above to give the builders a clear understanding of the platform or figure. In fact there are many categories of drawings from small sketches showing initial ideas to completed plans. Copies of the different drawings go to the director, the technical director, the stage manager, and the head of the construction crew.

After the planning, the scene designer's duties differ in various types of theatres. Particularly in educational and community theatres, the designer chooses the furniture and set dressings and supervises the set construction and scene painting.

Despite intensive training, the designer, like the actor, is never assured of success.

The Lighting Designer

Ultimately the lighting designer must be an artist! He must understand style, composition, balance, esthetics, and human emotions. He must also understand the science of light, optics, vision, the psychology of perception, and lighting technology. Using these tools the lighting designer must learn to think, feel, and create with his heart.[9]

When electric lights first came into use in the theatre, they simply illuminated the stage to enable the spectators to see the action. Modern lighting, like scenery, enhances the total production.

Oftentimes the quality of the light tells the story; the time of day, the weather, whether sun is streaming through the window. It can also help you appreciate what the actor is feeling, what the playwright wants you to feel. Any engineer can put a spot on someone. Lighting is not about function. It's much more about the mood and the emotion that the playwright and the director are trying to create. Our job is to support their poetic direction.[10]

9. Bill Williams, "Part I–An Introduction to Stage Lighting," *Stage Lighting Design*, 2nd ed., 1997-1999, http://www.mts.net/~william5/sld/sld-100.htm.

10. Jules Fisher quoted in Myrna Katz Frommer and Harvey Frommer, eds., *It Happened on Broadway: An Oral History of the Great White Way*, (New York: Harcourt, Brace & Company, 1998), 244.

There are two categories of stage lighting: general and specific. **General lighting** provides a well-lighted performance area. **Specific lighting** provides special effects, enhancing the playwright's message through intensity and color.

Dim lights can suggest a foreboding, mysterious atmosphere, whereas bright lights often mean "lightness" in treatment of subject matter. There are exceptions, however. Sledgehammer Theatre's production of Bertolt Brecht's *Drums in the Night*, presented in San Diego in 1991, focused "painfully bright" lights on the audience deliberately to make the spectators uncomfortable.

Functions of Lighting

Lighting complements the other areas of design and helps to convey the mood and message of the play. It provides **selective visibility**. Often only certain areas of the set are important to the action. In such cases, the lights can provide a point of focus by fading to black on the areas to be de-emphasized and coming up on the important areas. Large follow spots sometimes are used (particularly in musicals) to focus on the star performer.

Lighting can provide exposition by showing time and place. A bright light can indicate midday in a warm climate. Blazing chandeliers can indicate night time in a wealthy household.

Of course, lighting, like scenery, is a symbol. It suggests; then it is up to the audience to use imagination. For example, a common table lamp on-stage would not provide enough illumination. Its light must be intensified, usually by focusing additional overhead lighting on the lamp.

Another function of lighting is to reveal or define mass and form. Properly lighted, a papier-mâché rock can become real for the audience. Lighting also contributes to and complements the style of the production.

Lighting Components

Lighting consists of two components: a **source** and a **system of control**. The source is the lighting instruments. The two major kinds are **floodlights**, which are nonfocusable and have no lens, and **spotlights** (spots), which can be focused and usually do have a lens. Floodlights usually are for general illumination, such as for lighting backdrops, whereas the various types of spots are for specific illumination.

Spots come in various sizes and can focus from a very small area to a large one. Most have a metal frame into which color filters or transparencies can be placed to add color and thus emotional effect to the lighted area.

One of the most common spots is a **Fresnel** [frey-nel'] which provides a circular or oval area of light. The lens that covers the lamp (bulb) softens the edge of light so that it's difficult to define exactly where the lighted area ends. An advantage is that this same softness blends in with light from other instruments to provide a sense of continuity or evenness.

Another type of spotlight is the **ellipsoidal reflector**, which is brighter than a Fresnel and more controllable. It has a framing device that allows the area the light strikes to be specific. The edge, unlike that of the Fresnel, is exact. It can provide a contrast from intense brightness to total darkness with no "spill" into the unlighted area.

Another common source of illumination is the **striplight**, a long, troughlike instrument with lights a few inches apart along the length of the trough. Often, strips light the cyclorama, or circular curtain surrounding the sides and rear of the acting area in exterior scenes, providing the illusion of distance.

There are a variety of other instruments, which are used less frequently. One is the **beam projector**, which casts a narrow, intense light used, for instance, to simulate sunbeams. In effect, it is a tiny version of searchlights — those associated with shopping mall openings or film premieres in earlier eras, and which cast their rotating beams up into a night sky.

Becoming much more common are color scrollers or moveable lights (See page 202).

The control system is the **dimmer board** (or switchboard) — the panel from which the lights are operated. It is the "heart of every lighting installation." Primarily by means of dimmer controls, stage lighting is balanced to achieve the desired pictorial effect. All control boards provide this facility with various degrees of sophistication. But some instruments now allow "automated" remote control of focus and color.[11]

The control system or dimmer board allows the lighting technician to dim from one area to another and to control both the intensity of the light and the point of origination. It also can provide control over color. For example, if a play were to progress from noon to evening, the lighting technician could change the direction of the light by switching from one set of instruments to another. Various colors of filters could indicate increasing darkness.

---

11. Richard Pilbrow, *Stage Lighting Design*, (New York: Design Press, 1997), 373.

Virtually all newer boards are computer controlled, that is, they keep a record of each change, and so can come up with any combination or "cue" whenever necessary and can maintain the combination for as long or as short a time as needed. Lighting designer David Hays defines a cue as "the pace and orchestration of the shifting light."

> Do we want the audience to ponder a certain line? Should we therefore leave a glow on that actor's face as we fade? But is it the actor pondering the line, or the audience? Perhaps a simple pause before the next scene, without featuring the actor, is best. Or does energy and content demand a quick pickup on new entrants even as the old scene fades?[12]

Planning the Lighting

"The first rule of stage lighting," Designer Bill Williams says, "is ... there aren't any."[13]

> Since the lighting always has to be done after everything else, the lighting designer has to become used to working at any hour. All too often he will find himself focusing his lamps at the end of a long day, even perhaps at four o'clock in the morning. After hours on his feet, he may have to start lighting the production, beginning the really creative work, in a dirty, hungry, and exhausted state.[14]

People often think of the lighting designer as an expert electrician rather than as an artist. Certainly, designers know a great deal about electricity, and many of them do have an electrician's license. In addition, however, they are as creative and imaginative as the other theatre artists, and they possess a general knowledge of all areas of theatre production.

Lighting designers work closely with the director and the other designers to provide a cohesive image for the audience and to convey the mood of the play. They analyze the script to determine the source of light for each scene and plan how to indicate time, place, and even season. At the same time, they make certain that the lighting does not call attention to itself.

---

12. David Hays, *Light on the Subject: Stage Lighting for Directors and Actors and the Rest of Us*, (New York: Limelight Editions, 1989), 61.
13. Bill Williams, Part I, *Stage Lighting Design*, http://www.mts.net/~william5/sld/sld-200.htm, 1997-99.
14. Pilbrow, 49.

A lighting concept may seem obvious when a huge transformation is heaped on to a play. "Let's do it as if we've just been swallowed by a whale!" Hold it — is that a concept or just a locale? If the play is *Hay Fever* you've only switched it to a quirky set. Does it really change what happens between the actors? That's what the lighting designer must question. In this whale — are the characters trapped forever? Is there hope — light at the end of the gullet? Is there light only when the whale yawns, and it comes in striped by baleen strips like vertical Venetian blinds? Do we have flashlights with expiring batteries? Does an inrush of phosphorescent organisms supply us with a useful glow?

Silly, but not necessarily so if the play is *Pinocchio*, where Father Gepetto has come to the end of the world, the pit of despair, the belly of the beast. The symbol of the whale is right and profound. Perhaps his son comes to him as his candle, the shred of his remaining light, is used up and about to flicker out. Now you can get your teeth into it.[15]

Lighting designers understand where to hang lights for the best effect. They know that an actor or a set piece is lighted from various angles to appear three-dimensional. They know the psychological effects of lighting. For instance, people are more alert in high-intensity lighting, which the designer could use for a fast-moving comedy. At the same time the designers recognize that many quick changes in lighting tire an audience.

It is not widely appreciated that lighting needs framework, structure. Once this basic skeleton exists, it can then be fleshed out in any number of ways; but unless the structure is complete, the lighting design won't have integrity or depth. A series of exciting "looks" may be interesting, but they won't necessarily communicate an idea about the play. *Waiting for Godot*, for example, might have a simple structure of A, B, A, B (day, night, day, night). Another shape, say, one in which the light changes with the emotional state of the characters, would give a vastly different emphasis.[16]

15. Hays, 87 and 89.
16. Stephen Strawbridge, "Listening to Light," *American Theatre*, January 2003, 40.

The designer plans to control four aspects of lighting: **color, intensity, movement,** and **distribution.** Warmer colors, such as yellow to amber shades, generally are used in comedies, cooler colors in serious plays. For maximum visibility, yellow is best, whereas orange and red tend to inhibit visibility, as do blue and green. Colored light most often is used because white light glares and hurts the eyes.

The designer can plan color in lighting symbolically, but always in conjunction with the other elements of design. For example, focusing a red or pink hue on an actor could indicate a state of health, or it could be associated with shame, embarrassment, or passion. The color in lighting is directly related to the color of the other scenic elements. Most often a designer avoids green light, except for an eerie effect, because it suggests an unearthly or ghostlike quality. Mixtures of color in makeup, costuming, and lighting also can produce undesirable effects if the lighting designer does not take the other visual elements into consideration. "The designer should use strong color only with the greatest care, remembering that the first function of lighting is selective visibility. Under normal circumstances an actor cannot be considered truly visible if he has a bright green face."[17]

Overall, the designer is responsible for the design and also for overseeing the installation and operation of the lights.

The Lighting Plot

Lighting does not remain static, but becomes a new design with each movement of an actor or each change in intensity or focus.

Once designers determine what is needed to light a set, they make a lighting plot, a ground plan drawn to scale that shows a mixture of general and specific lighting for illumination and shadow, and an instrument schedule, which includes such information as the instruments to use (type, size, wattage, color, and dimmer connection), where to hang them, and where to focus them. They take a floor plan of the set and draw in the location of each instrument and the area the light will hit. In a proscenium theatre, the acting area most often is lighted from overhead, from the back, and from instruments placed somewhere in the auditorium. Designers also draw a lighting sectional which shows a composite side view of the location of the instruments and the set.

---

17. Pilbrow, 89.

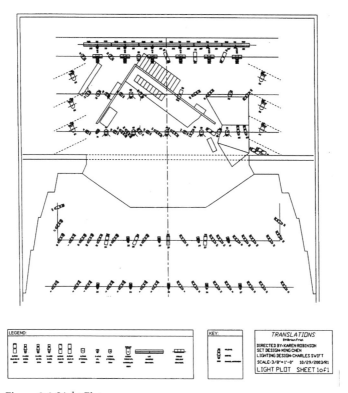

LEGEND:

KEY:

TRANSLATIONS
DIRECTED BY: KAREN ROBINSON
SET DESIGN MING CHEN
LIGHTING DESIGN CHARLES SWIFT
SCALE: 3/8" = 1'-0"   10/29/2003/R1
LIGHT PLOT   SHEET 1of 1

Figure 8-4: Light Plot.

The designer divides the stage into areas, using a minimum of two instruments for specific illumination in each area. Two or more are needed to eliminate long shadows and to light each side of the actor or set piece. The designer also prepares a list of the lighting cues, so the technician knows exactly what to change and when. These cues involve changes in intensity, movement, color, and/or distribution, indicating such things as differences in mood or in time and place. Once the lighting is set the way it will remain throughout the production, the designer's job in effect is finished, except that in many community theaters, for instance, he or she may be in charge of the lighting crew.

The lighting and scene designers work closely together since what each does strongly affects the other. Often, in fact, the same person serves both functions.

The designer works with various others besides the director, as seen in the following:

1. THE PRODUCER & DIRECTOR

Usually, it is the PRODUCER that is responsible for all aspects of a professional stage production. The DIRECTOR is usually engaged by the Producer. The Producer will usually impose restrictions on the Director, who must work with available time, budgets and resources.

2. THE DESIGNERS

The DESIGNERS (Set, Costume, Lighting, and Sound) are generally selected by the Director, to provide a cohesive team able to work well together on a particular production. Sometimes the Designers may be selected by the Producer, however, usually with the Director's approval.

3. THE LIGHTING DESIGNER

The LIGHTING DESIGNER is responsible for the design of all production lighting (and usually, special effects). This designer will prepare a lighting design, consisting of drawings and schedules and all information necessary for the lighting crews to fully install and connect all equipment. Further the lighting designer will supervise and direct all the artistic elements of the lighting design up until the opening of the production.

4. THE HEAD ELECTRICIAN

The HEAD ELECTRICIAN, (sometimes Master or Chief Electrician) heads and supervises the lighting crews during the set-up and "running" of a production. The Head Electrician will generally also run the lighting control console for each performance.

5. THE PRODUCTION ELECTRICIAN

A PRODUCTION ELECTRICIAN is sometimes engaged by the Producer, to facilitate the lighting set-up. This individual will assist with the ordering of all lighting equipment, coordination of crews and budgets, and provide general problem solving, up until "opening night."

6. THE LIGHTING CREW

The LIGHTING CREW is under the supervision of the Head Electrician. Under his direction, they are responsible for the installation, hanging, cabling, plugging, and coloring of all equipment. During the "focus," they are responsible for the precise aiming and adjustment of all fixtures, as directed by the lighting designer.

7. THE RUNNING CREW
The RUNNING CREW is responsible for the nightly operation of all production lighting. The Head Electrician will usually operate the lighting console, while the Running Crew electricians are usually responsible for followspot, projection, or special effect operation. It is also the running crew (and Head Electrician) that generally perform any lighting related maintenance, during the run of the production.[18]

The Costume Designer

Costuming in a play, like clothing in real life, conveys a lot of information, such as the character's occupation. An actor playing a businessman wears a different outfit than does an actor playing a Roman Catholic priest. Clothing also reveals personality. A formal person wears different clothing than an easygoing person. Costuming also can indicate how a character feels. In everyday life people often wear colorful clothing when they are in a positive mood. Conversely, a person who feels depressed is likely to dress in drab colors. Each person develops an individual style. One person may prefer to wear jeans and a T-shirt for relaxed occasions, while another feels comfortable only in dress slacks and a shirt or blouse that buttons. We associate each of these styles with different personalities.

A woman with dangling bracelets probably would be more outgoing than one with little or no jewelry. There is the old cliché of wearing a red carnation to be recognized. Most people don't wear red carnations, but many people do choose a distinctive touch — bow ties, big earrings, or a cowboy hat, for example. Such features in a costume tell us about the character's self-image.

Costumes can also tell the audience many things about a character's situation. If an actor entered wearing a tennis outfit, a playgoer might assume several things: the character plans to play tennis or has just finished playing tennis; he is athletic and competitive; he has free time; and he wants exercise.

---

18. Bill Williams, "Professional Lighting Procedure," *Stage Lighting Design,* 2nd ed. http://www.mrs.net/~william5/sid.htm, 1997-1999, pp. 1-2.

Costuming for the stage conveys the same sorts of messages as everyday clothing, but the effect is heightened. Of all the scenic elements, costuming and makeup provide the strongest clues to character. They are the most personal elements of design, and the audience perceives the character, costume, and makeup as a unity.

The designer takes into consideration the character and the way the actor is playing the character. In turn, the actor may be influenced by the costume to play a certain way. For instance, an 1880s dress suit may help an actor feel more completely the formality of the role.

The costume is that facet of the design that most identifies and supports the character, and thus, like the actor's gestures and movement on a vast stage, and like the oversized living room that is part of the set, the costumes often must be bigger than life to project personality and character to the audience. Generally, the more exaggerated the style of the production, the more exaggerated the costumes.

At the same time, a costume should give the actor freedom of movement ... unlike actual clothing worn in various historical periods.

Designing the Costumes

If you do a certain amount of work on your own before consulting with the director then the process starts with the script. I tend to do a certain amount of my own work before I go into a first meeting. It is important to be open minded in your first meeting with a director but I like to be well-prepared for that meeting because sometimes that time with your director can be limited. At the time of that first meeting, I will have read the play several times and from different points of view. I might read the play once to just check how many costume changes there are. I will read it again to make a prop list. I will read it again to analyze where the entrances and exits are and also to imagine where the furniture will be. It's difficult to concentrate on all of these things in one reading so I go through these processes in separate readings.

Once you have that under your belt, depending on the period of the production, I guess I start to do visual research based on my response to the text. Depending on where and when I might choose to look at photography of the period or I might choose to look at paintings or I might just look at history books and look for thematic influences.[19]

* * * * * * * * * *

I have two approaches and it depends which one has kicked off. I either will start drawing it and never think about color, think about character, think about design, think about you know, blocking all the scenes ... seeing what the look is, and then going in and carving it out. I may start with the leading lady. I may leave her till the very last. Just depends how the show hooks into me ... Then I will go back and I will palette the whole show. And I have thousands of five by three cards with fabrics stapled onto them that I make my palette out of. I go right into the fabric ...

If I start with, let's say, the overall color scheme, I will do that entire show, and if I'm working with a director who can abstract himself enough to understand — to look at the colors and see, I will share it with him. Try to. It's very hard to do, because it's like abstract painting. I'm painting with fabric. And then I will draw the show.[20]

The costume designer has to have a specialized background and a flair for style — not only the style of the character, but the style of the actor playing the part. What one actor feels comfortable wearing could inhibit another. The actor should feel at ease with the costume, both in characterization and in appearance. The designer keeps in mind what actions the actor will be performing, and whether a particular design will aid or hinder these movements. A gown that is appropriate for the straight play *The Importance of Being Earnest* might not work for the musical version *Earnest in Love*; yet both costumes must suit the historical period and the status of the character.

A designer keeps in mind the character's motives and personality. When we watch old Hollywood westerns, we can tell immediately who is the "good guy" and the "bad guy" by the color of their hats and horses. Stage costuming usually is not so blatant in its symbolism, but tries subtly to convey mood and personality. Often the audience is not even conscious of the design.

---

19. "Interview with Christina Poddubiuk," National Arts Centre, *ArtsAlive.ca*, October 16, 2002, http://artsalive.ca/en/eth/index.html.
20. Sponberg, "Patricia Zipprodt, Costume Designer," *Broadway Talks*, 110–111.

Figure 8-5: Design of a basic Hebrew tunic costume.

Like the other elements, costuming must be consistent with the overall concept of the play. There should be no incongruity of character — a conservatively dressed character, for instance, wearing gaudy jewelry (unless the playwright means for the character to be inconsistent).

> Any designer's job would be to approach the director and point out the clues in the story that affect your clothing of her in the performance. Now, the director could say to you as the designer, "I don't care; I want Blanche [in Tennessee Williams's *A Streetcar Named Desire*] to look like a street hooker, to look like a slut, to look like someone down on her luck and insane." Your job, if you continue to accept this contract, would then be to show the director the effect of his choice ... perhaps in a sketch or photograph, so that he could see how his idea would appear on-stage to an audience. However, you would also continue to show how you believe Blanche should look — e.g., like a traveling, sensuous, very womanly schoolteacher who is trying desperately to keep her life together despite the fact that she is a mess.[21]

---

21. Claremarie Verheyen in Luere, Jeane and Sidney Berger, *The Theatre Team: Playwright, Producer, Director, Designers and Actors*, (Westport, CT: Greenwood Press, 1998), 116.

The designer has to be aware of what a color usually signifies. Just as red light tells us any number of things, so can red in costuming.

Color also serves as a point of focus. Although all the dancers in a musical are performing the same step, the lead dancer is emphasized through costuming that differs in color or style from that of the chorus. Color and style help identify groups as well as individuals. Just as opposing basketball teams wear different colored jerseys, so do opposing sides in a play: The Sharks, one of the street gangs in *West Side Story*, dress differently from the Jets.

In many ways the costume designer's analysis of the script is similar to a director's or an actor's. Among the questions the designer asks are:

1. When and where does the action occur? Let's say it's 1888. But is the location New York or Russia? And is it a rural or metropolitan area?
2. What is the economic status of the characters? Are they blue-collar workers or business people?
3. What is the season and the time of day? Does the action take place largely indoors or out? If outdoors, is it late fall or the middle of July? What are the characters doing?
4. What are the characters like, and how does this influence their dress?

There are many ways to conduct research into period costumes — museums, newspapers and periodicals on microfilm, private collections of period clothing, and so forth. In addition, there are many books that treat fashion through the ages, such as Doreen Yarwood's *Fashion in the Western World, 1500–1990*. Some that focus on costuming tell how to adapt and then build period costumes for the stage.

A costume designer may be required to devise any type of clothing from any historical period, even though many times it often is impractical to duplicate period clothing exactly. In past periods, women's costumes often were cumbersome and difficult to change. In the theatre, quick changes often are required, so tearaway seams, snaps, and zippers are used. Fake furs take the place of heavy and hot real furs.

The costume designer meets with the director before designing a show. Together, they work out an overall concept to avoid a clash of colors and styles from one type of design to another. Although costuming complements the other areas of design, it also provides contrast. An actor wearing light blue clothing in front of a light blue wall would seem to fade into the background.

Also, the designer has a knowledge of texture and fabric. From a distance and under light, inexpensive fabric sometimes appears costly. The costumer also recognizes that different fabrics or textures drape or hang differently. Stiff fabric tends to be more angular and severe, and possibly would be better suited for a serious play or a formal character than would a clinging fabric.

The costume designer knows how a fabric will flow or cling as the performer moves. Properly designed costumes can help an actor to move in character. In the musical *Sugar* (The comparable film is *Some Like It Hot*), Joe and Jerry dress as women and join an all-girl band to escape pursuing gangsters. Because the play takes place in the thirties, the two "girls" wear spiked heels. The heels help them take shorter, mincing steps.

The Makeup Designer

Like costuming, makeup aids the actors in their portrayal of character and helps them "feel" the part. It also helps identify the characters for an audience.

There are three types or categories of makeup: straight, character, and stylized.

Straight makeup enhances or projects an actor's natural features. Under theatrical lighting a person's face tends to "wash out," so straight makeup brings out the actors' features more clearly.

Straight makeup begins with the application of a base or foundation, often redder in hue than normal skin color to compensate for the bright lights. The only considerations are that the makeup should be consistent with the actor's natural complexion and coloring and with the character. In earlier periods, grease paint was used for the foundation; now, however, the foundation is almost always water-based and is much the same as everyday street makeup.

After the base is applied, features of the actor's face may be highlighted or emphasized. Eyebrows usually are darkened, as are the eyelashes and rims of the eyes. Straight makeup is completed with a touch of rouge to the cheeks and lips.

Character makeup is used to alter appearance. An example is to make a person appear older. Then there are additional steps, such as adding wrinkles, after a base is applied. Character makeup also includes such things as fake scars or "beauty marks," or, as in *Cyrano de Bergerac*, a longer nose. Often, crepe hair is glued to the

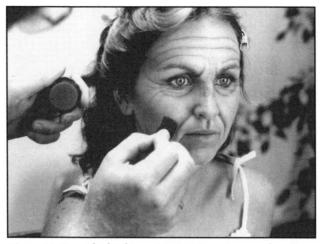

Figure 8-6: Use of highlights and dark makeup to age a character.

face to represent beards or moustaches.

Facial features can be made more prominent through the use of highlighting, or adding a touch of white. This can make eyes appear less sunken or a nose appear larger. The use of brown or black makeup, on the other hand, makes features seem to recede. It can make cheeks or eyes hollow, expressing illness or fatigue.

The face can also be changed through the use of latex, a sort of rubber that the makeup artist can build up on an actor's chin or cheekbones, for instance.

Stylized makeup, similar to character makeup in that it alters a character's appearance, also is nearly always planned by a makeup designer so that it meshes with the overall production style. This would be the case for the musical *Cats*, in which all the characters are cats. Other examples with which you may be familiar are the different alien beings in the various *Star Trek* movies and television series.

Planning the Makeup

Makeup designers, like the other designers, are acquainted with the theory of color and its symbolism. They know how each type of makeup will look under lights of a certain color. For instance, blue light will make rouge or lipstick appear black.

For any special needs, designers may prepare schematics — outlines of the head with the face divided into areas and planes.

They use the schematics to indicate the color and special features to apply to each area. Also, it may be necessary to change a character's makeup during the course of the play to correspond with different physical and emotional states.

The Property Master

Another theatrical artist is the property master, who analyzes the script to understand the style, type, and number of properties needed.

Next to the actor, properties and set dressings are among the most important physical elements on the stage. These are the objects actors use during the performance: the furniture they sit on, the articles they carry and handle, and the objects that decorate the space.[22]

The prop master and crew have the responsibility of determining, obtaining, and caring for all the properties of a production. Once the show closes, they are responsible for returning any borrowed or rented articles.

According to Broadway property master Abe Morrison:

The director tells you what he needs, the designer says how it should look, and the actor tells you how it should feel. Then the producer tells you how much you can pay for it. The prop person tries to please all of them.[23]

The work begins with the property master making a list of all the props. Next to be determined is whether they can be procured and used as is, whether they need to be modified or reconstructed, or whether they have to be built.

The property master then determines where to get the props — theatre storage, area businesses, other area theatres, and so on. During the run of the show the crew needs to see that the props are where they should be for access by the actors, and that they are in good repair.

There are three overall categories of props: set props, set dressing or ornamentation, and hand props. **Set props** include anything that stands within the set, such as furniture, trees, rocks, or, depending on the technical director's interpretation, even small

---

22. Harvey Sweet, *Handbook of Scenery, Properties, and Lighting, Vol I, Scenery and Props*, 2nd ed., (Boston: Allyn and Bacon, 1995), 220.

23. Jonathan Mandell, "Backstage at 'Journey.' A Diet Coke Distillery," *The New York Times*, June 1, 2003, http://www.nytimes.com/.

platforms. **Set dressing** includes wall fixtures, paintings, plaques, vases, and figurines. **Hand props** are those objects an actor either carries on-stage or handles while there. Often, the scene designer will choose the set dressing and sometimes the set props to make sure they are consistent with the overall design. At other times, the scene designer and property master work together in coordinating this aspect of the production.

Some productions require little in the way of props, while others list hundreds of items. For many shows the property master has to research historical items and build substitutes that appear accurate. More often, however, it's simply a matter of deciding what is needed and buying or borrowing it.

Properties are important for a number of reasons:

1. They add to a production's authenticity and/or style. An example is period furniture.
2. They augment characterization. Such things as constantly working on a partially knit sweater or twirling a cigar can go a long way in delineating personality.
3. They provide visual effects. The walls of a living room filled with paintings by Brueghel say something different about the occupant than do paintings by Pollock.

Although acting editions of previously produced scripts contain lists of properties by act and scene, for previously unpublished or unproduced shows the property master has no recourse except to go through the script carefully to determine all the properties needed.

In much the same manner as the lighting or costume designer, the property master makes plots. One of these lists where props are initially placed. Hand props may be placed, as required by the script, either on-stage or off-stage for actors to pick up and use; another shows how they are to be shifted during blackouts or intermissions.

Similar to the costumer, the property master often needs to do historical research, using many of the same facilities — museums, libraries, published historical material, and so on.

The Audio Designer

In recent times, sound for theatre is much more than ringing phones and doorbells. Now there often is a "soundscape" to do such things as provide exposition, set mood, or explain actions. Many audio designers came from backgrounds in music composition. According to designer John Gromada:

Doing sound design is a way for composers to make a living. As a composer in college, I saw sound design as a way to combine interest in music and theatre. I was always interested in electronic music and, as a way of getting my music into theatre, I learned about audio engineering and sound design. For sound designers, there isn't a heritage to inherit. There's a huge gap that started at the beginning of the twentieth century when naturalism and realism insisted we strip away artifice. That artifice never really resurfaced until, to some degree, technology and aesthetic tastes allowed it to. We're the people who are making that happen, I think.[24]

The audio designer provides the music and sound effects for a play.

We are beyond the era of sound "effects." Sound is no longer an effect, an extra, a *garni* supplied from time to time to mask a scene change or ease a transition. We are beyond the era of door buzzers and thunderclaps. Or rather, door buzzers and thunderclaps are no longer isolated effects, but part of a total program of sound that speaks to theatre as ontology. Sound is the holistic process and program that binds our multifarious experience of the world. Sound is our own inner continuity track. It is also our primary outward gesture to the world, our first and best chance to communicate with others, to become part of a larger rhythm.[25]

Determining the Sound Design

An audio designer needs to determine what sounds are necessary to represent the style or "reality" of the production. This is important because too little sound can leave an audience vaguely unsatisfied and too much intrudes on the presentation. Even the way a particular sound is used is important. Suppose the stage directions call for a doorbell to be heard. The designer first needs to decide on the type of doorbell — a buzzer, a chime, several notes of a tune. A buzzer can sound intrusive or jarring; notes of a song can come across as either individualistic or "cutesy."

---

24. Lenora Inez Brown, panel moderator, "Lend Us Your Ears," *American Theatre*, November, 2001, 31.

25. Peter Sellars, "Foreword," Deena Kaye and James Lebrecht, *Sound and Music for the Theatre*, (New York: Back Stage Books, 1992), vii.

The designer further needs to take into consideration why the doorbell is sounding. Is it to signify the arrival of an anticipated guest or an apartment manager bringing a previously threatened eviction notice? Should the sound seem angry, welcoming, frightening? Does it create a sense of anxiety or one of relief? Of course, these things go together to influence the volume of the sound, the length, the number of times the doorbell rings. In other words, when analyzing a script, the audio designer needs to pay attention to such things as mood, reason, style, and characterization.

The designer also needs to be acquainted with where specific sound effects can be acquired. Many designers maintain their own "libraries" of effects, gathered from such places as theatrical houses that sell recordings of particular sound effects, to private individuals who have specialized recordings, to various city or nature sounds the designers have taped themselves. This means, of course, that many of the sounds are prerecorded, but not necessarily all of them. The doorbell, for instance, can be "live."

The designer knows that an overall effect may include a combination of sounds. Suppose the action takes place outdoors in a rural area. The designer needs to ask what sounds a person would be likely to hear in such a setting, and maybe even go to a similar setting to experience these sounds — katydids, an occasional bird call, the far-off echo of a train whistle. But again, the designer has to determine the emotional or psychological content of the scene, and, subsequently, how to present these sounds and for how long. They'll call attention to themselves if they begin or end abruptly, if they're too loud, or even if they go on so long as to become intrusive or overwhelming.

No matter what the sound to be used, the designer must determine how to present it appropriately and in accordance with the style of the production and the genre, so that it matches the other elements of design — the pastel colors of the costumes, for instance, or the oppressive feeling of the setting.

Many effects are listed in the stage directions. Others may be indicated in the dialog. At any rate, the audio designer needs to go through the script carefully to see that everything essential to the story and the plot is noted.

Of course, the sounds have to be timed appropriately. If they don't mesh with the action — that is, if they occur too early or too late — most likely they will come across as humorous.

Purposes of Sound

With the continued development of audio systems and mixers, the use of sound is becoming a sophisticated process — much more a part of productions today than ever before in theatrical history. There are, in fact, a variety of reasons for using sound in a production. The most obvious uses are those things that are an integral part of the action, such as the ringing of a phone, the firing of a weapon, or a rainstorm. Sometimes a playwright will want a particular piece of music played at a certain time, maybe because a character is to turn on a song that has meaning to him or her, or so it catches a character unaware and brings up old memories when heard on the radio.

Sound also is used to introduce or frame the play (or even a scene in the play). Arthur Miller specifies that *Death of a Salesman* should open with the playing of a flute. Tina Howe is very specific with the music she wants used throughout her play *Painting Churches*, both as a frame and to establish mood and character:

Music in the Play

During the scene changes the opening measures of the following Chopin waltzes are played:
- As the house lights dim, the Waltz in A minor, opus posthumous.
- Setting up Act I, Scene 2, the Waltz in E minor, opus posthumous.
- Setting up Act I, Scene 3, the Waltz in E major, opus posthumous.
- To close Act I, the final notes of the Waltz in B minor, opus 69, #2.
- As the house lights dim for Act II, the Waltz in A flat major, opus 64, #3.
- Setting up Act II, Scene 2, repeat the Waltz in A minor, opus posthumous.
- To accompany the final moments of GARDNER's and FANNY's dance, the Waltz in D flat major, opus 70, #3.

Other effects besides music can introduce the action. David Rabe's *Hurlyburly* opens with a TV "droning out the early morning news."

A director or designer may only infer certain effects from what the playwright has written. In *Joe Turner's Come and Gone,* August Wilson, in part, has this to say after the list of characters and the setting and before the action begins:

It is August in Pittsburgh, 1911. The sun falls out of heaven like a stone. The fires of the steel mill rage with a combined sense of industry and progress. Barges loaded with coal and iron ore trudge up the river to the mill towns that dot the Monongahela and return with fresh, hard, gleaming steel. The city flexes its muscles. Men throw countless bridges across the rivers, lay roads and carve tunnels through the hills sprouting with houses.

From the deep and the near South the sons and daughters of newly freed African slaves wander into the city ...

This information might suggest using the sound of steel mills, barges on the river, men and women calling to each other, or trains unloading passengers.

Sound effects can serve to underscore a production or provide "atmosphere," like the country sounds on a summer's night. Very appropriately, this is how Alfred Uhry's *Driving Miss Daisy* opens:

In the dark we hear a car ignition turn on, and then a horrible crash. Bangs and booms and wood splintering. When the noise is very loud, it stops suddenly and the lights come up on DAISY WERTHAN's living room ...

Sounds and music may suggest a particular period, as would the old "Inner Sanctum" radio show or "The Charleston."

A designer may decide to use voice over. An example of this is the voice from the sound booth in the musical *A Chorus Line,* which tells the dancers on-stage what to do. Or it can be voices unrelated to the characters, but used to provide effect or to present characters' thoughts, which then is a device similar to the soliloquy.

Music or other sounds (old newscasts, for instance) added to a production can show the passage of time, or the movement from one place and/or time to another. Similarly, music or other sounds can be identified with a particular character. Arthur Kopit opens *End of the World* with these directions: "MUSIC: *lazy, bluesy music for a hard-boiled detective. It is 'Trent's Theme.' Curtain up.*"

The sound has to be convincing within the framework of a play. In Arnold Ridley's *The Ghost Train,* where a wrecked train supposedly passes a railway terminal, it would be unconvincing if the sound did not begin at one side of the stage and progress to the other as the train passes by. The designer has to determine how to convince the audience of the train's movement. After determining the effects, the sound designer then prepares a sound plot, just as the lighting designer prepared a plot.

A Multimedia Approach

The immediate presence of performer and audience member in theatre affects both. "In the movie theatre, we can watch a story and we can admire many things that actors do, but we cannot be caught up in a flow of living feeling that passes from actor to the audience and back again to the actor."[26]

Yet for today's audiences a film, a video tape, or a TV show has advantages that live theatre does not. It can appear more realistic. A setting for a TV show can more closely resemble a real room than a theatre setting can (even though the room may be constructed inside a large studio). Film or TV can take the spectator inside or outside or to far locations instantaneously.

Life in general has become much faster paced. Thus theatre is forced by other entertainment media to change its ways, to become closer in approach to these other media. To do this, it continues to incorporate techniques used in film or television. For example, *Alladeen* is a "cross-media theatre project by the New York City-based performance and media company, the Builders Association ..." and directed by Marianne Weems.

> *Alladeen* was created in collaboration with the London-based artists Keith Khan and Ali Zaidi, collectively known as motiroti pastiche of Hindi and Urdu (that means "big sandwich"). By drawing on fragments of the story of Aladdin, the street urchin who goes from a pauper to a prince in *The Arabian Nights*, *Alladeen* operates on two levels. It situates spectators in a call center in India, where performers portray phone operators, but actors and audience are also in a porous space and where threads from the myth of Aladdin occasionally bleed through. *Alladeen* explores how people operate as "global souls" caught up in circuits of technology and how our voices and images travel — and morph — from one culture to another.

---

26. Eric Bentley, *The Theatre of Commitment and Other Essays*, (New York: Atheneum, 1967), 59-60.

Created over three continents with an international array of artists, *Alladeen* takes several forms. In addition to live performance, there is a music video, directed by Ali Zaidi, featuring the music of the London-based DJ and composer Shri (Shrikanth Sriram), and a website (www.alladeen.com), also created by Zaidi, that investigates many additional aspects of Aladdin and our project as a whole.[27]

New Technologies
Additionally, the use of computers allows many other innovations.

It's not often that a graveyard steals the show, but then again, it's not often that a graveyard flies.

The cemetery in question is a six-ton piece of scenery in the new Broadway musical *Dance of the Vampires* ... The set piece makes its debut during a splashy second-act production number called "Eternity" in which a dozen campy vampires suddenly pop out of their coffins and break into song ...

But it is the way those coffins get there that is most likely to impress audiences. The graveyard, you see, descends some fifty feet from the theater's fly space, traveling vertically with the coffin lids facing the audience. The vampires' lair then tilts to a horizontal plane and magically eases onto the stage, even as the actors — complete with fangs, fright makeup, and capes — crawl into position underneath for their entrance.

As all this is happening, dozens of so-called intelligent lights — which can move, focus, and change color on their own — are spinning into position for the next cue overhead. At the same time, other set pieces are gliding in from the wings and fog is being pumped out of ten smoke ports hidden in the stage floor. The noise made by the changeover is covered by music mixed by a computer-assisted sound board and pumped through about 100 speakers strategically placed throughout the theater. The entire time allotted for the set change is under a minute.

---

27. Marianne Weems, "I Dream of Global Genies: The Builder's Association Rubs the Lamps of Identity and New Technology in Search of Transcultural Souls," *American Theatre*, December, 2003, 25-26.

How does all this work?

"You hit one Go button," said Peter Fulbright, the show's technical supervisor. "And everything goes ..."

[T]heatrical designers are stretching the boundaries of what is possible with a variety of new digital tools that allow them to coordinate and control dozens of independent elements — lights, sound, sets, and special effects — from a keyboard.[28]

Peter Feller, who owns the design company Feller Precision, says that "Forty years ago [the stagehand] was pushing on scenery with his own hand. Twenty years ago it was pulling a lever for each and every machine that had to move something. Today, it's hitting a Go button on a computer and making sure nothing goes wrong."[29]

A few decades back, sets raced in on grooves on the stage floor, twirled around a time or two perhaps, and stopped, providing almost a show in themselves. Shortly afterward, closed circuit television images appeared on various screens around or on the stage. The term *live theatre* took on new meaning, with special or multimedia effects often becoming an integral part of the drama itself.

Recent innovations now appear nearly simultaneously with the technology that allows their creation. Performances include such devices as videoconferencing and rear screen projections of pages from the World Wide Web.

A 1995 revival of *Red Horse Animation* by the avant-garde theatre company Mabou Mimes, directed by Lee Breuer and designed by Karen TenEyck, presented digitalized photographs (from the World Wide Web) projected one after another on a scrim at the rear of the stage.

In a New York performance by Ladysmith Black Mambazo and the "Rainbow Connection," an outreach program of the AMTF:

Ladysmith's founder and director Joseph Shabalala appeared on a large screen, where he could interact with performers on the stage, answer questions from the student audience, and sing along with children in a Spanish-language elementary school in Chicago. Dancers from the

---

28. Jesse McKinley, "Digital Magic on Broadway," *The New York Times*, October 17, 2002, http://www.nytimes.com/.
29. McKinley, "Digital Magic."

Rainbow Connection performed live on-stage in front of the screen. When the Chicago students were projected onto the screen singing Shabalala's "Nomathemba" (Zulu for "hope"), the Rainbow Connection performed a simultaneous dance routine. Seeing the dancers on their own monitor, the children in Chicago imitated them in an impromptu cross-continental call and response.[30]

Although we tend to think of the multimedia experience as relatively new, many of the technologies now in use have been available for years. A reason for increased usage of such devices as closed-circuit television, film, and other forms of screen projection is cost. It is much less expensive to project images of settings than to build the settings by conventional means.

Actually, screen projections have been used since the 1920s by such people as Erwin Piscator of Germany and Vsevolod Meyerhold of Russia. The Federal Theatre Project of the 1930s is well-known for its documentary series *Living Newspapers*. Tennessee Williams wrote directions for using slide projections in *The Glass Menagerie*.

One of the pioneers of multimedia stage settings was Josef Svoboda, born in Czechoslovakia, trained as an architect, and later appointed head designer at the National Theatre in Prague. With his designs, largely metaphoric rather than realistic, he sought to integrate all the technical elements into a changing and organic component of a production. One of his goals was to point up and/or de-emphasize scenic elements as is done in film.

Computer-Aided Design

Lately, more and more scene designers are using computers with a variety of software programs developed to make their work less tedious and the drawings and computer-generated models more easily understood by the technician. Perspective drawings are much easier to do, and the computer design has the advantage of being able to show the entire setting or any portion of it from various angles, drawn in three dimensions.

Computer programs, singly or in combination, are able to insert or take away portions of a design and show multilayered examples. It is possible to split a setting into its various parts and make computer drawings of each, as viewed from any angle.

30. Haines, 60.

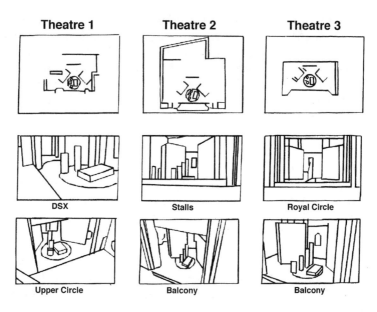

Figure 8-7: Computer-Aided Design sample screens.

There are two overall types of software. Drafting software aids in the drawing and provides templates for various types of stages or for furniture and costuming. The second category "automates the paperwork and preparation of schedules. Instrument, hook-up schedules, color and equipment lists may be easily generated in standard or customized forms ... [T]hese schedules may be directly linked to the drawings through database, so that any alteration to the drawing is automatically carried through to all the paperwork."[31]

"New processes now include building three-dimensional objects directly from a computer design by using liquid plastic which solidifies under ultraviolet light."[32]

Computers also are used for such other aspects of design as sound mixing and precision control of flying systems to move scenery in and out and for much greater control of projected scenery. Electronic pencils and brushes can aid in creating costume designs, and with the click of the curser a spotlight can shift

31. Pilbrow, 44-45.
32. Reid, 81.

position and angle. "Software programs are in an advanced state of development for the computer visualization of stage lighting on a video screen which displays pictorial images of costumed figures in the stage setting. These programs allow the direction, color, and intensity of the light to be manipulated on the screen to the same extent that it can be controlled in the theatre."[33]

CG Sets the Stage
Dynamic digital sets star in an innovative theatrical production
Diana Phillips Mahoney

Look out, New York, there's an up-and-coming actor planning to take the theater scene by storm, and this one doesn't have to wait tables before making it big. A theatrical group called The Zzyzx Studio will showcase the potential of what it's calling "The Living Stage" in a series of performances during the 1997-98 season, beginning this month at the Ohio Theater with a 50th anniversary production of Jean Genet's *The Maids*.

The Living Stage refers to the digitally projected environment in which the plays will be performed. More than static digital scenery ... The Living Stage combines projected, dynamic three-dimensional spaces with two-dimensional film and video imagery to visualize the memory and imagination of the play's characters, according to Zzyzx director and producer Frank De Luca. Rather than existing simply as a backdrop to the action of the play, The Living Stage is intended to be a character in its own right — one that is tightly integrated with the storyline, thus enhancing the understanding of the characters' actions and emotions.

The digital performance space for *The Maids* and for other upcoming Zzyzx productions is being designed and implemented by New York-based architect Peter Erni, founder of a digital media consulting company called

---

33. Reid, 82.

emergt. Erni is combining 3D animation, desktop video editing and large-screen projection to create the sets which can then be edited and manipulated up to the moment of performance ...

Each character [in *The Maids*] experiences [Madame's bedroom] differently, and as the characters move through the space, its appearance changes relative to the characters' perception of it ... [34]

Robotic lights that can follow an actor on-stage or change in color and intensity "are the major development of the nineties."

With increased availability of color scrollers, the color horizons from a single instrument can be greatly widened, but their expense can only be justified where there is a really potent reason to utilize a change of color. If available, a scroller not only allows a wider choice of color, it can be used dynamically to change the color "in view." Wonderful effects of sunset or dawn can be achieved with well-chosen series of hues in a slowly moving color string. Similarly, of course, automated fixtures liberate the designer. Some allow the slow (or rapid) cross-fading from color to color for dramatic effect ...

Now fluid control over not only the intensity of light but also the movement about the stage and its color is possible — all capable of sudden or subtle change as the action unfolds.[35]

Used with such lights are dichroic color filters which employ "thin layers of chemical on a sheet of glass that reflects selective wavelengths of light within the spectrum. Dichroics are effected by the angle of light to the filter, and color-changing devices have been made ... that, by turning the filters within the light beam, change the resultant color. Dichroics are found both in color filters as well as in reflectors, which also tint the light."[36]

---

34. http://emergt.com, reprinted from *Computer Graphics World*, March, 1997.
35. Pilbrow, 87-88.
36. Pilbrow, 366.

Summary

It is important for the director and designers to establish a good working relationship where there can be a free exchange of ideas. A set helps convey a play's theme and provides information essential to its understanding. The set fulfills the director's interpretation, provides an environment for the action, remains faithful to the playwright's intent, and complements the work of the other designers. It establishes both a framework for the action and a focal point for the audience, and it is designed for easy use by the actors. The set should be balanced, either symmetrically or asymmetrically, and its element should be harmonious.

There are two categories of stage lighting, general and specific. The former provides a well-lighted performance area, while the second provides special effects. Light complements the other areas of design and helps convey the play's mood and message. Lighting consists of two components: a source and a system of control, and lighting designers plan control of three aspects of lighting: color, intensity, and distribution.

Costuming is the facet of design that most identifies and supports the character. In analyzing a script, the costume designer has to consider such things as place and time and the economic situation of the characters.

There are three categories of makeup: straight, character, and special. The former involves enhancing or projecting an actor's natural features. The second and third alter an actor's appearance.

The property master is responsible for determining, obtaining, and caring for all the properties of a production. During the run of a show, the property crew is responsible for ensuring that the props are where they should be for easy access and that they are in good repair.

Audio designers provide the sound effects and music for a play.

Theatre always has been a combination of forms, and in the present day is often a true mixture of forms including live presentation, video, computer graphics, and television. New technologies for the theatre are developing rapidly. They include various uses of computers and the World Wide Web. Another type is the use of projections for special effects or even to provide entire settings. Computer-aided design is becoming common for such areas as stage settings, costuming, and audio design.

Questions for Discussion

1. What sort of background should a scene designer have?
2. What are the functions of scene design?
3. What are the requirements of scene design?
4. What kinds of information can an audience learn from a play?
5. What are the functions of lighting, and how might they be achieved?
6. In what way can lighting be symbolic?
7. What sorts of messages can costuming reveal to an audience?
8. What do the three different types of makeup — straight, character, and special— involve?
9. In what ways can sound be important to a production?
10. In what ways are computers becoming more and more important in theatre?

Chapter 9
THE BUSINESS SIDE OF THEATRE

Among those who work behind the scenes in theatre are the producers, the general and company managers, and the house and box office staffs. Others, whose work evolves directly out of that done by the director and the designers, are individuals and crews involved more closely with the production.

Before a play can be planned or presented, arrangements must be made for securing a theatre space, for promoting the show, for paying expenses, and, when required, for paying salaries. The producer can be an individual or a group. The manner of financing and the method of handling business arrangements depend on the type of theatre.

Producing in Educational and Community Theatres

In educational theatre, the school itself, or a department of the school, is the producer. Often, in elementary and high schools, one person is in charge of all the arrangements. Money may be advanced by the school or by an organization in the school. In college, the expense of producing plays comes out of the departmental budget and/or other sources. While the community theatre is also the producer of its own shows, the setup is somewhat different from educational theatre. Most often, an elected board governs the practical aspects of planning a season and is responsible for approving expenditures.

The important consideration for educational theatre is to plan a balanced season, whereas community theatre's major concern is selecting plays that draw well.

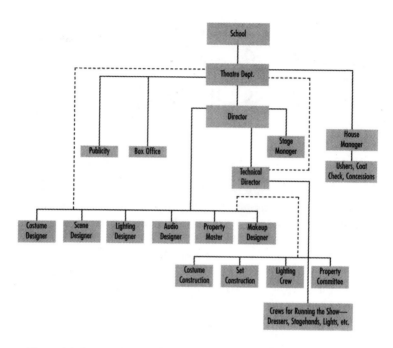

Figure 9-1: An organizational model for educational theatre.

Nonprofit Theatre

The commercial theatre in the United States, in the past and at the present, centers in New York City, with Chicago now considered by many to be the "second city." However, more and more professional theatres have been established throughout the country — repertory companies, various types of stock companies, dinner theatres, outdoor dramas, and children's theatre — in major cities as well as small communities.

Each year Theatre Communications Group (TCG) does a detailed survey of nonprofit theatre in the U.S. The following is an excerpt from the 2004 report.

The vast majority of nonprofit professional theatres did not exist fifty years ago. Despite struggling with a weak economy in 2003, these theatres continued to nurture and expand America's artistic cultural heritage, bringing the creative work of some 62,000 professional artists into communities around the country, where it was enjoyed by more than 34 million audience members ...

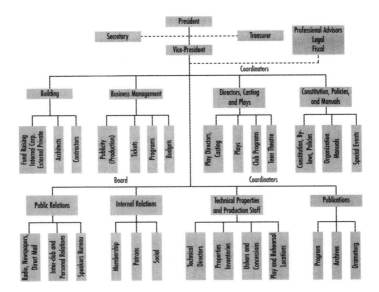

Figure 9-2: An organizational model for community theatre.

The 1,274 theatres in the U.S. nonprofit professional theatre field in 2003 are estimated to have:

• Added over one billion to the U.S. economy in the form of salaries and payments for goods and services.[1]

Until the late 1960s or early 1970s, most professional theatre existed to make a profit. Then came a change that gained impetus in the 1980s, totally changing the face of professional theatre. It was the establishment of nonprofit regional theatres that do not rely totally on box office receipts to fund their operation. Rather, they are supported in large part by grants and donations, which is more in line with the way it has been done in Europe, with governments of various countries subsidizing the arts.

Theoretically, this allows theatres more freedom in what they choose to present. Often, the producer in this sort of theatre is the organization itself, and most often the grants and other monies received are for overall operation rather than a single production.

---

1. Zannie Giraud Voss and Glenn B. Voss, with Christopher Shuff and Katie Taber, "Theatre Facts 2003," TCG annual report, 1.

These theatres are subsidized by foundations, government agencies, individuals or corporations, or often a combination of these sources. Many of these are "resident theatres" and hold membership in LORT (The League of Resident Theatres). LORT serves as a management association that negotiates contracts with professional theatrical unions including Actors Equity Association. Most resident theatres have a semi-permanent staff and company of actors.

Nonprofit theatre rarely existed in the first half of the twentieth century, and only lately has come to exist in nearly every major city in the United States. Included, for instance, are The American Repertory Theatre in Boston, The Goodman Theatre and the Steppenwolf Theatre Company in Chicago, The Mark Taper Forum in Los Angeles, and the Old Globe Theater and La Jolla Playhouse in San Diego. There are now more working artists in such theatres than in those that exist to make money for the producers. And the theatres, because they are culturally oriented and don't have to rely on box office receipts, are raising artistic standards. Yet, like their commercial counterparts, they are having problems with attendance and budgeting.

> There's a new and seminal thought bubbling up in American theatre, embracing both its for-profit and nonprofit forms. The thought is that the differences between the two have become blurred, increased collaborative actions between them is the handle for survival of both, and resentments from the past — each of the other — are too expensive to harbor. "Hang together or hang separately" is the gist of it. Considering that the nonprofit theatre arose in protest against the habits of Broadway and that Broadway has previously looked down upon the rest of us as the farm teams, this is an historic development.[2]

Broadway and Off-Broadway Theatre

When the booking of shows for a season and the casting for touring shows became centralized in the United States, the location was a small section of Manhattan on and around Broadway in New York City. Within the last few decades, rising costs have made Broadway a risky venture, even for the most courageous producer.

2. Zelda Fichandler, "The Profit in Nonprofit," *American Theatre*, December, 2000, 31.

Most shows are presented to appeal to a mass audience, and untried playwrights have little hope of production. The Broadway producer is concerned — and rightly so — with staging a show that will be a hit. Even at that, the majority of shows never regain their initial investment.

Yet to keep audiences interested, the theatre eventually must produce new plays.

New work is the lifeblood of the theater. The theater cannot flourish without new work; it cannot survive without it.

Yet as the third millennium turns, new work — and especially work that looks, sounds, and feels new — is not at the center of the American theater. On Broadway, Off-Broadway and throughout the country, the theater world, with some notable exceptions, is dominated by revivals and contemporary plays that have been audience-tested elsewhere.

The dream of the regional-theater movement, born in the 1960s as an alternative to the commercial arena of Broadway, was that each theater would have its own playwrights to nurture and develop — that each theater owner would have its own sensibility, its own concerns, its own plays. New work would be made across the country, propagating a lively, diverse theater culture bred of new voices and fresh ideas.

Today the regional theater exists in name only. What we find instead is that a small number of theaters are developing playwrights with actors, directors, and designers, while the rest pay lip service to development through dead-end readings and produce contemporary works that have played well at another theater. Instead of fifty new plays being produced at fifty regional theaters, those fifty theaters are producing the same new plays, often by an established writer ...

This is not a time for a risk-averse theater. This is a time for a vigorous, vital, thought-provoking theater, one that remembers its democratic roots in ancient Greece and envisions itself as a place for the community to gather to exchange ideas, pose questions, and purge emotions.[3]

---

3. Jennifer de Poyen, "A Bold Vision," *The San Diego Union-Tribune,* June 29, 2003, 1 and 4.

Although location has something to do with calling a theatre Off-Broadway (many are located in the Greenwich Village area), the main factor is size. According to standards set by Actors' Equity Association, the union for stage actors, an Off-Broadway theatre can seat no more than 299 spectators. Whereas Broadway appeals to the mass audience to make money, Off-Broadway producers, if they choose, can present plays that have limited appeal. There is the occasional show that becomes so successful it moves to a larger theatre. However, Off-Broadway, too, is becoming more commercialized than in the 1960s or 1970s, so that Off-Off Broadway has become in recent decades what Off-Broadway was in the 1950s and 1960s — a place for nearly any sort of theatre, and a wide range of experimentation.

The procedure for producing Broadway and most Off-Broadway shows is entirely different than for nonprofit theatre. Generally, a producer takes an **option** on a play. An option is a contract with the playwright, whereby the writer is paid a certain amount to give the producer exclusive rights for a limited time to produce the play. If the script is not produced within the time limit specified in the contract, the rights revert to the writer, who may seek another producer. Often, producers do take options on plays that they never present for one reason or another.

Once a producer takes an option — often after contact with literary agents who handle scripts — and definitely decides to produce the show, he or she makes the financial arrangements and rents the rehearsal space and theatre. The producer may provide all the money for a production, but more likely will seek backers, known as "angels," who form a corporation just for the run of a show. The producer receives up to half the profits.

If a play is accepted for production and arrangements are made, the producer reserves the right to make suggestions and changes. The same right extends to the backers. Actually, the producer may take an option on a script only if the writer agrees to changes beforehand.

Here's how producer Cheryl Crawford described her work:

Sometimes I think a producer is a person who is absolutely unable to do anything else, who has a strong interest in all the arts but the talent for none of them and enough business sense to know that sometimes you must dare to go to the edge of disaster to achieve what you desire. A producer is definitely a gambler. For the education of a theatre producer, the sky is the limit, which is what makes the profession so endlessly exciting ...[4]

Although producers have no direct working arrangements with the artistic end of a play in rehearsal, they approve any alterations that are made, because these changes will affect the show's audience-drawing potential. They are responsible for advertising to attract an audience. Yet according to actor Carroll O'Connor:

The producer blunders when he blows his backers' cash on advertising. Heavy advertising before opening is useless. Light advertising and a couple of good reviews will bring some customers to the box office; bad reviews will of course scare some of them away.[5]

O'Connor, of course, is speaking from a traditional point of view. Canadian producer Garth Drabinsky operated from an opposing position, that of "event marketing," as seen in the following:

In practice, the strategy goes like this: About a year before a show opens, an advertising rocket is released that announces a future event that will change people's lives. The messages goes out via an intensive multimedia advertising campaign. For the Toronto production of *Phantom of the Opera*, which is now in its ninth year and served as the template for the *Ragtime* campaign, that meant everything from an innovative billboard display to a major television documentary produced in partnership with Canadian Broadcasting Company.

Using this bazooka approach (what marketing people call "integrated packaging"), Drabinsky's Toronto-based company, Livent, Inc., draws on three advertising agencies to saturate the market with spot ads. The purpose of this early barrage of TV, radio, and newspaper advertising is to establish instant recognition of the show's logo and create a sense of anticipation about the upcoming "major event." In the model promotion for *Phantom*, special target promotions were created: movie trailers for the movie

4. Cheryl Crawford, *One Naked Individual: My Fifty Years in the Theatre*, (Indianapolis: The Bobbs-Merrill Company, Inc., 1997), 1.
5. Carroll O'Connor, *I Think I'm Outa Here: A Memoir of All My Families*, (New York: Pocket Books, 1998), 193.

crowd; "a multifaceted educational program" for children; a special box office that sold individual tickets for the singles crowd. Meanwhile, the merchandising machine cranked out *Phantom* jewelry, perfume, masks, mugs, dolls, and glow-in-the-dark underwear. By opening night, when you couldn't open a milk carton without seeing the *Phantom* mask logo, a then-record worldwide box office advance of $23.8 million had been set.

Six months before the opening of *Ragtime* there were already 200 print ads, two television ... spots and seventy radio spots.

Drabinsky tailored his campaign to the times. "During a recession, his sales campaigns sound the themes of 'romance, fantasy, and escape.'" For *Ragtime* the audience is encouraged "to 'enjoy' and to 'celebrate' the good times." From early on through the show's opening, Drabinsky shifts his advertising to a changing focus so potential audience members don't tire of a single faceted approach. "Needless to say, all this costs money — approximately fifteen percent of the show's potential Broadway gross ..."[6]

This sort of change in production and marketing had a lot to do with the approach taken by Cameron Mackintosh (producer) and Andrew Lloyd Webber (composer) with such productions as *Les Miserables*, and has spread to mega-advertising and investment by the Walt Disney Company. According to Sylviane Gold, Disney, with the musicals *Beauty and the Beast* and *The Lion King*, is transforming Forty-Second Street.

The lynchpin for all this transformation sits on the southern corner of 42nd and Seventh: a huge new Disney store, adjacent to (and, not coincidentally, adjoining the lobby of) the renovated New Amsterdam Theatre.

And along with the differences in the visible geography of Times Square have come changes in its invisible structure — its symbolic status as the center of the American theatre. Those changes, stirring behind closed doors at Broadway's production offices, union headquarters and talent agencies, and also at the area's many not-for-profit theatres, will be

---

6. Marilyn Stasio, "The Selling of Ragtime," *American Theatre*, December 1997, 20-23.

just as profound as those in the area's real estate; but for now, they are much harder to discern. What's certain is that as the theatre powers scramble to remain competitive in this new environment, the theatre itself will change ...

It's probably also safe to say that Disney's announcement that it had agreed to invest more than $30 million in the restoration of the New Amsterdam in exchange for a forty-nine-year lease and a low-interest loan from City Hall put the theatre world on notice: there was a mouse-shaped gorilla in its midst.[7]

Shortly after bringing *Ragtime* to New York, however, Drabinsky was one of four executives of Livenet charged with "fraud affecting the public market." After a long investigation, he and the others were charged with "accounting irregularities" and "insider trading." It remains to be seen if his type of operation can once again be successful.

A recent change in procedure is that:

Nonprofit theater companies are making their presence felt even more strongly on Broadway. People have been worrying about this for decades, ever since the New York Shakespeare Festival took *Two Gentlemen of Verona* to Broadway in 1971 and followed it with *A Chorus Line* in 1975, a move that wound up bankrolling that particular nonprofit company for years. What's new is the actual physical presence of the nonprofits in Broadway theaters, through long-term leases or outright ownership ...

While nonprofits will still account for only a small portion of Broadway tickets, their very presence rankles commercial producers. They fear that the nonprofits' relatively high-toned offerings and their subscription system, offering several shows a year, may lead to a disproportionate dominance of the Tony awards, prized both for prestige and for their stimulus to the box office.[8]

---

7. Sylviane Gold, "The Disney Difference," *American Theatre*, December, 1997, 14.
8. John Rockwell, "For Profit or Not, It's All Showbiz," *The New York Times*, September 22, 2002, http://www.nytimes.com/.

What has changed most of all in recent decades in the commercial Broadway theatre is that theatrical production now is big business. The unknown playwright, the playwright who has had a previous string of failures is no longer welcome. Rather, producers want only sure hits because of the big investments required. Producers and angels no longer want to take a risk; they want to be as certain as possible that what they are backing will give them a return many times over. And a mega-hit does just this. Once expenses are paid, an investor may make as much as a hundred percent of his investment for each year of the show's run.

However, this may not be the case. When the musical *The Producers* opened in 2001, "the critics loved the show, the producers loved the critics, the actors loved the producers, and the investors loved just about everybody. The next day, ticket buyers starting [sic] lining up before dawn." On that day about $3.3 million in tickets sold and everyone expected another mega-hit. However, three years later the show was suffering problems, though it did greatly recover from them.[9] Similarly, *Dance of the Vampires*, with a $12-million dollar budget, opened on December 9, 2002, and closed January 25, 2003, afer a run of about a month and a half with a total loss of the investment.

The producer's final responsibility is deciding when to end a show's run, whether it is after a day, a month, or several years.

If a production continues beyond opening night, it is up to the producer to meet all operating expenses and finally to begin splitting any profits among the investors. If the reviews are bad, the producer is the one who posts the closing notice, ending all arrangements.

It is becoming increasingly difficult to produce a play professionally in New York. It is not uncommon for budgets to run into the millions. The classics and other nonmusical plays with large casts are rarely produced. "These works have found a home as well as an audience in the nonprofit theatres, but there, too, producers are under constant pressure to keep expenditures low and ticket income high." Yet Broadway undoubtedly is expensive, and it's not unusual for the best tickets to cost a hundred dollars, with only a quarter of that going back to the investors.

---

9. Jesse McKinley, "The Case of the Incredible Shrinking Blockbuster," *The New York Times*, November 2, 2003, http://www.nytimes.com/.

The one relatively recent development that has forced Broadway to help finance serious, nonprofit theatre companies is the enticement of acquiring and transferring a production more or less intact from a nonprofit theatre as David Rabe's *Streamers* was transferred to Broadway from the Long Wharf Theatre, as Lanford Wilson's *Burn This* was brought to New York from the Mark Taper Forum. Or for that matter as *Les Miserables* was brought to London's West End and subsequently to Broadway from the Royal Shakespeare Company. In such cases, although other producers and investors may share in the profits, the originating theatre may also receive a percentage of the show's earnings which it may then use to help finance its on-going activities. Commercial producers may also provide "enhancement money" in the form of contributions which may enable the nonprofit group to develop and stage a particular production.[10]

Many people feel, as does Dramatist Guild president Peter Stone, that Broadway is in a "crisis period" for several reasons. Producers have "negotiated contracts somewhat carelessly," young people are more interested in television, videos, cable, and movies, and current audiences think a play is a failure if the seats at a performance are not all filled.

So the sad fact is we have developed a paradox: We have a theater that is way out of line economically, and we have houses that are much too big for the available audience. And we have an audience that is so success-oriented that they won't consider a play that has three quarters of a house in it.

Stone states that perhaps the only possible solution is to concentrate on a unified New York theatre, instead of Broadway and Off-Broadway.[11]

Playwright Terrence McNally flatly proclaims: "'Where are the new American producers?' playwrights ask. We complain that there are no new American producers. We're right." He goes on to say that "if you're talking about serious American theater today you're

10. Stephen Langley, *Theatre Management and Production in America*, (New York: Drama Book Publishers, 1990), 11.

11. Peter Stone, "Peter Stone on Broadway: Let's Call the Whole Thing Off," from "The State of the Theatre 1994," *The Dramatists Guild Quarterly*, Spring 1994, 8–9.

no longer talking about on Broadway or off. You're speaking about the not-for-profit regional theater," whose "corporations have replaced the commercial producers who made Off-Broadway happen in the '60s."[12]

It isn't only playwrights who feel this way. Producer Richard Horner states that costs are getting out of hand due to "featherbedding" — having, under union rules, to hire many more people than are necessary.

> I know that actors used to rehearse for no money, without being paid. Actors were commonly stranded in other cities when their shows closed on tour with no way to get home. There were great abuses. There's no question about it ... But, unfortunately, the pendulum has swung far in the other direction.[13]

One solution, of course, is a closer relationship among nonprofit and commercial theatres.

> On her installment ... as new chairman of the National Endowment for the Arts, Jane Alexander called for wider collaboration by commercial producers and nonprofit resident theatres. The call ... rekindled a debate launched formally at the First Annual Congress of Theatre (FACT) in June 1974, when Broadway producer Alexander Cohen invited 220 representatives from nonprofit and commercial theatres to convene in Princeton, N.J. His goal — which was not wholeheartedly embraced by the nonprofit emissaries who attended the meeting "on scholarship" — was to formulate cooperative solutions to the problems afflicting both theatrical sectors: growing financial needs in the burgeoning nonprofit community, and a moribund climate on Broadway ...

> Twenty years after FACT [First Annual Congress of Theatre], delegates mulled prospects of greater union between the commercial and noncommercial sides of the theatre, industry trends and strapped finances have forced

---

12. Terrence McNally, "Terrence McNally on Off-Broadway: The New Establishment," from "The State of the Theater 1994," *Dramatists Guild Quarterly*, Spring 1994, 10–11.

13. Arvid F. Sponberg, "Richard Horner, Producer," *Broadway Talks: What Professionals Think About Commercial Theater in America*, (New York: Greenwood Press, 1991), 12.

both groups to live together under common law if not by holy matrimony. Forged out of necessity, the partnership shows signs of promise: Hope seems to lie in nurturing a cautious collaboration between commercial producers sympathetic to aims of nonprofit theatres, and managers of nonprofit theatres who can work these relationships to advance traditional goals — service to the community and fidelity to artistic purpose — without indulging foolish expectations of limitless cash flow ...

Cooperation doesn't guarantee harmony, however, even after details of financial arrangements are hammered out. On-Broadway and elsewhere, commercial producers are quick to yell foul when tax-advantaged, nonprofit theatres pose competition. Inside the nonprofit environment, the old debate persists: Do commercial aspirations constrain creativity and stifle voices that are not commercial enough?[14]

Members of the Business Staff

Besides the producer and the theatrical artists, there are many others involved in presenting a play. In New York theatre there are a general manager and a company manager. The former is the first person involved in the show after the producer decides to go ahead with it, negotiating agreements with the director, the theatre owners, the designers, and the stars. The general manager develops the production budget and sees that it's followed and that any profits are distributed among the investors.

The company manager is the producer's representative in the day-to-day business operations of a production, including seeing that everything associated with the project is on schedule and running smoothly. He or she oversees expenses, payroll, and ticket sales. Overall the job involves seeing that everything functions properly.

The house manager supervises a host of people, including ushers, doormen, and cleaners; checks box office statements; and oversees house maintenance. The business staff also is extensive, with various secretaries, accountants, an attorney, and a press agent.

Although community and educational theatres generally do not have so extensive a staff as do professional theatres, there still are

---

14. S. L. Mintz, "A Marriage of Convenience," *American Theatre*, November 1994, 26–28.

many members. The house manager usually is responsible for all front-of-the house matters. This work includes seeing that the theatre and the grounds are in proper order, arranging for ushers and ticket takers, sometimes arranging for the printing and delivery of programs, handling the checking of coats, and often being in charge of the concession stand.

Publicity managers or press agents also have many duties. The most important, of course, is to sell tickets. Second, they are responsible for projecting a good image of the theatre and for increasing public awareness of its existence and program. Last, they are responsible for publicizing each show. Although they have several others working with them, they have the final responsibility for all press releases for radio, television, and public appearances. Publicity managers work directly with the box office personnel, because both are responsible for ticket sales.

Summary

The producer can be an individual or a group. The manner of financing and the method of handling business arrangements depend on the type of theatre. The important consideration for educational theatre is to plan a balanced season, whereas community theatre's major concern is selecting plays that draw well.

Until the late 1960s or early 1970s, most professional theatre existed to make a profit. Then the change to nonprofit regional theatres changed the face of professional theatre. In Off-Broadway theatre, there need not be so great a concern about staging a hit show.

For most Off-Broadway and Broadway shows, a producer takes an option on a play. The producer then is responsible for raising money to stage the show and for making all the financial arrangements, including the renting of a rehearsal space and theatre. Producers have no direct working arrangement with the artistic end of a play, but they approve any alterations since these affect the show's audience-drawing potential. They also are responsible for advertising. A producer's final responsibility is deciding when to end a show's run.

The business staff of a theatre includes a general manager, a company manager, and publicity managers. The former negotiates agreements with the director, the theatre owners, the designers, and the lead performers. The general manager also develops the production budget. The company manager is the producer's representative in the day-to-day business operations of a production. Publicity managers and press agents are responsible for selling tickets, for projecting a good image of the theatre, and for publicizing the show.

Questions for Discussion

1. What are the responsibilities of a producer?
2. How are shows financed and produced in educational, community, and professional theatre?
3. What work on the business end falls to people other than the producer?
4. Why is it becoming so difficult to produce a play on Broadway?
5. What are the basic differences between for-profit and not-for-profit commercial theatre?
6. In what way is production of for-profit theatre changing? Do you think such a change is good? Why?

Chapter 10
THE AUDIENCE AND THE CRITIC

There is an unknown quality in every theatre presentation: the direct contact between artist and spectator. Even with the same script, setting, and performers, a play differs from night to night. Not only do the performers' attitudes and actions change, the audience changes as well. Each group of theatregoers brings new expectations and perspectives. The size of an audience affects the flow of communication to a certain degree, but even two audiences of the same size may react much differently to a production.

An audience brings an indispensable ingredient to the theatrical event. It brings a contemporary consciousness. Theatre does not — in fact, cannot — exist in a vacuum. It reflects as well as modifies the world around it. In order to be truly effective, it must speak to an audience in ways that the audience can readily understand and it must be able to sustain an audience's attention for the duration of the performance.[1]

This direct flow of feeling between audience and artist sets theatre and other live arts apart from film and television. Eric Bentley observes that film has many of the same qualities as theatre, including a theatre building, actors, and an audience. But "we cannot be caught up in a flow of living feeling that passes from actor to the audience and back again to the actor."[2] Similarly, when asked if a performance depends on the audience's reaction, Julie Andrews said, "It's almost the biggest part of the challenge. Nobody knows you were good last night except the people who were there."[3]

---

1. Bloom, Martin, *Accommodating the Lively Arts: An Architect's View*, (Lyme, NH: Smith and Kraus, 1997), 3.

2. Eric Bentley, *The Theatre of Commitment and Other Essays*, (New York: Atheneum, 1967), 59-60. Reprinted by permission of the author.

3. Roy Newquist, *Showcase*, (New York: William Morrow & Co., Inc., 1966), 41.

The interaction between performers and audience can ignite sparks which glow with unparalleled brilliance. Performers cannot help but be encouraged by the signals which come from an audience reacting positively to their performances. For an audience, urging performers on to the best of their capabilities and rewarding their achievements with commensurate demonstrations of approval can provide tremendous satisfaction. In fact, the ultimate success of any act of theatre — whether it occurs within a formal enclave like Lincoln Center, or along Main Street, or on the side streets leading from Times Square or Piccadilly Circus — depends as much upon the degree of receptivity of a live audience as it does upon the talents of those on the stage.[4]

An audience affects not only the performers but also itself. Whether we call what happens "reinforcement" or "mob psychology," as part of a group, we partially lose our own identities and inhibitions. We somehow sense what the group wants and what direction it will take, although our own purpose or response may not be fully defined before we join with others. Generally, as part of a theatre audience, we are willing to experience more of a release of our emotions than we will by ourselves or with one or two others. Director Sidney Berger writes:

> I can't direct for the audience ... because they are total strangers to me ... I can work with the play and I can work with the actors as my collaborator and partners. Ultimately the audience comes into the theatre and then they become my collaborator. Because when they are there and reacting to that play, I have got to alter my work depending on what I sense from that, and they become the last stage.[5]

It is difficult to appreciate a theatre performance if there are few members in an audience, or even if they are isolated from one another. If there are several rows of empty seats directly in front of the stage, the members of the audience will tend to retain some of their individual inhibitions. For the audience to merge, the members must experience physical closeness.

---

4. Bloom, p. 2-3.
5. Sidney Berger in Luere, Jeane, ed., *Playwright Versus Director: Authorial Intentions and Performance Interpretations*, (Westport, CT: Greenwood Press, 1994), 42-43.

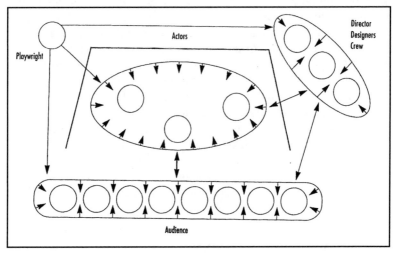

Figure 10-1: The communication process among theatre audiences and artists.

A bonding occurs. That is why, for example, we often hear a burst of laughter at a line that strikes the audience as funny. The members trust each other, and so most responses encompass the group and are immediate.

The idea of involving the audience in the performance is founded on the principle that theatre is based in ritual. This theory has been part of the theatrical vocabulary since the reform movement of the early twentieth century. Reformers, then and now, have been opposed to the illusionistic theatre and its architectural home, the picture-frame proscenium. The aim of the illusionistic theatre is for the audience to believe, with willing suspension of disbelief, that the performance is real, and to diminish the audience's awareness of the theatricality. But the audience-involvers want the spectator to perceive the performance as an artistic — even artificial — theatrical event. Theatrical performance is seen as a ritualistic interaction between two groups of people: spectators and performers. Therefore, performance and architecture should highlight and reinforce this interaction, and the open stage is considered to be the most conducive to this effect.[6]

---

6. Condee, 22.

Of course, different types of plays will attract different audiences. What draws audiences in New York City may leave empty seats in the South or Midwest. Not only do moral and sociological outlooks differ from one area to another, but a larger city has a larger potential audience of any particular type from which to draw than does a small community.

Thus, the theatre audience has half a contract to fulfill. Their responsibility includes becoming acquainted with theatre in order to understand it as an art form. Only by attending and experiencing a variety of plays — from current tragicomedy to Elizabethan tragedy — can an audience member learn to judge the worth of a production. The more effectively we can judge a production, the more it enriches our lives. More prosaically, they have a responsibility to arrive at the production on time, and to be quiet and attentive.

Why Audiences Attend the Theatre

There are many reasons for attending the theatre, but people most often attend to be entertained. Theatre offers a chance to escape into a make-believe existence and to forget everyday cares. As dramatist Bertold Brecht once said, the theatre "needs no other passport than fun."[7]

The theatre also offers us the opportunity to learn of recent, present, and imminent change. Theatre, like other arts, not only mirrors the society in which it is produced, but often judges the social, economic, and political climate in which it is presented. Norwegian playwright Henrik Ibsen stated that the artist must be a few years ahead of the average person in thinking. Artists must anticipate what changes will occur in their society. Art gauges the undercurrents of society and predicts the future. Rather, they show what is likely to occur or is already afoot.

Audiences also attend the theatre to confront social problems. Since World War II, theatre has changed in content and style as it has tried to alert us to the needs of society. Frank D. Gilroy's *The Subject Was Roses* (1964) shows the discouragement and disillusionment faced by a young man home from World War II. This production foreshadowed the increasing discontent over the Vietnam conflict, seen, for instance, in David Rabe's *Sticks and Bones* (1972), a violent antiwar play that attacks the silliness and hypocrisy

---

7. Berthold Brecht, "A Short Organum for the Theatre," John Willet, trans., in *Playwrights on Playwriting*, Toby Cole, ed., (New York: Hill and Wang, 1960), 74.

of middle-class America. Whereas Gilroy's play uses realistic subject matter, characterization, and dialog, Rabe's play uses strong new devices: a phantom Vietnamese girl, present only in the memory of a returning Vietnam veteran; characters patterned after the Nelson family on the old (1950s) *Ozzie and Harriet* television show; and dialog that often is purposely inane or "corny."

In past ages, the theatre presented problems about isolated individuals or groups far removed from the experiences of the audience, such as the nobility in Greek tragedy. Most of the audience members could empathize with the characters, but also could feel secure in the knowledge that the productions presented someone else's particular troubles.

In the recent past through the present, theatre has tried to come closer to its audience's problems and needs, even placing the dilemmas squarely in the laps of the audience. David Henry Hwang's *FOB* shows how difficult it is for people of a different culture to adapt to living in the United States. Lucy Gannon's *Keeping Tom Nice* is about a family's attempts to deal with a severely disabled son/brother who is unable to communicate. Lanford Wilson's *Burn This* is about the accidental death of a young gay man and the effect on the lives of others, including his parents (who didn't know he was gay) and his boorish brother.

Earlier plays, such as Ibsen's social dramas, did not neglect universality or **immediacy** (the quality of a work of art that makes it important or relevant to the time in which it is presented to the public), but more recent theatre has tried consciously to dramatize the concerns of its audience. One group to attempt this was the Living Theatre. In its production of *Paradise Now* (1968), the group openly confronted audiences and demanded responses to such issues as war and "establishment" rules. The Open Theatre, under the guidance of Joseph Chaikin, presented such plays as van Itallie's *America Hurrah* (composed of three one-acts), which ridiculed the treatment individuals often receive in impersonal job interviews and protested the disregard we often show for others' property.

From the 1980s through the early part of this century came plays that honestly explored the base and basic feelings of humankind. These include McNally's *Frankie and Johnny in the Clair de Lune*, the story of the love between two lonely middle-aged people, a short-order cook and a waitress; David Rabe's *Hurlyburly*, about two divorced casting agents caught up in a frenzy of cocaine and booze and abusing the women in their lives; and Andrea Stolowitz's *Knowing Cairo*, that addresses problems of dealing with an aging parent.

A fourth reason audiences go to the theatre is to learn about individuals and their personalities. Shakespeare's *Othello*, for instance, deals with jealousy — an emotion we all experience at one time or another. By contrast, the characters of Henrik Ibsen often face the immediate concerns of their own time. In *Ghosts*, for example, Mrs. Alving is a woman who, because divorce was frowned upon at the time, stayed with an unworthy husband, now dead. Written in 1881, the play shows the mental anguish a person may have to suffer in choosing the "safe" route. She continues to suffer when she learns that her son Oswald has a venereal disease, inherited from his father — something that she tries to keep hidden.

Another reason audiences are drawn to the theatre is to learn from the past. A play can acquaint us with the past in order to provide new interpretations of the present. Such is the case with Peter Shaffer's *The Royal Hunt of the Sun*, which deals with Pizarro's conquest of the Incas of Peru. Although it presents historical events, the play also portrays a loss of faith. Pizarro has lost faith in Christianity and wants to believe in the immortality of the Indian emperor, Atahuallpa. The emperor believes that because the Sun is his father, he will be resurrected if he is put to death. Of course, when Pizarro kills him, the emperor is not resurrected. August Wilson often deals with a more recent past in such plays as *Joe Turner's Come and Gone* and *Gem of the Ocean* because, he says, he wants to write about issues that have confronted and will continue to confront black people.

Attending the theatre can also serve to reaffirm the audience's beliefs about an issue. A playwright has a better chance of reaching his or her audience by beginning with a common premise — something that most potential theatregoers already believe. For example, if an audience did not feel at the beginning of a production that war is inhumane, a play with an antiwar theme, such as Laurence Stallings and Maxwell Anderson's *What Price Glory?* (1924), would have little chance of success. According to theatre critic John Gassner, the play "did more than any other dramatic piece to promote the cause of realism and freedom on the American stage ... In its day ... [it] was also considered the last word in pacifism because the authors described fighting as grimy business ... and refrained from attributing exalted sentiments to its warriors."[8]

---

8. John Gassner, editor, *Twenty-Five Best Plays of the Modern American Theatre: Early Series*, (New York: Crown Publishers, 1949), 58.

Plays sometimes are simply observations of life. The absurdist movement, which reached its height in the 1950s, stated only that life is absurd, thus reaffirming a belief many people shared, though they hadn't necessarily thought much about it.

Often an audience is willing to be led in a certain direction, but doesn't want a decision forced upon it. *West Side Story* pleads for understanding among individuals of different cultural backgrounds by showing how prejudice can destroy. One of its messages is that understanding, caring, and love should begin on an individual basis.

An audience attends the theatre simply to feel — to experience emotion. The playwright, the designers, and the actors all work together to try to elicit certain responses. A serious play allows empathy or identification more often than does a comedy. Yet almost any subject can be treated humorously or seriously. For instance, compare how seriously the idea of greed is treated in Lillian Hellman's *The Little Foxes*, a serious play, and in Molière's *The Miser*, a comedy.

The Little Foxes
Lillian Hellman

The members of the Hubbard family, united against the outside world, often hate one another. They attempt to raise money to establish a cotton mill in a nearby town. When the play opens, Regina's husband Horace, president of the local bank, is in Johns Hopkins, a Baltimore hospital, being treated for a heart ailment. When letters to him fail to bring the money necessary for the Hubbard's venture, Regina sends her daughter Alexandra to bring Horace back home.

Weakened by the trip, Horace refuses to provide the money Regina and her brothers need, so Benjamin and Oscar steal securities belonging to Horace and cut Regina out of her share in the entrepreneurial venture. She becomes enraged.

The shock of realizing what his wife is really like causes Horace to have a heart attack. By giving him medication, Regina could save his life. She refuses, and he dies. Regina confronts her brothers with the theft and demands seventy-five percent of the business not to expose them.

The Miser
by Molière

Harpagon, a widower and father of an adult son and daughter, lets his miserliness rule his life, which in turn frustrates his two children and makes him the dupe of everyone who recognizes his all-consuming weakness. The two children plot to select their own marriage partners rather than the ones Harpagon chose out of greed.

Harpagon's own son Cléante, Harpagon's rival for the affections of Marianne, forces his father to choose between her and his cash box. Of course, he chooses the money.

Who Attends the Theatre

More people attend the theatre in metropolitan areas than in urban areas since more theatre is available in larger cities. The average or typical attendee is caucasian, middle-aged or older, and has a college education, a white-collar job, and better-than-average income. Attendance is higher in the Northeast, due no doubt to the fact that theatre is more readily available in such cities as New York, Boston, and Philadelphia, and in the West where the average level of education is the highest in the nation. Also, it seems to follow that audiences are much more likely to attend the theatre in areas where more live theatre of various types is available. Supply, in fact, often creates new demand.

There are many exceptions to the average. Audiences differ for experimental or ethnic theatre and for other productions that cater to a special group. Nor does the average apply to college or university theatre. "The profile is also radically altered when there is a free-admission policy — a practice made feasible when subsidization is available and made desirable by the alarmingly urgent need to attract a wider and younger segment or the population."[9]

According to a survey published in 1996, "American participation in theater or 'non-musical stage plays' increased from

9. Stephen Langley, *Theatre Management and Production in America*, (New York: Drama Book Publishers, 1990), 49-50.

11.9 percent of all adults in 1982 to 13.5 percent in 1992." This adds up to about 25.1 million people as compared to about 20 million ten years earlier. They attended an average of 2.4 times in the twelve months preceding the survey with a third expressing interest in attending the theatre more often. Slightly more than 53.2 percent said they also had attended musical theatre, "although only 45.1 percent of the musical theater audience also reported attending stage plays — indicative of the relatively broader appeal of musicals."

The survey concluded that education continued to be "the single most important predictor of stage play participation. While 35 percent of those with graduate school education reported theater attendance, only 4 percent of those with high school education did so. Frequency of attendance also increases with education level."[10]

Those of higher–than-average income also were more likely to attend. As higher expenses drive up ticket prices, consumers in the lower income brackets, including most people under thirty years of age, are excluded from the audience.[11] And in regard to age, those in the forty-five to fifty-four age group attended the theatre more than any other age group, though the AMS survey did find that "theater participation is somewhat more constant across age groups."[12]

"One of the most significant findings" was that "participation rates for African Americans more than doubled from 5.8 percent in 1982 to 12.0 percent in 1992," and "Hispanic participation" "rose from 5.5 percent to 8.6 percent." This may in part be attributed to efforts in the nonprofit theatre to bring about a diversification among audience members and on a "renewed focus on ethnically and culturally specific works" and increased funding. "The growing popularity of performance art and solo performance (i.e., storytelling and monolog) undoubtedly had a positive impact on theater participation, particularly among young audiences."[13]

How will the theater make itself relevant to an increasingly diverse public? Much depends on the resources made available to theaters, playwrights, and performers to develop new work and attract new audiences. Most likely,

---

10. AMS Planning & Research Corp., "Research Division Report #35," *American Participation in Theater*, (Santa Ana, CA: Seven Locks Press, National Endowment for the Arts, 1996), 1-2.
11. Langley, 11.
12. AMS survey, 2.
13. AMS survey, 3.

the rising cost of production and touring professional theater — coupled with changes in the funding mix for nonprofit theaters — will create even more pressure on earned income. However, it is the developmental component of theater, free from commercial expectations, that ultimately creates renewal. Audiences will continue to change and grow as new works (and old works infused with new relevancy) bring the lives of more Americans close to the theater. Responsibility for creating new work rests not only with the nonprofit theater but also with commercial producers, the funding community, and ultimately the audience itself.[14]

Still, most would agree that the theatre needs to attract a wider audience, particularly a younger one since many feel that most of those under eighteen or twenty are too interested in television and films and videos to be attracted to theatre. Here is what a number of those whose work is related to professional theatre say on the subject:

> **Lee Roy Reams [actor]:** Unless you are a megahit and become a tourist attraction, you can't make money. *Beauty and the Beast* personifies the tourist attraction Broadway has become. You have the Disney name. You can bring your children — and thank god you can, because maybe those are going to become the people who are going to sustain the audience.

> **Howard Kissel [critic]:** Up to the 1960s, New Yorkers went to the theater all the time. These days they go for a birthday, an anniversary — if then — or because they have to entertain people from out of town.

> **Joseph Traina [house manager]:** After the initial rush, your normal theater-goers are the tourists and people who are used to going to amusement parks, the circus, the movies. They've been raised on television, and they're very casual. They'll sit on the arms of the chairs, put their feet up on the seats, throw their coats and jackets on the railings.[15]

---

14. AMS report, 4-5.

15. Myrna Katz Frommer and Harvey Frommer, eds., *It Happened on Broadway: An Oral History of the Great White Way*, Reams, Kissel, Traina, (New York: Harcourt, Brace & Company, 1998), 277-278.

However, a more recent survey of New York Theatres showed "... that the Broadway audience under twenty years of age has grown dramatically" with 21.7 percent of attendees under the age of twenty-five.[16]

Attracting Audiences to the Theatre

There have been many attempts of various sorts to attract a larger theatre audience. These range anywhere from lowering ticket prices, to cultivating minority audiences, to presenting programs in elementary schools to try to instill in youngsters an appreciation for the medium that they will then carry with them throughout their lives.

Despite continuing research into why more people don't attend plays, there seems to be no sure answer to the problem, though:

Most artistic directors look for tomorrow's audience in today's classroom. They agree that it is the responsibility of the theatre community to condition audiences from school age on to see theatre as an important part of their lives ...

A number of theatres have proved that attracting minority audiences is an artistic issue; the plays a theatre chooses to produce can make a significant difference in the cultural make-up of its audience. The Negro Ensemble Company ... has helped boost black attendance at theatres across the country by circulating national touring companies of such acclaimed shows as *Home* and *A Soldier's Play*. The critical and box office success of these productions — in addition to the heavy attendance of black audiences primarily for black musicals on Broadway has sent strong signals to theatres that minority audiences exist and that they will attend theatre if the theatres show an interest in their art and culture.[17]

Ellen Zisholtz-Herzog, executive director of Art Synergy in Nashville, feels that one answer to attracting audiences to minority theatre is collaboration. "What group," she asks, "is a minority? What group is a majority? Maybe what we're talking about is how

---

16. "Just What Is the Theatre Development Fund, and What Is It Trying to Tell Us About Broadway and Ourselves," *What's New on the Rialto*, October 8, 1998, www.audienceresearch.com/News/TDF.htm.

17. Todd London, *The Artistic Home: Discussions with Artistic Directors of America's Institutional Theatres*, (New York: Theatre Communication Group, Inc., 1988), 51.

you can involve the entire spectrum of ethnic groups in what you're doing. We should start thinking differently and speaking differently. We should think about how the various ethnic groups can work together."[18]

And, of course, attracting audience members involves presenting shows that meet their expectations, which is tied in with the reasons for attending the theatre. What exactly can a theatre do to meet audiences' interests and expectations? How can the theatre then make sure potential audience members know that certain shows are designed to appeal to them directly? These are some of the questions that each producer or board or artistic director must attempt to answer.

The Audience Member as Critic

All members of a theatre audience are critics whether they think so or not. Their response is subjective. One may be thrilled by a production of a recent Broadway hit while another wishes to be home playing computer games. These reactions, in effect, are criticisms since criticism does imply opinion. Yet we tend to look upon a critic as someone set somewhat apart, someone who's a writer, who has a strong background in whatever medium he or she is reviewing. In all probability, we think our opinions are important only to ourselves and maybe to family and friends.

What Makes a Critic a Professional?

Professional critics usually have much more knowledge on which to base opinions than does the average theatregoer. They have more experience and a more discerning eye, as well as having the ability to write an entertaining piece that will be read by hundreds or maybe thousands of newspaper subscribers. As such, they must be able to pinpoint why they, and perhaps the rest of the audience, have responded a particular way. Was it because of something specific the actor did, the lighting accomplished? Was it that everything in the production meshed or else clashed? If the latter, what were the reasons? In other words, the critic must have the training and the background to know why something is good or bad and be able to articulate the reasons, rather than saying, "The show was great, the acting terrific, and the set beautiful." That may be the overall audience reaction, but what makes these things so?

---

18. Nathaniel Graham Nesmith, moderator, Dramatists Guild Symposium, "Marketing to a Minority Audience," *The Dramatist*, November-December, 1998.

The critic is the one who should be able to tell us, that is, if we agree with the assessment. Often we do not; even critics don't agree. Each of them, as each audience member, has a slightly different perspective. Each brings all of his or her background and experience to a production, everything that has helped shape the person each is. Still, if critics are to do their job effectively and well, they need to recognize their mind sets — their prejudices — just as you do when attempting to state your reasons for liking or disliking a production. Put yourself in their place.

Suppose, for instance, you will attend a production of Kramer's *The Normal Heart*. What are your feelings about AIDS? About gay men? Why? How will this affect the way you view the show? With such views, can you be objective in your critique?

What genres do you like or dislike? Why? Would you rather see a comedy, or do you prefer something you can "sink your teeth into"?

Take into consideration why you are attending a performance. Is it because you want to be there, because it's a class requirement, or because you have been given an assignment of writing a review?

You need to consider the audience the playwright intended to see the work. Does the play fit the audience? Another basis for judgment is whether the producer or director really paid attention to the type of audience the theatre usually draws.

You need to ask yourself: How did the presentation affect me personally? Emotionally? Professionally? You should try to be honest in your judgment of the production. Yet your opinion is bound to differ from someone else's.

The following appeared after the opening of August Wilson's *Joe Turner's Come and Gone:*

New chapter in Wilson saga of black life
John Beaufort
The Christian Science Monitor, March 30, 1988

"Joe Turner's Come and Gone" is the most searching of the growing cycle of August Wilson dramas about the black American experience. It was preceded on Broadway by "Ma Rainey's Black Bottom" (the 1920s) and the current "Fences" (the 1950s), winner of the Pulitzer Prize and other awards. The transcendent new work further explores the personal sufferings and struggles born of a diaspora that began with slavery and continued with the post-emancipation of blacks to the industrial North.

In the present work, the struggle is as much for self-identity and self-realization as for lost kinfolk. "Joe Turner" is set in Pittsburgh in 1911. Swinging in mood from the richly comic to the poignantly tragic, the play constitutes what Mr. Wilson has described as "a boardinghouse play." Its inspiration comes from a painting by the late Romare Bearden and its title from a W. C. Handy blues ballad about the actual Joe Turner ...

While Wilson's dialog abounds in folk-flavored vernacular, his lyric flights ... give "Joe Turner" its extra dimension of poetic drama. The author also proves once more that he has moved far beyond the conventional "race play." The crimes of Joe Turner are presented as merely part of the pattern of subjugation that black Americans have historically endured ...

It is obvious that Beaufort liked both the play and the production. Yet not everyone agrees. In talking about Wilson's collection of work, *The Oxford Companion to American Theatre* says:

This profusion of awards is baffling, for while the plays have powerful scenes or moments, they are basically an unhomogenized melange of styles and techniques. Wilson employs realism, mysticism, some extremely eccentric characters, musical segments, and anything else that might work for immediate effect. As a result, the plays, except possibly for *Ma Rainey*, lack a sense of tone and a legitimate, sustained dramatic thrust.[19]

19. Gerald Bordman, ed., *The Oxford Companion to American Theatre*, (New York: Oxford University Press, 2nd ed., 1992), 718.

Critic Versus Reviewer

Although both write about theatrical productions, there is a difference between a reviewer and a critic. Generally, the reviewer must write a critique or evaluation of the production very quickly so it can appear in the next day's edition of a newspaper. It is more likely to deal only with the elements directly affecting the production. Critics, on the other hand, have more time and so can be more reflective. Their work may appear days or even weeks after a production which means they have more time to consider the production's impact and value. They might compare a particular production to a writer's entire body of work, to a theatre's season as a whole, or perhaps even to other productions of the same play. For example, the following is from the magazine *American Theatre* where Hulbert most certainly had more time to think through what he wanted to say than does a reviewer with a deadline of hours.

The Disney Company's recent premiere of *Elaborate Lives: The Legend of Aida* at Atlanta's Alliance Theatre raised an intriguing question: As it developed this pop-rock musical by Elton John, Tim Rice, and Linda Woolverton, would Disney continue the classy, risky path it had forged with *The Lion King* or fall back on the safer more conventional track that led to 1994's *Beauty and the Beast*?

On one level, *Elaborate Lives* can't help but be more original than *Beauty and the Beast* in that it is Disney's first straight-to-stage musical sans animated forebear. Billed as a more sophisticated musical that's still appropriate for family audiences, it takes off from the legend that inspired Verdi's opera about the doomed love between a black Nubian slave and the Egyptian soldier who vanquished her people ...

What's troubling is that not only does *Elaborate Lives* fail to break new ground, but it was staffed as if Disney never seriously intended it to. [Director Robert Jess] Roth, Woolverton, [Choreographer Matt] West, and [Set Designer Stanley] Meyer are all alumni of the theme-park follies of *Beauty and the Beast*. Nowhere is there an innovator even close to the caliber of *Lion King* auteur Julie Taymor.[20]

---

20. Dan Hulbert, "Safety First: Disney makes a timid but expensive foray into ancient Egypt" in "Critic's Notebook, *American Theatre*, December, 1998, 52.

Purposes of a Review

A review fulfills a number of purposes:

1. It acquaints a potential audience with the production and directs them either to attend or not.
2. It allows those who have seen the show to compare their own opinions with that of the reviewer and perhaps to help them clarify their own thinking about the play's worth or significance. At the same time, it refreshes their memory.
3. It helps the audience member to relive the experience of attending the production.
4. It promotes and helps publicize a production and maybe the theatre itself.
5. It provides instruction for those who may be interested in the production or in theatre itself but who have limited knowledge of it.
6. It can influence the theatre artists to change and improve their work.
7. It can be entertaining.

A reviewer can exert powerful influence. Many Broadway and Off-Broadway productions have closed due to adverse criticism from one or two powerful or respected critics writing for major New York publications. Generally, a reviewer's condemnation is so powerful that few New York productions have been able to succeed after receiving bad reviews, particularly from *The New York Times*.

Merle Debuskey relates the power of one reviewer over those waiting to see what he said:

> After the show, people used to assemble at Sardi's.[21] It's around the corner from the *Times*, and when the second edition, with Brooks Atkinson, came out, the papers would be dropped off. The place could either be filled with excitement or empty out in a flash. I can't tell you how quickly a restaurant can empty out.[22]

---

21. It's been traditional for those connected with a Broadway show to gather after opening night at Sardi's Restaurant to await the reviews.

22. Merle Debuskey, quoted in Myrna Katz Frommer and Harvey Frommer, eds. *It Happened on Broadway: An Oral History of the Great White Way* (New York: Harcourt, Brace & Company, 1998), 43.

Standards for Criticism

The critic/reviewer, whether a student writing a paper for a theatre class or a professional, needs a set of standards on which to base his or her criticism. This again comes from experiencing theatre — from seeing plays, both good and bad. German playwright and director Johann Wolfgang von Goethe suggested three questions by which to judge a production. These are a good starting point for the reviewer:

1. What is the artist or production trying to do?

If the play is a comedy, is it truly comedic? If it's a tragedy, does it fulfill these functions? In other words, do not try to judge a comedy by the standards of tragedy, or a tragedy by the standards of melodrama.

2. How well was it done?

How would you judge its quality? For instance, was the acting outstanding or merely adequate? Did the setting contribute to the overall effect the production seemed to be trying to achieve? Did all the elements of the production mesh?

3. Was it worth doing?

This is perhaps the most important and also the most subjective of the three questions. Do we view a show as accomplishing whatever purpose it set out to do? And if so, was this purpose important enough? Unique enough? Entertaining enough to hold our attention?

In reviewing a production, the critic or reviewer needs to stay focused and involved. Of course, this is hard to do if the acting is poor, the designs inappropriate, or the blocking sloppy. Most likely you will then have to step back from what is going on and view it more from the "outside." At the same time, you have a right to be demanding of a good choice of play, a well-written script, and a well-executed production. To judge this, you need to be knowledgeable and sensitive — as to what can realistically be expected of a performance, given the company and the theatre, and in regard to your openness in evaluating what you are perceiving.

What to Consider in a Review

One of the first things to consider is that a review, unlike a news story, both describes and judges. It is not a review if the writer expresses no opinion or evaluation. But the critique should include both the positive and negative features. At the same time, they need to avoid giving mixed signals — implying at one point that the production is worthwhile while implying at another that it falls below par. Reviewers need to decide which outweighs the other, the positive or the negative. Implied, of course, is that the reviewer needs to look at the production as a whole and at each of its parts.

Unless reviewers are seeing a premiere presentation of an original play, they generally spend much more time on the production itself than on the writing of the script. Critics, on the other hand, may spend as much or more time discussing the playwright since they often compare the present work to past works.

Besides knowledge of theatre in general, reviewers can prepare themselves specifically for a production they will see. They can, for instance, learn ahead of time as much as they can about the play, the theatre structure, and the company that will present it. Some of the questions they might consider are:

1. What is the play's genre? This is important for knowing what to expect.

2. In what time period is the play set? The reviewer then can consider if the production conveyed a proper sense of the time.

3. Is this a professional or nonprofessional organization or company? If this is a community theatre or a repertory theatre, for instance, is the play consistent with their past aims, or is this a departure?

4. Is the production being presented in an open or proscenium stage? What part does the building itself play in the productions? In what part of town is it located? Is it easily accessible? Does the location influence the sort of play that is likely to be successful? What are the positive aspects of the structure itself? Does it place any handicaps on the actors or the production?

5. What sort of audiences does the theatre draw — middle class? Minority? Those under thirty?

The more prepared reviewers are, the better able they will be to concentrate on the production. Some reviewers like to read the play ahead of time; others insist this is detrimental because a person cannot help but have certain expectations of how a play should be presented.

According to Campbell Titchner, "dramatic criticism can be divided into two broad categories. These are the physical (or mechanical) and the artistic (or creative) ones ... Physical considerations deal with tangibles, with fixed objects, with the things that cannot be easily changed."[23]

> The emphasis of the review is almost always on the creative aspects of the offering, and probably begins with acting. The reviewer knows that in theater, the audience should feel that the actor is indeed the person he or she is playing, a good starting point, and is not walking through the part for the hundredth time ...[24]

It is hard to imagine a theatre review that does not discuss acting, directing, and writing. Acting normally occupies most of the reviewer's time, whereas the critic is more concerned with writing and direction, because in her arena the actors are usually well known, and their particular talents well documented.

Some Questions Asked by Reviewers

Some specific questions to answer about the actors and their performance follow. There are any number of others a reviewer may wish to consider.

Does the actor: Fit the role? Communicate the lines well? Relate well to the other characters? Use his or her voice effectively for the stage and the character? Pick up cues quickly and have a good sense of timing? Move, stand, and gesture expressively and in character? Interpret the character effectively? Have stage presence and a high energy level? Perform consistently?

A reviewer also considers the directing: Is stage movement motivated by the situation? Does the performance overall appear spontaneous? Is the interpretation of the script appropriate? Is the style appropriate and effectively carried throughout? Is the stage picture aesthetically pleasing, the blocking logical and natural? Is the overall pacing appropriate? Is the company a true ensemble or simply individual actors?

---

23. Campbell B. Titchner, *Reviewing the Arts*, 2nd ed., (Mahwah, NJ: Lawrence Erlbaum Associates, Publishers, 1998), 88.
24. Titchner, 92.

The reviewer also may want to include the theatre itself. Things to consider are the acoustics, the size of the stage and theatre in relation to the style or type of production, whether the stage is used effectively, and whether it presents any special problems to the action (such as support columns blocking the view of some spectators)?

Also to be considered are the various areas of design. Does the scenery provide the necessary exposition? Does it maintain the production style consistently? Is it "actor friendly"? Are any scenery changes handled in a timely manner, and are they necessary and effective? Is the scenery interesting and aesthetically pleasing? Does the scenery help establish mood? Is any symbolism presented and carried out effectively?

Is the lighting appropriate? Does it provide good visibility? Is the lighting plan effectively executed? Does the lighting enhance the other elements of design? Does it provide necessary exposition? Is there use of lighting as symbolism? If so, is it carried out well?

Are the costumes appropriate for each character, the time period, and the circumstances? Are they easy to wear, or do they hinder movement and characterization? Is the style consistent with the rest of the production? Do the costumes help project the mood of the production?

Are sound effects appropriate? Is the sound effectively executed, and does it support the overall production? Is the makeup appropriate to the character, the period, the circumstances, the mood, the theme, the style?

Remember that all artistic elements should be subjugated to the whole. None should stand out or overwhelm but rather should be only a single part of the overall production. In effect, this involves a production's style. So the reviewer needs to consider if the overall style is appropriate to the play and consistent in the acting, the directing, and the elements of design.

Also to consider is how well the production stands up as a whole. How does it compare with other productions the critic has seen?

Even if the production involves a previously presented play, as most do, reviewers may want to touch on the writing. These are some of the things they may want to consider: When and where did the dramatist live? What were the economic and social conditions, and did they influence the subject matter and approach? What were the social influences? Is the viewpoint honest? Truthful?

What sort of structure does the play have? Is it easy to follow? What is the play's central message? What does the dramatist want the audience to think or feel after seeing a production of the play?

Did the play hold the reviewer's attention? Were the ideas, the story, the plot, the characterization interesting? Was the critic able to suspend disbelief and put himself or herself into the world of the play? Was the writing flawed?

Were the theme, the characters, the situation universal? Was the theme worthwhile?

Many plays — particularly those that are political in nature — often do not hold up beyond a certain period. This is the case with much of the AIDS drama of today. In fact, much of it already seems dated. On the other hand, playwrights are still dealing with many of the same social issues Ibsen dealt with in his plays about women's rights or individual rights.

Is the treatment of material appropriate?

How well does the play stand up as a comedy, a tragedy, a farce? If it's a comedy, is it really funny? What comic devices are used? Is the conflict logical?

What symbolism, if any, does the writer use (in contrast to that imposed by the director and designers)? Is it appropriate?

Is the background information clear and presented unobtrusively? Is there adequate foreshadowing?

Are the characters well drawn, and is there enough contrast among them to make the situation and conflict interesting? Are the protagonist's goals logical and worthwhile? Can you easily determine the purpose each character serves? Is there a balance between the main characters' individuality and typification?

Is the dialog appropriate to the situation? The mood? The characters? Does it give clues to personality and background?

The final consideration is whether or not you would recommend the production to others.

Summary

Since audiences and performers affect one another's reactions, a theatrical production differs from night to night.

Different types of plays draw differing audiences who attend the theatre for a number of reasons: to be entertained; to learn of recent, present, and imminent change; to confront social issues; to learn about people; to learn from the past; to reaffirm the audience's beliefs; to feel or to experience emotion.

The major difference between the average theatregoer and the professional reviewer or critic is that the professional generally better articulates the reasons for a production's success or failure.

A review fulfills a number of purposes. First it acquaints potential audiences with the production. It allows those who have seen a show to compare their opinions with the reviewer's. It helps audience members relive the experience of attending the production; it helps publicize the production and/or the theatre; it provides instruction; it sometimes influences theatre artists to improve their work. It entertains.

Questions for Discussion

1. In what ways do audiences and performers affect one another during a production? Why do you suppose this happens?
2. What does it mean to say that the audience has half a contract to fulfill in attending a theatrical production? What is involved in this contract?
3. What are the major reasons for attending the theatre?
4. In what ways does theatre mirror society?
5. In what ways do audiences at a college or university theatre differ from audiences at a community theatre? At a nonprofit theatre?
6. What would you consider to be the best ways to attract an audience to the theatre?
7. What is the difference between a play reviewer and a critic?
8. Do you think a critic or reviewer can be considered a theatre professional? Why?
9. What sorts of things should you consider about a production before attending? About yourself and your background? In general?
10. If you were to write a review of the next production at your school, what things would you consider to be most important to include? Why?
11. What purposes does a play review serve?

Part III
THEATRE HISTORY

Chapter 11
THEATRE'S BEGINNINGS

Theatre, or at least a form of reenactment, most likely began with a ritualistic "worship" long before the advent of recorded history. In all probability, early human beings became aware that outside forces controlled their food supply, weather conditions, and the movement of animals. To appease these forces the people developed prayers, hymns of praise, and reenactments of rituals that seemed to bring success in the hunt or in battle. Often, rituals were concerned with the changing of the seasons or with re-creating past deeds in order to preserve the history and beliefs of the tribe. Only when humor or comedy was introduced was theatre likely to develop.

In places such as Crete or Mesopotamia, no advances were made in theatre; instead, what "drama" was presented dealt with mythology and religion. In others, such as Peru, Indians developed both tragedy and comedy which they composed in blank verse.

Theatre in Asia

India

Drama and theatre developed in a number of Asian countries, one of which was India. Classical or Sanskrit drama was based on the concept of two types of emotions: deep mainsprings such as love and fleeting emotions such as anger. Through witnessing a blending of the two in facial expression and movement, the audience was expected to feel a sense of joy or aesthetic pleasure.

The earliest Sanskrit drama of which we are aware can be traced to 320 AD. Rather than centering on character development or philosophical issues, it dealt with fundamental moods, or rasas, such as the furious, the peaceful, or the heroic, to which all the other dramatic elements were subordinate.

China

Another country to develop drama and theatre was China where, in the ninth century, Emperor Tan Ming Huang established the first school of scenic art and music. During the Sung Dynasty (960–1279 AD), as in India, song, dance, and dialog were melded into a story in which gestures and movements were used to express various emotional states. Spectators came and went as they wished since the plays were based on traditional and familiar stories.

Japan

Drama in Japan evolved from ritual dances, increasing in importance after the seventh century AD. From these beginnings came **Noh**, or doll theatre, and **Kabuki**, of which the latter is the more important and lasting. Noh theatre reached its apex in the fifteenth century while Kabuki dates from the seventeenth century, and is the more popular of the two. Both forms included a drama-music-dance mixture and were highly stylized and therefore completely presentational.

The name Kabuki comes from the ideographs: *ka* meaning song, *bu* meaning dance, and *ki* meaning prostitute or later — due to nineteenth century objections — skill. Early on, the troupes were made up of women, but due to their loose morals, in 1629 the shogun banned their appearance. Then came troupes made up of male prostitutes, which in 1652 also were banned on the same grounds as the women's companies. Finally came troupes made up of men, who were required to shave their foreheads and relinquish any emphasis on physical charm.

Between 1675 and 1750, Kabuki Theatre evolved into the form that still is prevalent. Developed to appeal to popular tastes, it originally consisted of improvised sketches introduced into performances of dance. After 1650, more elaborate presentations began to develop with the first two-act form presented in 1664. Soon emphasis shifted to the drama itself, and each company now included a playwright and a number of apprentices.

There are three categories of presentation: **jidaimono**, which usually deal in great spectacle with events in the distant past; **sewamono**, which feature tales of ordinary people such as lovers or merchants, and **shosagoto**, dance plays, which often deal with spirits or animals. The plays essentially are melodramas with loosely connected episodes.

Dance is the basis of Kabuki and is expected to mirror the verbal text by distilling emotions and actions into stylized movement and posture. A presentation, with stock roles, all played by men, in bold, patterned makeup and traditional costumes, traditionally lasts for hours. Men train for much of their lives to be able to perform, and their style of acting is stylized. Many consider that true Kabuki ended in 1868 when it began to be influenced by Western theatre.

Greek Theatre

After the Persian wars (500-448 BC), Athens became the most influential Greek state. Sparta, which had had superior military strength, lost its prestige as a result of the victories of the Athenian naval fleet. Consequently, Athens set about wielding power over the other members of the Delian League, a formation of Greek states, to such a degree that these other states became its subjects rather than its allies. This period became known as Athens's Golden Age. With emphasis on the intellect and intellectual pursuits, the city became widely known as an artistic and cultural center. It isn't surprising then that Athens should develop the world's most advanced theatre up to that period.

No one knows, of course, how long it took for drama and theatre to develop, but it must have been centuries before the appearance of the playwrights whose work we know today.

The Development of Drama

Greek theatre, from which the rest of Western theatre developed, began some time before the sixth century BC with **dithyrambs**, or hymns, to Dionysus, the god of wine and harvest. The hymns related episodes from his life. According to legend, Dionysus — son of Zeus, the greatest of Greek gods, and of the mortal Semele — was killed, dismembered, and then resurrected. His life thus signified rebirth of the seasons with a yearly return to spring.

Theatre's development from the Dionysian hymns to the appearance of full-scale drama was gradual. First, there was only a chorus speaking or singing. Later, an individual actor appeared. According to legend, the first such person was Thespis (from which comes *thespian*, a synonym for actor), who thus is given the distinction of being the first playwright, the first actor, and the first director in Western theatre. There is record that he first performed in 534 BC when he is credited with winning the prize at the first tragedy contest in Greece. Even though the introduction of an actor added dialog to the dithyrambs, the chorus itself remained the unifying force.

After a time, the chorus dressed as satyrs — creatures that were half goat and half man — and the worship then became known as the "goat song," or **tragoidia**, from which comes the word *tragedy*. It was not until the work of the playwright Aeschylus, however, that the Dionysian presentations could be called drama since up until then they contained no conflict.

Out of the ecclesiastical part of the celebration came both tragedy and the **satyr play**. Only one complete satyr play survives — *The Cyclops* by Euripides. Because of this, we know little about the genre, except that it was a ribald form of comedy in which appeared the folkloric figure of Silenus, a water spirit, accompanied by the satyrs, and that it was written by a playwright to be presented in the afternoon of the day on which his tragedies also were to be produced.

Although we know that tragedy and satyr plays grew out of religious celebration, the origin of comedy is not known. It may have developed from dances and songs improvised by Dionysian revelers or from farces enacted at various places in Greece and Italy. Another theory is that a group of young men (**komos**) began to join the processions to the altar of Dionysus, improvising songs and witticisms to the crowd, which answered back, with both groups becoming increasingly insulting.

Throughout, the chorus continued to serve as a character, or sometimes as two characters discussing events with each other, or as a messenger. Not much action occurred on-stage, and most information about events was presented through dialog and choral songs. The plays were written in verse and consisted of scenes among characters alternating with choral songs.

Theatre Festivals and Theatrical Production

The three festivals at which Greek drama developed were the City Dionysia, held in Athens at the end of March each year; the Lenaia, held in Athens each January; and the Rural Dionysia, held in December. The festivals had a master of revels, called the **archon**, who selected the plays and the order in which they would be presented. He chose wealthy citizens to bear the expense of room and board for the chorus members. These citizens, called the **choregoi**, paid for training the chorus, for the costumes, for the musicians, and for any additional expenses. While the *archon* was elected, the *choregoi* were appointed to what was considered a prestigious position. Sometimes there was a strong rivalry among the *choregoi* to see who could spend the most money.

A playwright applied to the *archon* for rights to present plays. If selected, he was given a chorus and was expected to present music as well as drama. Many playwrights directed their plays and appeared in them. The actors (the Greek word for them is *hypocrites*, which at first meant simply "answerer") were paid by the state. There is indication that admission to the festivals was free, and everyone was expected to attend.

All of the plays still in existence were written for the City Dionysia. It was the most important festival, and some believe that all prisoners were freed and no legal proceedings were allowed to continue during the festival. Frequently attended by dignitaries of other states, it began with a processional and pageant in which the statue of Dionysus was taken from the temple at the foot of the Acropolis, carried outside the city of Athens, and then carried back with great celebration. Then ten dithyrambs were presented, five composed of choruses of boys and five composed of choruses of men. For the next few days, plays were presented. Three writers of tragedy were chosen every year, and each was expected to present a trilogy plus a satyr play — all taking place the same day.

At first, awards were presented for the best tragedies and, later, for the best tragic actor and comedy. The festival ended with the presentation of the prizes and a meeting of governmental leaders to discuss affairs of state.

During the fifth century BC, all the most important developments in playwriting and production occurred.

Plays and Playwrights

From its beginning, comedy formed a complete whole, performed separately from other plays. On the other hand, tragedy was presented in trilogies comprising a cycle of legends, each telling a story complete in itself, but connected both chronologically and through subject matter.

The first important dramatist of whom we have record is Aeschylus (525–456 BC), who wrote eighty to ninety plays, seven of which are still in existance. He relied largely on the chorus and primarily used traditional themes based on myths and Olympian law. Although his plays had a plot line, they were mostly choral. He introduced a second actor into his plays, not to provide dramatic conflict, but for the sake of variety. His best work is considered to be the *Orestian Trilogy* (458 BC), in which all three plays — *Agamemnon*, *The Libation Bearers*, and *Eumenides* — deal with revenge.

The next major writer of tragedy was Sophocles (496–406 BC), who wrote well over a hundred plays. He is credited with introducing a third actor and with reducing the size of the chorus from fifty to twelve.

Sophocles was more interested in the interplay between characters than in the telling of religious myths. His plots are much more realistic than those of Aeschylus, and he is concerned with human beings as the determiners of their own fate, rather than as subject to the gods. His characters are complex, strong, and believable, and the central character always has a tragic flaw that brings about his or her downfall. Sophocles' plays, better developed than those of Aeschylus, have a skillful and believable climax. His work includes *Oedipus Rex*, *Oedipus at Colonus*, and *Antigone*.

The third major writer of tragedy was Euripides (480–406 BC), who is credited with ninety-two plays, of which seventeen tragedies and a satyr play survive. Concerned largely with the human being as an individual, Euripides dealt with the inner conflict of good and evil — that is, human beings against conscience — and questioned many of the ideals of Greek society and religion. He was admired for his ideas and the presentation of realistic characters, but criticized for the structure of his plays, which often were melodramatic and contrived.

The chorus is of much less importance in Euripides' plays, serving largely as a mouthpiece for the playwright rather than as a part of the action.

Euripides' most widely performed play is *The Trojan Women*. Produced in 415 BC, a few months after Athenian forces had massacred all the males on the neutral island of Melos, the play takes a strong antiwar stand, no doubt a reaction against the toll taken by the Peloponnesian Wars.[1] Although the women and the city itself already have suffered tragedy as the drama opens, the intensity mounts throughout. Adding more power to the idea of "man's inhumanity to man" is Hecuba's vengeance in begging Menelaus to kill his wife, Helen.

---

1. In 415 BC Aristophanes (See Page 252) wrote *Lysistrata* as a plea to end the continuing war between Athens and Sparta. The women of Athens, led by Lysistrata, meet with women from all over Greece. Those from both Athens and Sparta promise to withhold sex from the men until peace is declared.

The Trojan Women
Euripides

The city of Troy is burning and in ruins, its men dead. The women and children are to become slaves to the victorious Greeks, commanded by Menelaus and Agamemnon.

The play tells of the suffering and despair of the women, including Queen Hecuba, who has become a slave to Odysseus, the man she most despises. Now she learns that one of her daughters, Polyxena, and her grandson Astyanax have been murdered. Another daughter, Cassandra, has been made Agamemnon's mistress.

Cassandra, half crazed, rejoices in her fate because it has angered the goddess Athene, who thus will wreck the Greek fleet in a storm.

Andromache, mother of Astyanax, is forced to set sail with her new master, leaving Hecuba to bury the baby. The queen encounters Menelaus and Helen, his beautiful spouse, who caused the war by deserting Menelaus for Hecuba's son Paris. Hecuba pleads with Menelaus to execute Helen, which he agrees to do.

As Hecuba prepares to bury the small body of her grandson, the Greeks burn Troy and, amidst the wailing, Trojan women set sail for home.

Comedy: Old and New

Throughout the history of classical Greece, tragedy dealt with the gods and heroes, while comedy related to current events and people. Greek comedy was developed after tragedy and was considered inferior, yet it was important to Greek citizens, who stressed the concept of "a well-balanced man in a well-balanced state."

Although comedies were presented at the City Dionysia, they were given more support at the Lenaia. Choruses of twenty-four members were used, and often there were more individual actors than appeared in tragedies.

The plots of Greek comedies were more complicated than those of tragedies, but were more episodic. Unlike tragic heroes, comic characters were ordinary people. In essence, tragedy dealt with what humankind should be, while comedy dealt with what it actually is.

There are two categories of comedy, Old and New. **Old Comedy** (454–404 BC) is characterized by its emphasis on an idea rather than on a cause-to-effect relationship of events. The episodes often seem unrelated. However, they do build in comic intensity. Often broad satires based on well-known people and events, comedies parodied the same subjects treated seriously in tragedy.

Old Comedy also made use of a chorus, from whom the play took its name, such as *The Wasps* or *The Frogs*.

The major and only extant writer of Old Comedy was Aristophanes (c. 448–385 BC). In *The Clouds* (423 BC), Socrates (and philosophers in general) becomes the scapegoat of Aristophanes' biting wit. The story concerns Strepsiades, who decides to seek Socrates' advice about how he can avoid paying back money he owes as a result of his unscrupulous son running up huge debts. The dialog is filled with pseudo-intellectual babbling about science and logic, which Aristophanes sees as a "narrow-minded effort to stifle the breadth, complexity, beauty, and joy of experience, for it substitutes clever thinking for full wholesome living."[2] When the play was produced, according to legend:

Socrates ... stood up so that the spectators could compare him with the image on the stage. But in 399 BC, when he showed himself to a court of 501 Athenians, he could not convince them that he was not the dishonest and irreverent creature whom they had seen in Aristophanes' comedy.[3]

2. Sylvan Barnet, Morton Berman, and William Burto, eds. *Eight Great Comedies*, (New York: New American Library, 1958), 15.
3. Barnet, 16.

The Clouds
Aristophanes
Translated by William James Hickie

SOCRATES: Do you, yourself, first find out and state what you wish.

STREPSIADES: You have heard a thousand times what I wish. About the interest; so that I may pay no one.

SOCRATES: Come then, wrap yourself up, and having given your mind play with subtilty, revolve your affairs by little and little, rightly distinguishing and examining.

STREPSIADES: Ah me, unhappy man!

SOCRATES: Keep quiet; and if you be puzzled in any one of your conceptions, leave it and go; and then set your mind in motion again, and lock it up.

STREPSIADES: *(In great glee)* O dearest little Socrates!

SOCRATES: What, old man?

STREPSIADES: I have got a device for cheating them of the interest.

SOCRATES: Exhibit it.

STREPSIADES: Now tell me this, pray; if I were to purchase a Thessalian witch, and draw down the moon by night, and then shut it up, as if it were a mirror, in a round crest-case, and then carefully keep it —

SOCRATES: What good, pray, would this do you?

STREPSIADES: What? If the moon were to rise no longer anywhere, I should not pay the interest.

SOCRATES: Why so, pray?

STREPSIADES: Because the money is lent out by the month.

SOCRATES: Capital! But I will again propose to you another clever question. If a suit of five talents should be entered against you, tell me how you would obliterate it.

STREPSIADES: How? How? I do not know but I must seek.

SOCRATES: Do not then always revolve your thoughts about yourself; but slack away your mind into the air, like a cock-chafer tied with a thread by the foot.

STREPSIADES: I have found a very clever method of getting rid of my suit, so that you yourself would acknowledge it.

SOCRATES: Of what description?

STREPSIADES: Have you ever seen this stone in the chemist's shops, the beautiful and transparent one, from which they kindle fire?

SOCRATES: Do you mean the burning-glass?

STREPSIADES: I do. Come what would you say, pray, if I were to take this, when the clerk was entering the suit, and were to stand at a distance, in the direction of the sun, thus, and melt out the letters of my suit?

SOCRATES: Cleverly done, by the Graces!

STREPSIADES: Oh! How I am delighted, that a suit of five talents has been cancelled!

SOCRATES: Come now, quickly seize upon this.

STREPSIADES: What?

SOCRATES: How, when engaged in a lawsuit, you could overturn the suit, when you were about to be cast, because you had no witnesses.

STREPSIADES: Most readily and easily.

SOCRATES: Tell me, pray.

STREPSIADES: Well now, I'll tell you. If, while one suit was still pending, before mine was called on, I were to run away and hang myself.

SOCRATES: You talk nonsense.

STREPSIADES: By the gods, would I! For no one will bring action against me when I am dead.

New Comedy, popular in the time of Alexander the Great, is associated with Menander (c. 342–291 BC), the most celebrated writer of this form. He wrote more than one hundred plays, with the first performance of his work in 321 BC.

New Comedy dealt with middle-class citizens because the government, perhaps due to the theatregoers' changing tastes, no longer allowed playwrights to poke fun at leaders or other well-known people. As a result, the characters are more types than individuals. To make them interesting, the writer had to place them in situations where their follies could be exposed and ridiculed.

The Physical Theatre

Plays were presented outdoors, on a flat place, or **orchestra**, at the base of a hill. At first, this was an open space with no walls or ceiling. The auditorium, or **theatron**, was the hillside itself where the audience stood to watch the plays. In time, permanent seats were constructed of stone.

An altar to Dionysus, called the *themele*, was located in the middle of each site. Some time during the fifth century BC, a **skene** building, or scene house, was added to provide a dressing area and a place for actors to wait before going on-stage. It eventually came to be used as a background for the dramatic action and later became a two-story building with various openings on both stories. The second story was used for the appearance of the gods, while the doors below were for the protagonist and the other characters. One of the openings, the *thyromata*, which framed action that occurred within the building, may have been the predecessor of our proscenium stage. Actors used doors in the *proskenion* to make entrances and exits.

The theatre of Dionysus, the most famous Greek theatre, seated about fourteen thousand spectators. Since most of the action in Greek drama takes place outside, little scenery was used. Some believe, however, that painted flats occasionally were leaned against the exterior walls of the scene house. A later form of scenery was the *periaktoi* — tall prisms with three sides on which different scenes were painted. Mounted on poles at each side of the stage, they could be rotated to show the appropriate scenes.

After the fourth century BC, much more elaborate stone theatres were built, yet the drama itself never came close to matching the quality of that of the fifth century theatres.

Stage Machinery

There were various types of stage machinery. One was the *mechane*, or **deus ex machina**, a device or crane of some sort that lowered the gods when the play called for them to intervene in characters' lives. In contemporary times, *deus ex machina* has come to mean a less-than-desirable literary device in which a playwright has fate solve the protagonist's problem, rather than having the character solve it.

Another piece of stage machinery was the **ekkyklema**, a cart or platform that rolled out of the *thyromata*. It may have been used to carry the bodies of actors portraying warriors killed in battle since, so far as is known, the Greeks did not show violence on-stage.

The Actors

The actors in the Greek theatre were highly respected. They were trusted as diplomats, were exempt from military service, and were considered servants of Dionysus. The Greek actor also was highly trained and skillful, because he was expected to assume many different roles.

Masks and Costumes

Every type of character that appeared in a Greek play had a specific mask, making it easy for the audience to recognize a servant, a young woman, or an old man just by the mask the actor wore. This was particularly important because all the performers were men. The tragic actor also wore a boot, or *cothurnus*, (which in the latter part of the fourth century became more stylized with the soles thickened by several inches to give the actor added stature), and possibly a *chiton*, an ankle-length embroidered robe.

Costumes for comedy were less cumbersome, since the comic actor was required to be nimble. Usually he wore slippers, flesh-colored tights, a short tunic, and, in Aristophanes' plays, a large leather phallus. For satyr plays, the actors wore a tail and a phallus.

Aristotle

Perhaps the most important contribution of the Greek theatre to that of our own era were the writings of Aristotle. (See a discussion of *The Poetics* in Chapter 1.) Though much of his work is lost and so cannot be interpreted exactly, Aristotle's approach continues to influence the writing of drama.

Roman Theatre

During the First Punic War (264–241 BC), the Romans became exposed to the drama of Greece and began importing Greek plays even though they regarded the Greek culture as decadent. Roman playwrights imitated Greek plays, particularly those written by Menander. Roman citizens also saw **mimes** that were performed by Greek citizens who had settled in Sicily. Loosely improvised plays, with suggestive action and dialog, sensational elements, and stereotyped characters, mimes first appeared in Rome in the third century BC.

Despite the many similarities between Greek and Roman theatre, some differences existed. Whereas the Greeks viewed drama as reflecting moral values and important issues, the Romans regarded it strictly as entertainment. In addition, the Greeks made more use of a chorus both for speaking and singing, while music in the Roman theatre was associated with single actors and was more equally distributed throughout the play.

There was no real connection between plays and religion, although shrines to various gods often were part of the theatre buildings and sacrifices were made to them during the festivals. At first, drama was presented during festivals held only four times a year, but later was included for occasions such as military victories or funerals of noted citizens. The festivals also featured chariot races, gladiatorial displays, enactments of sea battles, boxing, and public crucifixions. Slaves were forced to participate in gladiatorial battles to the death. Jugglers, acrobats, trained animal acts, and pantomimes in which dancing played the most important part were also presented.

Acting Companies

A magistrate in charge of the festivals received aid from the state, but also might contribute some of his own money. He then contracted with an acting company and a manager for the plays, which it is believed were bought outright from the writers and may have been viewed beforehand to check for appropriateness rather than for artistic quality. Several acting companies participated in each festival, and admission was free. The companies that were judged the best (that is, received the most applause) were given prizes in addition to being paid.

Roman actors (*histriones*) usually specialized in playing certain types of characters, although Roscius, Rome's most famous actor, played in both comedy and tragedy.

The acting style of Rome was more improvisational in nature than that of Greece. The movements were broad and exaggerated, because in large theatres many spectators could not discern small movements. Costumes for tragedy were similar to those worn by Greek actors. Costumes for comedy were Greek if the play was based on Greek life, or Roman if it dealt with everyday Roman life. Both tragic and comic actors wore masks with attached wigs. Men played female roles, except in the mimes.

Theatre Buildings

Initially, Roman theatres were temporary structures made of wood, with only a platform and a scene (Greek *skene*) building. Not until 55 BC was the first permanent theatre erected, at Pompeii. Others followed at various locations in the empire, each more elaborate than those preceding it. There were stone columns and arches and intricate statues and friezes. Often, the buildings were covered to protect the artistry as well as the actors.

Playwrights

Titus Maccius Plautus, Rome's first major playwright (254 – 184 BC), wrote a large number of comedies, twenty-one of which still exist. Although he borrowed his plots from Menander, he adapted and changed them. Two of his best-known works are *The Menaechmi* and *Amphitruo*, both of which deal with the complications of mistaken identity. Shakespeare based his *Comedy of Errors* on *The Menaechmi*.

Plautus's plays differed from Greek comedies in that they did not satirize the government, but pointed up the idiosyncrasies of individual characters, often dealing with misunderstood motives and deceptions. A prologue outlined the plot, and the plays, though coarse, remained popular long after his death due to their broad humor, improbable situations, and lively spirit.

Second in popularity was Publius Terentius Afer, known as Terence (about 195–159 BC). His dialog was written in the style of everyday conversation, and his plays showed a sympathetic treatment of character. A black slave who had lived in Athens, Terence wrote six plays, all of which survive. *The Brothers* is one of his better known works. He based his writings on Menander, but attempted to improve the form and structure, often combining several Greek plays into one drama. Each of the plays had a double plot and was more polished and more skillfully written than those of Plautus.

The only Roman tragedies still in existence were written by Lucius Annaeus Seneca (4 BC–65 AD). Although adaptations of Greek tragedies, his plays differed markedly from their sources. Because they were written to be recited rather than produced, they contained much violence that would have been nearly impossible to present on the stage and were characterized by elaborate speeches, soliloquies, asides, and sensationalism in general.

After the fourth century AD, largely because of the influence of the Christian church, the theatre existed only in a very limited way until the tenth century, when it once more began to gain popularity.

258

Summary

Theatre in many different cultures most likely began with a ritualistic form of worship. India developed Sanskrit drama which was based on the concept of moods or rasas. Japanese drama included Noh theatre and the more popular Kabuki.

Greek theatre developed in Athens and was a blending of ritual and imitation that began in the sixth century with hymns to Dionysus. Drama was presented at three festivals, each of which had a master of revels or *archon* who selected the plays, and a *choregoi* who footed any expenses.

Aeschylus, the first important playwright relied largely on the chorus and used traditional themes for his writing. Sophocles was more interested in the interplay between characters, while Euripides was concerned largely with the human being as an individual.

Greek comedy related to current events. The only extant writer of this form is Aristophanes. The most celebrated writer of New Comedy was Menander.

Plays were presented outdoors in a flat area. In the fifth century BC, a *skene* building was added. Later a second floor was used for the appearance of the gods.

Roman writers imitated Greek plays, particularly those by Menander. Drama in Rome was first presented at festivals held four times a year. The most popular Roman playwrights were Plautus and Terence. The only Roman tragedies in existence were written by Seneca and were adaptations of Greek plays.

Questions for Discussion

1. Why do you suppose theatre developed in a similar way in many different cultures?
2. Why do you think dance became such a large part of theatre in some areas?
3. What are the major differences between Sanskrit drama and Western drama?
4. Kabuki actors were in the same class as prostitutes while Greek actors were honored and respected. What do you think accounts for this?
5. There is no way to determine how comedy originated. How do you think it might have? Why?
6. Why do you suppose the Greeks did not show violence on-stage?
7. Roman theatre generally is considered inferior to that of Greece. Why do you suppose that is so?

Chapter 12
MEDIEVAL THEATRE

"The theatres," Augustine said in 400 AD "are falling nearly everywhere, the theatres, those sinks of uncleanness and public places of debauchery. And why are they falling? They are falling because of the reformation of the age, because the lewd and sacrilegious practices for which they are built are out of fashion." That the theatres were falling is an indisputable fact; that the age had reformed is far less certain. Barbarian attacks on Italy had contributed much to theatre's devastation.[1] After the fall of the Western Roman Empire, overrun by invaders in 476, little in the way of drama or theatrical entertainment was presented for several hundred years. Yet, a fondness remained. Minstrels (itinerant troubadours), acrobats, singers, jugglers, and animal trainers traveled through the countryside, stopping to perform in towns and villages.

There were mimes and pantomimes, pagan rites, and festivals. But the Christian church was a powerful institution, growing more so year by year, gaining in strength since before the fall of Rome. The church was against theatre, declaring it was sacrilegious, evil, and immoral, so it was difficult for drama to exist. Those few actors who continued to perform were forbidden the sacrament of communion.

Apparently, however, this didn't seem to matter a great deal to the occasional performers who continued to present their fare, nor did it bother their audiences. This is apparent from the order given repeatedly by the church to stop presenting and attending all theatrical performances.

---

1. Sylvan Barnet, Morton Berman, and William Burto, eds., *The Genius of the Early American Theater*, (New York: New American Library, 1962), 10.

Rebirth

Ironically, when drama was reborn it appeared as a part of the church service in much of Western Europe. In the ninth century, the cross and the Resurrection of Christ became increasingly important symbols of the church. At about the same time, the liturgy was expanded to include Latin sequences, or hymns. The person responsible for this was the St. Gall monk Notker Balbulus, the Stammerer (c. 840–912). A colleague of his named Tutilo (c. 850–915) then changed the liturgical insertions into dialog delivered by priests. One priest impersonated an angel and three others impersonated the three women visiting Christ's tomb. Thus **liturgical drama** came into existence one Easter morning in the form of a playlet — a **trope** designed to teach and to provide visual examples of the biblical story of Jesus' crucifixion and rising from the dead:

> ANGEL: *Quem queritis in sepulchro, o Christicole?*
>
> [Whom seek ye in the sepulcher, O women of Christ?]
>
> MARYS: *Jesum Nazerenum crucifixum, o caelicolae.*
>
> [Jesus of Nazareth, who is crucified, O heavenly one.]
>
> ANGEL: *Non est hic, surrexit sicut praedixerat. Ite, nuntiate quia surrexit de speculchro.*
>
> [He is not here; He is risen, as was foretold. Go, proclaim that he has risen from the sepulcher!]

This trope was the source of the Passion play still performed today.

The tropes (from the Latin *tropus*, melody) continued to be a part of the mass at the church's major yearly events, such as Easter, Advent, and Christmas, and thus became a tradition throughout Western Europe. The widespread use of such playlets is not surprising since the church, rather than national governments, ruled the actions of the people. Thus, drama was similar from Holland to France to Italy to England, with only local customs and tastes dictating slight differences.

Gradually, the playlets were expanded until they became more elaborate and were included extensively in church services. In one trope Mary Magdalene, at Christ's tomb, mistakes Christ for a gardener. In another the Marys buy perfume from a stall that has been set up outside Christ's tomb.

At first, the lines were delivered in Latin. Later, each was repeated — as in the previous example — in the language of the country. Beginning in the eleventh century the Latin was dropped, and the lines were spoken in the local language.

The Staging of Liturgical Drama

In the beginning, tropes were presented only by clergymen in the larger churches and cathedrals. The staging or scenery consisted of "mansions," or **sedes**, and an acting area, or **platea**. A *sede* represented a specific place, such as Christ's tomb, which was most often at the altar of the church. After the dramatizations became more lengthy and elaborate, additional tropes showed events leading up to and following the Resurrection.

Now there were several different *sedes* — one for each locale — placed at various points around the interior of the sanctuary. Since each mansion was small, the *platea* could be a central area or the entire open space. The action would start at one mansion or *sede* (the specific location) and move into the *platea* (the nonspecific or central location). After the play switched to another mansion, the same general central area again became the playing space.

Figure 12-1: Sedes from Medieval Theatre.

As time went on, the staging became more elaborate. At first, chairs or the altar indicated the different mansions. Later, more elaborate *sedes* were built, such as a sepulcher for Christ's tomb, large enough for several people to enter.

The presentations grew longer, with more and more mansions added. The dialog departed from that recorded in the Bible, becoming more secular and even including humor. In addition, more people were participating, and the costuming and scenery were becoming increasingly spectacular.

Moving Outside the Church

By the thirteenth century, the presentations had become too elaborate and disruptive to be presented inside the church buildings, which by now were overcrowded with spectators. Thus, the drama, usually still acted by clergymen, came to be presented on the west side of the church. Here, in many cases, was a porch — a ready-made stage of sorts — opening onto the town square, where local residents could stand and watch.

Many church officials began to have doubts about whether the plays should be presented at all; they were becoming more and more what the leaders had earlier feared. One edict about their presentation followed another, so that gradually laymen began acting in them, and by the fourteenth and fifteenth centuries, all the responsibilities of the production were assumed by secular groups. By this time, the dialog was spoken entirely in the local language.

One of the most popular forms that developed was the *Corpus Christi* (Body of Christ) play, presented from about 1350 to about 1550 on the Thursday following Pentecost, that is, some time between late May and late June. This drama emphasized transubstantiation, or the mystery of communion bread and wine becoming Christ's body and blood. The productions grew to include dozens of scenes, encompassing all of creation, and were presented in towns and villages all across England.

The Producing Groups and the Productions

The secular play-producing groups were largely trade guilds or special societies, the latter formed just for this purpose. In France, one such group was the *Confrérie de la Passion*, established in 1402 by Charles VI at the Hôpital de la Trinité, thus becoming the first permanent company to have a particular theatre to call its home. Although the church no longer participated to any great extent in the productions, its approval was still necessary. Each guild had a patron saint, its own priest, and a chapel. Sometimes several small guilds joined together to produce a single play.

Later, the drama moved from the west door of the church to other locations. Various types of structures were used. Some plays, for example, were produced on a platform pushed against a building, while others were presented in old Roman amphitheatres or in town squares.

Production and Spectacle

In England, there were two major means of production. One was to present plays in "rounds" or ancient amphitheatres, and the other was to use **pageant wagons** as stages. A pageant wagon carried two or more mansions, and some historians believe that at times several were placed next to each other. The acting may have taken place entirely on the wagons or on the ground in front of them. The wagons were designed to be moved from place to place, with each site marked by flags indicating where they were to stop. Some wagons symbolized particular locations, such as the mouth of hell belching fire. One was shaped like a ship for a play about Noah.

Typically, the mansions were positioned to represent the planes of heaven, earth, and hell. Heaven usually was at one end of the playing area and hell at the other, with a series of mansions between. The more mansions there were, the longer and more elaborate the presentation. It is recorded, for instance, that in 1501 at Mons, France, a play was given with sixty-seven mansions. It took forty-eight days to rehearse, and one performance lasted four days.

The scenes were really short episodes that had no connection with one another except that they dealt with biblical subject matter. Each episode was complete in itself, and the overall presentation had no continuing plot.

Of great concern were special effects. There are records of professionals being hired to invent all sorts of startling "secrets" (as they were called) including Christ's walking on the water and smoke and fire billowing from the mouth of hell. There were earthquakes and clouds. Thunder roared. Actors and objects were raised and lowered by means of ropes and pulleys, allowing the audience to watch as monsters and animals flew freely through hell. There is even record of an effigy being filled with bones and animal entrails to provide a realistic scene. Fountains sprang up, water turned into wine, and the miracle of the loaves and fishes was enacted.

Unlike the drama of Greece, medieval religious drama involved much violence, including sword fights and battles. The lists of battle regalia and other properties were often long and costly.

Most of the actors dressed in contemporary costumes they supplied themselves, but angels wore white robes with wings, and God was dressed as an official of the church. Satan, wearing wings, horns, claws, and a tail, was designed to be both humorous and awe-inspiring. In fact, beginning in the sixteenth century, the plays included many comic elements. Unfortunately, not many of the texts of these works survive. Of the hundreds given in England, only those from Chester, York, Coventry, and Wakefield exist in complete form.

Cycle Plays

At the end of the fourteenth century, all the plays that had been presented throughout the church year were combined into a single presentation, or cycle. The Wakefield Cycle contained thirty-two episodes, while the York Cycle comprised forty-eight. Elaborate productions such as these continued until the middle of the sixteenth century, all the while changing in content as old sections were deleted and new ones were added.

Further, more and more humor, often centered on wives, crept into the presentations. For example, in each of two plays about the flooding of the earth, Noah has a shrewish wife. There also is humor in *The Second Shepherd's Play*, part of the Wakefield Cycle. (Its title is in reference to the fact that of the thirty-two plays that make up the cycle, this is the second dealing with the Nativity.) Mak complains about his wife and how he can ill afford to support his family. He casts a spell on three shepherds so that they fall asleep. Then he steals one of their sheep. Among his complaints, which sets up what happens later, are that his wife:

> Lies wallowing — by the rood — by the fire, lo!
> And a house full of brood. She drinks well, too
> There's no other good that she will do!
> But she
> Eats as fast as may be,
> And every year that we see
> She brings forth a baby —
> And, some years, two.

Were I even more prosperous and richer by some,
I were eaten out of house and even of home.
Yet is she a foul souse, if ye come near;
There is none that goes or anywhere roams
'Worse than she ...

Mak then proposes the idea of passing off the stolen sheep as a newborn baby. His wife agrees to go along with the deception.

The play presents a parallel between the tale of Mak, his wife, and their newborn "baby" and the nativity story of Joseph, Mary, and their newborn "lamb." First, each of the two births is preceded by song, with Mak singing out of tune and the angels singing sweetly. The shepherds also offer gifts to both of the newborns. The humor was not intended to be sacrilegious, but rather to point up humankind's follies. Thus side-by-side exist a realistic world of bad weather, lack of money, and less-than-ideal family relationships — often treated humorously — and a world of faith, innocence, and awe at the birth of Jesus.

The Second Shepherd's Play
Anonymous

FIRST SHEPHERD: Gave ye the child anything?
SECOND SHEPHERD: I swear not one farthing.
THIRD SHEPHERD: Quickly back will I fling;
　　Abide ye me here. *(He runs back.)*
　　Mak, take it to no grief if I come to thy son.
MAK: Nay, thou dost me great mischief, and foul hast
　　thou done.
THIRD SHEPHERD: The child will it not grieve, that
　　daystar one?
　　Mak, with your leave, let me give your son
　　But sixpence.
MAK: Nay, go way! He sleeps.
THIRD SHEPHERD: Methinks he peeps.
MAK: When he wakens he weeps.
　　I pray you, go hence!
　　(The others return.)

THIRD SHEPHERD: Give me leave him to kiss, and lift up
the clout.² *(He lifts up the cover.)*
What the devil is this? He has a long snout!
FIRST SHEPHERD: He is shapèd amiss. Let's not wait about.
SECOND SHEPHERD: "Ill-spun weft," iwis, "aye comes
foul out."³
A son! *(Recognizes the sheep.)* He is like to our sheep!
THIRD SHEPHERD: How, Gib, may I peep?
FIRST SHEPHERD: "How nature will creep
Where it cannot run!"
SECOND SHEPHERD: This was a quaint gaud and a far cast;⁴
It was a high fraud.
THIRD SHEPHERD: Yea, sirs, was't.
Let's burn this bawd and bind her fast.
A false scold hangs at the last;
So shalt thou.
Will ye see how they swaddle
His four feet in the middle?
Saw I never in a cradle
A horned lad ere now.
MAK: Peace, bid I. What! Leave off your care!
I am he that begat, and yond woman him bare.
FIRST SHEPHERD: How named is your brat? "Mak?" Lo,
God, Mak's heir.
SECOND SHEPHERD: Let be all that. Now God curse his fare,
This boy.
WIFE: A pretty child is he
As sits on a woman's knee;
A dillydown, pardie,
To give a man joy.
THIRD SHEPHERD: I know him by the ear-mark;
that is a good token.
MAK: I tell you, sirs, hark! — his nose was broken.
I was told by a clerk a spell had been spoken.

2. Cloth
3. "An ill-spun weft always comes out foul," meaning that the parents' deformity appears in the child.
4. A clever prank and a sly trick

FIRST SHEPHERD: This is a false work; my vengeance
  is woken.
  Get weapon!
WIFE: He was taken by an elf,
  I saw it myself;
  When the clock struck twelve
  Was he misshapen.
SECOND SHEPHERD: Ye two are most deft,
  but we're not misled.
FIRST SHEPHERD: Since they stand by their theft,
  let's see them both dead.
MAK: If I trespass eft,[5] strike off my head.
  With you will I be left.
THIRD SHEPHERD: Sirs, let them dread:
  For this trespass
  We will neither curse nor fight,
  Strike nor smite;
  But hold him tight,
  And cast him in canvas.
  (They toss MAK in a sheet and return to the field.)
  For, iwis, thou break my heart in three.

On the other hand, *Abraham and Isaac* is serious and completely reverential in tone, with the intent of showing what Christian behavior should be like.

The guilds, or town councils, hired directors who were in charge of the technical aspects of the production as well as the acting. A director also was responsible for collecting admission fees and welcoming the audience. Until laymen began appearing extensively in the plays, the actors chanted their lines. Later, their speech became more natural.

For the most part, actors were amateurs. Some received minimal pay, and sometimes those playing leading roles were paid large sums of money. All were given food and drink during the rehearsal and performance periods. At first, all the performers were men, though later women and children appeared in some of the

---

5. Again

plays. For example, in 1498 at Metz, one young woman delivered 2300 lines as St. Catherine. The actors typically were local citizens of the working class.

The three most important forms of drama to evolve from the church presentations were **mystery plays**, **miracle plays**, and **morality plays**. The mystery play dealt with the life of Christ and depicted scenes from the Creation to the Second Coming. This is the form that began in the church, but later moved outdoors. Miracle plays (also called saint plays) dealt with the lives of saints and martyrs, but could include topical scenes involving family troubles. These dramas emphasized such things as miraculous power and divine intervention in people's lives. In some parts of Europe, such as Coventry, the miracle plays lasted until the late sixteenth century. At this time, however, morality plays were gaining in importance.

Morality Plays

The morality plays, which developed later than the mystery and miracle plays, were most popular between the beginning of the fifteenth century and the mid-sixteenth century. The subject matter concerned moral instruction — particularly man's attempt to save his soul. All the characters were allegorical. The central figure usually was called Everyman, and such characters as Virtue and Vice fought over his soul. The first morality play of which there is record was the *Play of the Lord's Prayer*, presented in York, England, in 1384. Another is *The Castle of Perseverance*, presented in about 1425. The latter shows the battle between a Bad Angel and a Good Angel for the soul of Humanum Genus.

Often, morality plays dealt with a person's entire life, presenting humorous or mischievous characters in the form of the Devil and Vice. Most had humorous scenes satirizing current social and political conditions, somewhat similar to Old Comedy in Greece. Scenes such as these were not the main point of the drama, however, but existed to capture and direct the audience's attention to the crux of the play — the need to live a virtuous life.

Morality plays were more popular in England than anywhere else, although they also were presented on the continent of Europe. Unlike the cycle plays, morality plays generally were performed by professional actors. They are important in that they were a step toward secularization of drama. Further, they had a great influence on Elizabethan playwrights such as Christopher Marlowe, who relied heavily upon the morality play for his *The Tragical History of Doctor Faustus*, in which the title character makes a pact with the devil.

An example of the morality play is *Everyman*, although it is different from most in that it is shorter and contains no humor. On the other hand, the characters have more depth than in most plays of this sort. The tale concerns God's calling death to come for Everyman. Trying to find someone to accompany him to his grave, Everyman turns to Fellowship, Kindred, Cousin, and Goods, but each turns him down. It then appears at first that Knowledge, Confession, Discretion, Strength, Beauty, or Five-Wits may agree to go along. Yet all forsake him. Only Good-Deeds is ready to enter the grave with him.

During the sixteenth century, morality plays became more secularized, at first arguing for either the Catholic point of view or the Protestant. Eventually, some became entirely secular, relating to current concerns.

Secular Drama

Along with the church plays, several forms of secular drama developed during the Middle Ages. The most important was the **farce**, typically presented in France, Germany, and England. Usually bawdy and risqué, this form was concerned with humanity's depravity, and was not more than a few hundred lines in length. A second secular form was the **interlude**, a comic play performed by professional traveling players for wealthy citizens at celebrations.

For a number of reasons, medieval drama began to decline during the sixteenth century. First, the social structure of Europe was changing and the plays could no longer be presented effectively as community undertakings. Second, there was an increased interest in classical learning, and new forms of drama combining both medieval and classical influences were beginning to develop. Third, there is evidence that many of the actors began to travel as professionals or semiprofessionals. Fourth, and perhaps most important, there was dissension in the church. Queen Elizabeth I of England forbade religious plays in 1559, and the church itself forbade such plays in continental Europe. By the beginning of the seventeenth century medieval drama was at an end except in Spain, where the style continued well past the middle of the eighteenth century.

Summary

After the fall of the Roman Empire in 476, little in the way of theatre was presented for several hundred years. Drama was reborn as part of the church service in the form of tropes. As the tropes became more elaborate, the staging consisted of *sedes* (mansions) for each separate scene and a *platea*, or central acting place. By the thirteenth century, presentations moved to the west side of the church. In the next couple of centuries, secular groups assumed responsibility for their production.

In England, plays were presented using ancient amphitheatres and pageant wagons and often consisted of a great number of episodic scenes. There were numerous special effects and a great deal of violence. By the end of the fourteenth century the plays were combined into a single presentation or cycle.

The three important forms of drama to evolve from the church presentations were mystery plays, miracle plays, and morality plays. Secular drama that developed during the Middle Ages included the farce and interludes. Medieval drama began to decline during the sixteenth century.

Questions for Discussion

1. Why do you suppose the church was so opposed to theatrical presentation?
2. And since the church was opposed, why do you think drama was reborn inside the Roman Catholic church?
3. Why do you think there was so much emphasis placed on "secrets" or special effects? On humor?
4. Why do you think the use of pageant wagons became very popular?
5. Why do you think the church had such control over secular drama during the Middle Ages?

Chapter 13

RENAISSANCE THEATRE

Renaissance, or reawakening, aptly describes what occurred throughout Western Europe during the fifteenth century. There was renewed interest in classical learning and in looking toward humanity, rather than solely the church, for the salvation of the human race.

A Time of Great Change

The Renaissance brought great changes. Although the causes and effects are complex, three events are important in the rebirth of learning. First is the fall of Constantinople to the Turks in 1453. Facing an end to their way of life and even to those lives themselves, monks and scholars fled by the scores, taking with them all the ancient manuscripts they could carry. For the first time, many ancient Greek writings became available to those in the West — particularly in Italy. A collection of independent states with courts and academies where the arts were patronized, Italy became the major focus for the new interest in classical learning and the new sense of humanism. The middle class had begun its rise and guilds and academies were becoming the lifeblood of culture.

Another event that led to change was the invention and spread of the printing press. This became particularly important in 1467 when Pope Paul II established Rome's first press, which then issued works in Greek. The third occurred in 1429 when Nicholas of Cusa, a young graduate in law, discovered twelve Senecan tragedies, hitherto known only by name.

From the early 1500s, when small bands of professional actors performed in the homes of noblemen or in booths in the town square, to the early 1600s, when Shakespeare's company was playing at the Globe, the changes were vast. In Italy in the early 1500s, actors played on stages with draw curtains; by late in the century, "Florentine spectators were being enchanted by productions in which richly painted scenes continually changed, by seeming magic" so that "within the course of a single century the theatre was brought from the ancient medieval world into a world perceptibly modern."[1]

The change in theatre took two nearly opposing directions — one that looked backward, the other forward. The first grew out of attempts by writers and architects to reach what they considered to be the perfection of the classic form. This meant imitating Greek and Roman plays and changing and adapting recently discovered principles of perspective to scenery, framing it behind a proscenium arch.

The second approach, which grew out of medieval drama and staging, established a looser form that relied on sensational effects and romantic adventures.

The Italian Renaissance

Because Latin was understood by scholars of the time and because classical learning was greatly admired, the works of the Roman playwrights Plautus, Seneca, and Terence influenced the beginnings of drama in Italy. In particular, the works of Terence were well regarded for his purity of language. Among the first plays of the Renaissance were adaptations of translations of these writers' works. Of the three, Seneca was most admired, and thus it was largely due to his influence that an inflexible framework of rules was established under the name of **neoclassicism**. Rigid rules dictated that all plays must be written in five acts; that tragedies had to teach a moral lesson; and that all drama, in fact, should be viewed as a vehicle for instruction. Furthermore, the depicted events had to be those that could occur in everyday life. Tragedy was to deal with nobility, and comedy with the middle and lower classes. There could be no mixing of comic and tragic elements.

In addition to the Roman dramatists, other influences affected the formulation of neoclassic rules. Most important were Aristotle's *The Poetics* and Horace's *Art of Poetry*, the latter written during the first century BC. One of the most binding and ridiculous rules was that every drama had to adhere strictly to the unities of time, place, and action. That is: a play had to occur in the space of one day; the setting, once established, could not change; there could be no subplots. The latter actually is the only one of the unities insisted upon by Aristotle.

1. Allardyce Nicol, *The Development of the Theatre*, 5th ed., (New York: Harcourt, Brace & World, Inc., 1966), 69.

Such rules were stifling, allowing for little creativity, so that during the entire period of the Italian Renaissance very little good drama appeared.

One of the first writers of comedy was Lodovico Ariosto (1474–1533). Until this time plays had been written in Latin. His *La Cassaria*, produced in 1508, marks the true beginning of Italian drama in that it was the first play to be performed using the language of the time.

Another playwright was Niccolò Machiavelli, better known for his writings on political philosophy. His play *La Mandragola*, written between 1513 and 1520 and often considered the masterpiece of Italian Renaissance drama, followed the classic format, but was much more original, as well as highly cynical in its subject matter, which relied on medieval farce.

For the most part, neoclassic plays were too strictly structured to provide much entertainment. Thus, several new forms of drama began to develop. The pastoral, for example, was widely popular during the sixteenth century. The characters were shepherds and shepherdesses, nymphs and fauns, and the plots involved romantic love.

Another drama form, the **intermezzi**, was originally a series of short scenes or plays with singing and dancing that was presented between the acts of a neoclassic tragedy. The subject matter often was drawn from mythology, and the stage effects were elaborate, making the form a favorite of theatregoers. At first, the intermezzi presented at a single performance were unrelated. Later, they were tied together, usually with the neoclassic tragedy with which they appeared.

By the seventeenth century, opera, first written and produced in the 1590s, replaced the intermezzi in popularity. Begun as an attempt to add music, dance, and choral singing to tragedies, in much the same way (the Italians believed) as had been done in ancient Greece, opera became popular so quickly that by 1650 it had spread through much of Europe.

Theatre Design and Architecture

The Italian Renaissance contributed most to theatre, not through drama, but through its staging. There was a strong movement toward the presentation of spectacles and spectacular effects, influenced by Vitruvius, who, near the beginning of the first century AD, had written a book about constructing buildings. *De architectura* was rediscovered in 1414 and translated into Italian in 1521. This led Sebastiano Serlio in 1545 to write *Architettura*, in which he showed how a theatre should be planned and how scenery was to be erected and used. He assumed that theatres would be constructed in existing buildings and recommended following the Roman style, with seating arrangements at one end of a hall and a stage at the other.

Serlio described three settings that could be used for all plays: tragic, comic, and pastoral. All three used false perspective. The floor of the stage was to be painted in squares, which became smaller and smaller toward the back. The stage floor itself was to be **raked**, that is, it sloped upward from front to back. All of this was to give the impression of distance. This use of false perspective became characteristic of all theatres constructed in Italy during the Renaissance.

The use of perspective scenery marked the start of a movement away from the formal or fixed stages of the Greek and Roman theatre to much more flexible settings where changes from one location to another could be shown by shifting the scenery.

New Theatre Structures and Scenery

After a time, the idea of adapting existing halls was abandoned in favor of erecting permanent theatre buildings based on Roman models. The oldest still in existence is the Teatro Olimpico, constructed for the Olympic Academy in Vicenza and first used in 1585. Begun in 1580 by Andrea Palladio, who died before it was erected, it was finished by his pupil Vincenzo Scamozzi, who followed the Roman plan, but added false perspective in the raked floors and the three-dimensional background, which shows openings for streets. The aisleways, or streets, gradually decrease in size, giving the effect of great distance. The seating area was elliptical, providing excellent sightlines from any seat in the house.

The Teatro Farnese, built at Parma in 1618, was the first to use a proscenium arch, or framing device. The action, however, could not be portrayed realistically due to the false or forced perspective. If actors walked too far Upstage, they dwarfed the buildings, ruining the effect. Yet the proscenium arch was important in providing a definite separation of audience and action.

Although scenery still provided background rather than an environment, various methods could be used to show changes in location. One was based on Serlio's work and involved a modified use of the Greek *periaktoi*. These "Serlion wings" were two flats fastened together in a V-shape. Later a third side was added. Each three-sided wing was placed slightly more toward the center of the stage than the one in front of it. The side facing the audience could be painted to give the effect of walls or any specific location. To change the scene, the wing could be rotated to expose another view to the audience.

Another means of changing scenes was developed by Nicola Sabbattini. He used the two-sided, V-shaped wings — one very close behind the other — in groups. One of the sides faced the audience. The other was angled Upstage to support the wing so it could stand alone. Since the wings were in groups, it was a simple task to pull away the front wing of each group to reveal a new scene behind. From these two approaches the wing and drop system was further refined, spreading throughout Europe and to the United States.

Stage machinery provided almost miraculous effects. Buildings rose and descended through trapdoors, and mechanical animals and chariots, called "glories" and constructed of wooden frames covered with canvas, flew over the stage, manipulated by ropes and pulleys. Professional artists, among the best of their day, were hired to paint the scenery. Candles provided lighting, with special effects achieved by placing them behind colored bottles.

Commedia dell'arte

In addition to the drama presented in buildings, another form developed in Renaissance Italy — the *commedia dell'arte*, believed to have evolved either from ancient pantomimes or from the plays of Plautus and Terence. Definitely an actors' theatre, it involved improvising from outlines called scenarios, thus making it adaptable to changing locations and situations. Performed by professional troupes, *commedia dell'arte* attracted audiences from the mid-fifteenth to the mid-sixteenth centuries.

Although the actors built lines and actions from basic outlines, they were free to add whatever they wished. Since the troupes moved from village to village, the performers adapted their material to specific places by referring to current events and residents of each locale.

Stock characters, similar to those in Roman comedy, were divided into three groups: the lovers, who played straight characters; the professional types; and the servants. The latter two types were always comic. Some were Pantalone, the old miser; Il Capitano, the braggart soldier; and Il Dottore, the academician or "Ph.D.," who used a sort of gibberish in substituting incorrect words and phrases for the proper ones. The comic servants as a group were called **zanni** (from which our word *zany* derives) and included Pulcinella, a hunchback with a hooked nose similar to the character of Punch in Punch and Judy shows, and Arlecchino, who performed comedy similar to that of the modern-day Three Stooges.

Once actors were accepted as members of a troupe, they played the same character the rest of their lives, so a "young lover" might remain a romantic figure up until retirement. At the core of each troupe was a family, with the children trained from an early age to take the places of the elderly. Most troupes performed in the marketplace, although those with the best reputations, such as the Gelosi or the Accesi, sometimes were invited to play in court theatres for the nobility. Generally, however, a wagon with a piece of cloth as background served as the stage.

A major part of the show consisted of **lazzi** — verbal or visual business — in which a character went into a certain comedy routine whenever he or she wished. By using prearranged signals, the others let the person know when they felt the routine should end and the troupe should get on with the performance. The *commedia dell'arte* had a strong influence on later forms of drama, as did other Italian theatre practices.

Figure 13-1: Commedia dell'arte characters.

Spanish Theatre

During the time that neoclassicism was gaining a foothold in Italy, drama and the theatre were developing in Spain. Although influenced to a certain degree by neoclassicism, Spain, because of its independence and isolation from the rest of Europe, developed a drama of greater literary value than that of Italy. Since a great number of plays were written between 1580 and 1680, this era became known as Spain's Golden Age.

The most popular drama, the **auto sacramental**, was akin to the medieval mystery and miracle plays in subject matter, yet similar to the morality play in the use of allegorical characters. Although they had religious themes, many of the early plays contained references to contemporary events.

Spain's best known and most prolific playwright was Lope de Vega (1562–1635), believed to have written more than eighteen hundred plays — quite a feat in the days of the quill pen! His drama, which was secular, was characterized by a mixing of form, vigorous action, and suspense, with most of his characters drawn from history or mythology.

By the end of Spain's Golden Age, more than thirty thousand plays had been written, many of which dealt with the themes of love and honor. Produced largely between 1623 and 1654, they were presented either in court theatres or **corrales**. The latter, typical of northern Spain, were open courtyards formed by the outer walls of houses. Spectators filled the balconies and rooms of the houses, sat on benches in the courtyard, or, for a small admission fee, stood behind the last row of seats. The stage itself was wide and uncurtained, with a large apron extending into the courtyard. A balcony above the general playing area also could be used for scenes. Though there existed some crudely painted scenery, most of the changes of locale were indicated through dialog.

Unlike companies in the rest of Europe, some troupes included women, even though actresses were not licensed to appear in plays until 1587. By 1700, Spain's power began to decline.

The Theatre of Elizabethan England

Although there were traveling players in England before the Elizabethan era (1558–1603), their performances were infrequent and scattered since in the fifteenth century they had been defined by law as vagabonds and rogues. Then during the reign of Queen Elizabeth, actors were legally recognized by a 1572 law that required a license from two justices of the peace or the patronage of a nobleman in order to perform. Two years later, a Master of Revels was appointed to license acting companies.

Patronage by a nobleman did not guarantee success, however, since no financial support was involved. It meant only that he protected the troupe, which in turn was expected to present entertainment for him. In general, despite legal recognition, actors were little more than tolerated by the middle class, which distrusted the theatre. It was, in fact, the nobility who helped to establish the theatre as a respectable form of entertainment for everyone, not just the upper classes. Yet, it took time before the general public ceased to regard theatre as only a means of camouflaging more undesirable activities. Even after the government's recognition of acting as a profession, there was strong opposition from local leaders in smaller towns. Sometimes actors were paid not to perform. Still, theatre was firmly established in England by the 1580s.

Because of the religious discontent brought about by the conflict between Catholics and Protestants, the queen sought to unite the country by making the citizens aware of their cultural heritage. This spirit of nationalism in turn affected theatre in that dramatists now often chose patriotic themes for their plays.

Origins

The English theatre had several origins. First were the schools, where plays were read, and sometimes performed, in Latin. Students then wrote in imitation of the models. Although influenced by the classical style of writing, they dealt with English locations and subject matter.

Second was the Inns of Court, schools and places of residence for lawyers. Because the residents were from the upper class, they were exposed to classical learning and influenced by the plays of ancient Rome.

A third source was professional acting companies whose plays were a mixture of various classical and medieval practices. Even so, playwrights were not bound by the unities of time, place, and action, as can be seen in Shakespeare's plays, which have subplots, switch time and place, and sometimes mix comic and tragic elements.

Playwrights

English drama did not achieve greatness until such plays as Thomas Kyd's *The Spanish Tragedy* (c. 1587) set an example for such other gripping "revenge" tragedies as Shakespeare's *Hamlet*. Wholly different was the work of England's first writer of sophisticated comedy, John Lyly, who was noted for his use of mythological themes and pastoral settings.

The three greatest writers of Elizabethan drama were Ben Jonson, Christopher Marlowe, and William Shakespeare. Jonson's first comedy, *Every Man in His Humor* (1598), presented the eccentricities of the English middle class. *Every Man Out of His Humor* (1599) satirized all that Jonson detested in society. Thus he used comedy to denounce middle-class vices and foolish actions with the purpose of correcting England's social ills. His most widely read play, *Volpone*, or *The Fox* (1606), is a bitter satire of human greed. Volpone, with the help of his "parasite" Mosca, tricks three men into promising him their wealth in the hope of inheriting his estates and fortune. One of them even pledges his wife to Volpone. In the end, she is saved after Volpone is exposed to the justice of a Venetian court.

Christopher Marlowe often is called the father of English tragedy. His *Tamburlaine the Great* (c. 1587), written in blank verse, ushered in the first great age of drama in England. He wrote only four important plays and was considered a greater poet than a dramatist. A member of The Admiral's Men, an acting company for whom he wrote, Marlowe may also have been a secret agent, and both he and his friend Thomas Kyd were accused of heresy and atheism. Kyd served a term in prison and later died in disgrace, but Marlowe was stabbed to death in a tavern brawl over the price of a meal before he could be imprisoned. Although his early death prevented the full development of his powers, he helped to free Elizabethan drama from the restrictions of medieval forms.

His *The Tragical History of Doctor Faustus* owes much of its inspiration to the medieval morality play. Based on a German legend, the plot concerns a man, Faustus, who summons up Mephistopheles and sells his soul in return for twenty-four years in which all his wishes will be fulfilled. Scene 16 occurs as the agreed-upon time is ending.

The Tragical History of Doctor Faustus
Christopher Marlowe

From Scene 16
FAUSTUS: Ah, Faustus.
Now hast thou but one bare hour to live,
And then thou must be damn'd perpetually!
Stand still, you ever-moving spheres of heaven,
That time may cease, and midnight never come;
Fair Nature's eye, rise, rise again, and make
Perpetual day; or let this hour be but
A year, a month, a week, a natural day,
That Faustus may repent and save his soul!
O lente, lente, currite noctis equi![2]
The stars move still, time runs, the clock will strike,
The devil will come, and Faustus must be damn'd.
O, I'll leap up to my God! — Who pulls me down?
See, see, where Christ's blood streams in the firmament!
One drop would save my soul, half a drop: ah, my Christ! —
Ah, rend not my heart for naming of my Christ!
Yet will I call on him: O, spare me, Lucifer! —
Where is it now? 'tis gone: and see, where God
Stretcheth out his arm, and bends his ireful brows!
Mountains and hills, come, come, and fall on me,
And hide me from the heavy wrath of God!
No, no!
Then will I headlong run into the earth:
Earth, gape! O, no, it will not harbour me!
You stars that reign'd at my nativity,
Whose influence hath allotted death and hell,
Now draw up Faustus, like a foggy mist,
Into the entrails of yon labouring clouds,
That, when you vomit forth into the air,
My limbs may issue from your smoky mouths,
So that my soul may but ascend to heaven!
(The clock strikes the half-hour)

---

2. "Oh, run slowly, slowly, horses of the night," From Ovid's *Amores*.

Ah, half the hour is past! 'twill all be past anon.
O God,
If thou wilt not have mercy on my soul,
Yet for Christ's sake, whose blood hath ransom'd me,
Impose some end to my incessant pain;
Let Faustus live in hell a thousand years,
A hundred thousand, and at last be sav'd!
O, no end is limited to damned souls!
Why wert thou not a creature wanting soul?
Or why is this immortal that thou hast?
Ah, Pythagoras' metempsychosis,[3] were that true,
This soul should fly from me, and I be chang'd
Unto some brutish beast! All beasts are happy,
For, when they die,
Their souls are soon dissolv'd in elements;
But mine must live still to be plagu'd in hell.
Curs'd be the parents that engendered me!
No, Faustus, curse thyself, curse Lucifer
That hath depriv'd thee of the joys of heaven.
(The clock strikes twelve)
O, it strikes, it strikes! Now, body, turn to air,
Or Lucifer will bear thee quick to hell!
(Thunder and lightning)
O soul, be chang'd into little water-drops,
And fall into the ocean, ne'er be found!
(Enter Devils)
My God, my God, look not so fierce on me!
Adders and serpents, let me breathe a while!
Ugly hell, gape not! come not, Lucifer!
I'll burn my books! — Ah, Mephistopheles!
(Exeunt Devils with Faustus)

---

3. Transmigration of souls.

The greatest Elizabethan dramatist was William Shakespeare. Not much is known about his early life other than that he was born in 1564 and was the son of John and Mary Shakespeare. Records show he was married to Anne Hathaway in 1582. By the 1590s he was a dramatist and actor in London. In 1595 he was a shareholder or part owner in the Lord Chamberlain's Men, later called the King's Men upon the ascension of James I to the throne, at the Globe Theatre. He began writing around 1590 and wrote thirty-eight plays, some as collaborations, before he died in 1616. Although he borrowed many of his plots from other sources, the plays he based on these plots were original and entertaining. He wrote in various genres, though his tragedies as a whole constitute his best work.

Hamlet, if not the best-known, is certainly one of the most widely-read of Shakespeare's plays and "seems to have been his favorite play."

> When he wrote it, he was, with all thinking men of his age, in a period of profound disillusionment and pessimism, and he made it the vessel into which he poured his thoughts on all kinds of problems: on fathers and children, on sex, on drunkenness, on suicide, on mortality and corruption, on ingratitude and loyalty, on acting, on handwriting even, on fate, on man and the universe. There is more of Shakespeare himself in this play than in any of his others.[4]

This tragedy, as many of his best plays, was written during the first ten years of his company's occupation of the Globe, that is 1598 to 1608. The play leaves many questions unanswered about the title character's reasons, motivations, and beliefs. In fact, actors and theatre scholars continue to debate how to interpret the role. The first excerpt that follows includes the first third or so of one of Hamlet's soliloquies. The second is taken to be Shakespeare's feelings about acting and presents his own company's style contrasted to the more impassioned or overly dramatic approach of the well-known actor Edward Alleyn.

---

4. G. B. Harrison, *Shakespeare: The Complete Works*, (New York: Harcourt, Brace and Company, 1848 and 1952), 884.

HAMLET: To be, or not to be — that is the question.
Whether 'tis nobler in the mind to suffer
The slings and arrows of outrageous[5] fortune,
Or to take arms against a sea of troubles
And by opposing end them. To die, to sleep —
No more, and by a sleep to say we end
The heartache and the thousand natural shocks
That flesh is heir to. 'Tis a consummation
Devoutly to be wished. To die, to sleep,
To sleep — perchance to dream. Aye, there's the rub,
For in that sleep of death what dreams may come
When we have shuffled off this mortal coil
Must give us pause.

* * * * * * * * * * * *

HAMLET: Speak the speech, I pray you, as I pronounced it
to you, trippingly on the tongue. But if you mouth it,[6] as
many of your players do, I had as lief the town crier spoke
my lines. Nor do not saw the air too much with your hand,
thus, but use all gently. For in the very torrent, tempest,
and, as I may say, whirlwind of passion, you must acquire
and beget a temperance that may give it smoothness. Oh, it
offends me to the soul to hear a robustious periwig-pated
fellow tear a passion to tatters, to very rags, to split the ears
of the groundlings, who for the most part are capable of
nothing but inexplicable dumb shows[7] and noise. I would
have such a fellow whipped for o'erdoing Termagant[8] — it
out-Herods Herod. Pray you, avoid it.

I. PLAYER: I warrant your Honor.

HAMLET: Be not to tame neither, but let your own
discretion be your tutor. Suit the action to the work, the
word to the action, with this special observance, that you
o'erstep not the modesty of nature. For anything so
overdone is from[9] the purpose of playing whose end, both

---

5. Cruel.
6. Ham it up.
7. Outdated dramatic device of miming the action that was to follow. This was still being done by Alleyn's Admiral's Men.
8. God of the Saracens, often presented as a roaring despot.
9. Contrary to.

at the first and now, was and is to hold as 'twere the mirror up to Nature — to show Virtue her own features, scorn her own image, and the very age and body of the time his form and pressure. Now this overdone or come tardy off, though it make the unskillful laugh, cannot but make the judicious grieve, the censure of the which one must in your allowance o'erweigh a whole theater of others. Oh, there be players that I have seen play, and heard others praise — and that highly, not to speak it profanely — that neither having the accent of Christians nor the gait of Christian, pagan, nor man, have so strutted and bellowed that I have thought some of Nature's journeymen had made men, and not made them well, them imitated humanity so abominably.

I. PLAYER: I hope we have reformed that indifferently[10] with us, sir.

HAMLET: Oh, reform it altogether. And let those that play your clowns speak no more than is set down for them. For there be of them that will themselves laugh, to set on some quantity of barren spectators to laugh too, though in the meantime some necessary question of the play be then to be considered. That's villainous, and shows a most pitiful ambition in that fool that uses it.

The Theatres

During the Elizabethan era there were two types of theatres, public (outdoor and operating in the summer) and private (indoor and operating in the winter), although the private theatres were open to anyone who could afford the price of admission. The indoor theatres, which played to more exclusive audiences, accommodated only one-fourth to one-half as many spectators as did the public theatres. Audience members sat in the pit (the main floor of the auditorium), in galleries, or in private boxes. Usually the stage was three to four feet above the level of the pit, and there was no proscenium arch or front curtain. The first private theatre was built in 1576 in Blackfriars, a residential section of London.

All the popular public theatres, such as the Swan, the Fortune, and the Globe, were located outside the city because at that time London was disease-ridden. The theatres varied in size, but usually held two to three thousand spectators. They were constructed in

---

10. Moderately.

Figure 13-2: An illustration of the Globe Theatre.

various shapes, from circles to squares. The Globe, where Shakespeare's plays were performed, was believed to have been eight-sided. Excavations in 1989 indicate, however, that this may not have been the case. It is impossible to be certain about the shape and dimensions because other buildings now cover much of the site.

It is conjectured that in the public theatre the pit was a large, unroofed open space where the groundlings, or those paying the lowest admission fee, stood to watch the plays. Around the pit (or yard, as it sometimes was called) were galleries, which formed the outer portion of the building and contained boxes for spectators who paid a higher admission fee. The stage projected into the pit, so that spectators could view the action from three sides. Audience members even sat on the stage itself, forcing the actors to move around them.

Action could take place on three levels. At the rear of the stage was an area called the "inner below" — a large room to conceal or reveal characters and locations. There also was an upper stage where, for example, the balcony scene in *Romeo and Juliet* could have been performed. A third level was for musicians. It is generally believed that scenery was not used in the public theatres, and there was no artificial lighting since the plays were presented in the afternoon. Night scenes were suggested by having the actors carry lanterns or candles. The stages contained trapdoors, as used in the gravediggers' scene in *Hamlet*.

Acting Companies

Acting companies at the public theatres consisted of ten to twenty men and three to five boy apprentices. The boys played female parts until they reached maturity, then were taken in as permanent members of the company. Each actor specialized in a certain type of role, but almost all wore contemporary costumes unless they played unusual roles such as foreigners or supernatural beings. About half the members were shareholders.

Each playwright wrote for a specific company. Some were salaried, while others sold their plays outright. The playwright thus often wrote for particular actors and frequently helped with the rehearsals of the plays. The companies all had a repertoire of plays they had rehearsed, and hence could change the bill frequently.

After the death of Queen Elizabeth, the English theatre lost popularity for a time; then, nearly sixty years later, it again began to emerge as a lively form of entertainment.

Summary

Three events are important in the rebirth of learning during the Renaissance: the fall of Constantinople, the spread of the printing press, and the rediscovery of Seneca's tragedies.

Italy contributed most to theatre through staging. Sebastiano Serlio described three settings — tragic, comic, and pastoral — which used false perspective. Early theatres were constructed in existing halls. The first permanent theatre was the Teatro Olimpico.

Various methods were developed to change scenery. One was Serlion wings or modified Greek periaktoi. Another was V-shaped wings that stood one behind the other and were developed by Nicola Sabbattini.

The *commedia dell'arte*, popular for a century, involved stock characters and improvisation.

Although Spain was influenced to a degree by neoclassicism, its drama developed somewhat differently and had a more lasting literary value than that in the rest of Europe. The most popular Spanish drama was the *auto sacramental*. Spain's most prolific playwright was Lope de Vega, believed to have written more than eighteen hundred plays.

Elizabethan theatre had its basis in several sources, schools, Inns of Court, and professional acting companies.

The three greatest Elizabethan dramatists were Ben Jonson, Christopher Marlowe, and William Shakespeare. Jonson used satire to denounce middle class vices and foolish actions. Marlowe wrote few plays, but helped free Elizabethan drama from the restriction of medieval forms. Shakespeare wrote in various genres, but his tragedies are considered his greatest work.

There were two types of theatre in Elizabethan England, private and public. The former was more exclusive. The popular theatres, such as Shakespeare's Globe, stood outside of town.

Questions for Discussion

1. What do you think accounts for the theatre's taking two opposite approaches in its development?
2. Why do you suppose neoclassicism encompassed such rigid rules?
3. What do you feel is the most important contribution of the Italian Renaissance to contemporary theatre. Why?
4. In what ways is the comedy of the *commedia dell'arte* similar to comedy on television or in film today?
5. Why do you think Shakespeare often is regarded as the world's greatest playwright ever?

Chapter 14
SEVENTEENTH- AND EIGHTEENTH-CENTURY THEATRE

By the mid-seventeenth century, Europe was developing a greater sense of nationalism, with governments becoming centralized within each nation rather than the rulers' owing allegiance to the Pope. With the spirit of nationalism, however, came civil strife in France, Spain, and England.

On into the eighteenth century, Italy still dominated the technical aspects of production, and its influence spread across the continent. Most often, the spectacle was used for opera or for a new drama form called the **masque**, which used elaborate costumes and staging to tell allegorical stories of well-known people or events.

In England, the Puritans gained control, beheaded Charles I, and banned theatre. Thirteen years later, in 1660, Charles II was restored to the throne and lifted the ban. The **Restoration**, which lasted for the next forty-two years, was a time of dazzling comedy addressing the foibles of the upper classes.

With the beginning of the eighteenth century and the Age of Enlightenment, a wave of intellectual activity spread across Western Europe, bringing further change to theatre. The idea of "sensationalism," that knowledge comes only from sense perceptions, as advanced by philosopher John Locke, already had taken hold in England and now began to spread across Europe.

Nature (as instinct), rather than reason, was seen as civilization's ruling force. The world was becoming more and more industrialized, in large part as a result of the invention of the steam engine, which provided a sure and steady source of power. Mass production made manufactured goods more widely available, so that wealth shifted away from agriculture toward commerce.

After mid-century, the theatre began attracting large numbers of spectators. Old theatres were remodeled and new ones erected. Growing cities became more able to support theatrical activity.

In England came a surge of new plays. Germany began to produce her own playwrights. In France, neoclassicism persisted in certain theatres, based largely now on Greek models rather than Roman, while opera dropped the use of stock characters and began to use original music and sentimentality in its plots. There was a resurgence of humorous comedy and a renewed interest in the plays of Shakespeare. Acting styles changed from an emphasis on declamation to an emphasis on movement and variety.

English Theatre

At the beginning of the seventeenth century, the theatre of England was not much different from that of the Elizabethan era. Not only did public theatres continue to exist when James I assumed the throne (1603), but all the acting companies came under royal patronage. Shakespeare's own company was now known as the King's Men.

Soon the government was overthrown by the Puritans under Oliver Cromwell and Charles was beheaded, establishing conditions similar to those existing in the Middle Ages, when the church viewed theatre as sinful and degrading. In 1642 the theatres were closed and all theatrical entertainment forbidden.

The Restoration

At the beginning of the Restoration, actresses appeared for the first time on the English stage and by the mid-1660s were an accepted part of the theatre. New theatre buildings had proscenium arches and proscenium doors (on the walls at the sides of the proscenium arch) through which actors could enter and exit. An apron stage projected into the audience, providing the advantage of intimacy between spectator and performer, but the disadvantage of actors performing in front of rather than amidst the scenery. Scenery was painted in perspective on wings and backdrops.

The eighteenth century ushered in the era of "actors' theatre," so that performers outranked playwrights in importance. The most significant dramatic genre was **comedy of manners** (also called Restoration comedy), which satirized the social customs of the time. The underlying theme was that humankind is less than perfect, but that this is to be expected, since nothing can bring about change in basic human nature. The plays most often satirized those persons who were self-deceived or who made an attempt to deceive others. The most notable playwright was William Congreve, important historically for refining and developing comedy of manners to a high style of art. His best play was *The Way of the World* (1700).

Intellectual in approach, with a complicated plot and names descriptive of the characters' personalities, it deals with the intrigues of love — specifically the wooing of Millamant by Mirabell. Congreve uses a sparkling wit and writing style.

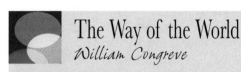

The Way of the World
William Congreve

Mirabell and Fainall are opponents, first at cards and second over the matter of inheritances. Both are sharp-witted at repartee, but there the similarities end. Mirabell is a generous man, while Fainall is ruthless.

Mirabell and the stunning Mrs. Millamant (every female, married or single, was addressed as Mrs.) are in love, yet Mirabell has alienated Lady Wishfort, Mrs. Millamant's aunt, by pretending romantic interest in her to conceal what he feels for her niece.

Mrs. Wishfort, who controls Mrs. Millamant's fortune, has determined that she will marry Sir Wilfull. Yet when Fainall and his paramour Mrs. Marwood try to blackmail Lady Wishfort by threatening to expose the reputation of her daughter Mrs. Fainall (Mirabell's former mistress), Lady Wishfort seeks Mirabell's help.

He already has acted to protect Mrs. Fainall's fortune, ruining Fainall's scheme. Sir Wilfull says he would rather travel than wed, so Lady Wishfort agrees to Mirabell and Millamant's marriage.

By the end of the Restoration period, England was becoming industrialized. The middle class, with more money and leisure time, began attending the theatre regularly. New playwrights, such as George Farquhar, whose work resembled comedy of manners, but was more riotous than witty, were helping to bring about change.

Theatre in the Time of Queen Anne

Queen Anne, who assumed the throne at the beginning of the eighteenth century, was interested neither in art nor theatre. But the theatre went on, reflecting the changes in the social and economic structure of England. The emergence of the middle class as the major theatre audience led to romanticism and melodrama. The new audiences wanted sensationalism, but in plays that taught a moral lesson. Thus perseverance was rewarded, and dishonesty and laziness resulted in defeat.

The type of drama most prevalent was **sentimental comedy**, characterized by false emotions and sentimentality over the misfortunes of others. The major characters bore their ills with a smile, and always were rewarded in the end. The plays were referred to as comedies — not because they were funny, but because they ended happily. The situations often were too deplorable to be believed, and the characters too noble. The prevailing viewpoint was that humanity is basically good and has only to heed an inner conscience to reap just rewards.

A similar form was **bourgeois tragedy**. Written in much the same style, the plays ended unhappily when the leading characters yielded to temptation. The playwright with the greatest influence in this form was George Lillo (1693–1739) whose *The London Merchant* (1731) shows how a good man can be led astray through love of an undesirable woman. Produced frequently, it influenced the writing of sentimental drama in France.

The London Merchant
George Lillo

A young London merchant named George Barnwell falls prey to the lure of the villainous seductress Millwood. At her urging, he robs his master and kills his uncle. Remorseful, he is arrested and sentenced to death. The characters are wooden stereotypes and the dialog sounds like a parody. It would be extremely difficult for today's audiences to take the play seriously.

From Act V, Scene 5
BARNWELL: Trueman — my friend, whom I so wisht to see! Yet now he's here I dare not look upon him.
(Weeps)
TRUEMAN: Oh Barnwell! Barnwell!
BARNWELL: Mercy, Mercy, gracious Heaven! For death, but not for this, was I prepared.

293

> TRUEMAN: What have I suffer'd since I saw you last!
> What pain has absence given me! — But oh! to see thee
> thus!
> BARNWELL: I know it is dreadful! I feel the anguish of thy
> generous soul — but I was born to murder all who love me.
> *(Both weep)*

Another form was **burlesque farce**, which made fun of the other dramas of the day. The prime example is Henry Fielding's *The Tragedy of Tragedies, or, the Life and Death of Tom Thumb the Great.*

Pantomime, as performed by John Rich, was the most popular of all. Featuring dances and mimicry to the accompaniment of music, it presented both comic and serious scenes with elaborate scenery and effects. Also popular was **ballad opera** such as John Gay's *The Beggar's Opera* (1728), which burlesqued Italian opera and satirized the current political situation. All the characters are criminals of one sort or another, yet all live by a binding code of honor. Like the characters of sentimental comedy, they believe that only through hard — though illegal — work can a person succeed.

A major dramatist was Oliver Goldsmith (1730–1774) whose play *She Stoops to Conquer* was an attempt to return to comedy that was truly funny, rather than sentimental. He based his plays largely on those of Elizabethan writers. Another playwright was Richard Brinsley Sheridan, who wrote *The Rivals* and *The School for Scandal*, returning to comedy of manners.

Possibly the most famous theatrical figure of the time was David Garrick (1717–1779). As manager of the Drury Lane Theatre, he was credited with introducing a natural style of acting to the English stage. He believed in closely-supervised rehearsals in which he took charge of directing the actors, something not done before this time. Garrick brought French scene designer Philippe-Jacques de Loutherbourg to England to design three-dimensional settings. Moreover, Garrick insisted that the audience could no longer sit on the stage and was responsible for concealing stage lighting from the audience.

By the end of the eighteenth century, there was a definite movement toward realism in sets and staging. This move opened the way for the modern era of the theatre.

French Theatre

Because civil wars divided the country from the 1560s to the 1620s, French theatre developed later than the theatre of England.

Cardinal Richelieu and the French Academy

Cardinal Richelieu, who came to power in 1625, looked to Italy as a model for improving France's cultural image. In 1641, as part of his effort to raise awareness of the arts, he had a theatre built in the Palais Cardinal. (After his death it was renamed the Palais Royal.) Built in the manner of Italian theatres, it later became home to the company led by Molière. Previously, only the Hôtel de Bourgogne and another theatre, the Théâtre du Marais, had been operating in Paris.

In 1629, Cardinal Richelieu established the French Academy, where various playwrights gathered to write, adhering to the rules of neoclassicism even more rigidly than had their counterparts in Italy. They felt that comedy's aim was to ridicule, while tragedy's purpose was to show the results of humankind's misdeeds and errors. They were particularly concerned with the three unities and with purity of form. They believed an important element of drama should be verisimilitude — the appearance of truth.

The two most important writers of the French Academy were Pierre Corneille and Jean Racine. Corneille began writing in the late 1620s, and in 1636 he wrote his most successful play, *Le Cid* (the word *cid* is comparable to *lord*). It was a tragicomedy, so-called because it deals with a serious theme but ends happily. It became one of the most popular plays of the century. Staged with multiple settings, it harkened back to medieval drama. Corneille did not follow the unities of time, place, and action, but apparently believed the play to be neoclassic, but closer to the rules adapted in Spain.

Racine (1639–1699) was the greatest writer of French classical tragedy. His best-known play, *Phèdre*, deals with the internal conflict of a single character — a woman who wanted to do right but was prevented from it by circumstances and emotions.

Molière and Other Playwrights

Jean-Baptiste Poquelin (1622–1673), known as Molière, often has been called the French Shakespeare. Born in 1622, the son of the private upholsterer of Louis XIV, Molière grew up close to the court, received the education of a nobleman, and later studied law. At the age of twenty-one he helped found the Théâtre Illustre, which failed after two years. As a result, Molière was thrown into debtor's prison. Upon his release, he and his troupe toured the provinces for the next dozen years, at which time he became the group's principal playwright. When the company was invited to Paris in 1658, Louis XIV saw one of Molière's plays and granted him the right to perform at a small theatre, the Petit Bourbon, and later at the Palais Royal.

Credited with introducing literary comedy into France, Molière based his plots on a variety of sources, including Greek, Roman, Italian, and Spanish drama, although he adapted the material for specific actors in his company. His plays deal with types, based on Roman comedy and the *commedia dell'arte*, but he gave them individual characteristics. He always played his own leading roles, and many of his plays contained elements of autobiography. In *The School for Husbands*, an early satire, for instance, he ridiculed himself for his marriage at the age of forty to Armande Béjart, who was eighteen.

One of his most humorous plays is *The Miser*, which owes its stock characters and comic routines to the *commedia dell'arte* and its misunderstandings and lack of communication to Roman comedy. The protagonist Harpagon is ruled by greed, which affects every aspect of his life. Yet he is a human being, an individual, "vivified by a few details — he has a cough, he is subject to flattery, he wishes to wed a pretty girl — but always he is the essence of avarice."[1] (See the synopsis in Chapter 10.) *The Miser* was first performed in Paris in 1669 with Molière playing the title role. In the following, the miser Harpagon, who is sixty years old, is meeting with the matchmaker Frosine. Her flattery, of course, has no basis in fact.

---

1. Sylvan Barnet, Morton Berman, and William Burto, eds., *Eight Great Comedies*, (New York: New American Library, 1985), 175.

From The Miser
Molière

HARPAGON: ... Frosine, there is one more thing that makes me uneasy. The girl is young, you know; and young people generally like those who are young like themselves, and only care for the society of the young. I am afraid that a man of my age may not exactly suit her taste, and that this may occasion in my family certain complications that would in nowise be pleasant to me.

FROSINE: Oh, how badly you judge her! This is one more peculiarity of which I had to speak to you. She has the greatest detestation to all young men, and only likes old people.

HARPAGON: Does she?

FROSINE: I should like you to hear her talk on that subject; she cannot bear at all the sight of a young man, and nothing delights her more than to see a fine old man with a venerable beard. The oldest are to her the most charming, and I warn you beforehand not to go and make yourself any younger than you really are. She wishes for one sixty years old at least; and it is not more than six months ago that on the very eve of being married she suddenly broke off the match on learning that her lover was only fifty-six years of age, and did not put on spectacles to sign the contract.

HARPAGON: Only for that?

FROSINE: Yes; she says there is no pleasure with a man of fifty-six; and she has a decided affection for those who wear spectacles.

HARPAGON: Well, this is quite new to me.

FROSINE: No one can imagine how far she carries this. She has in her room a few pictures and engravings, and what do you imagine they are? An Adonis, a Cephalus, a Paris, an Apollo? Not a bit of it! Fine portraits of Saturn, of King Priam, of old Nestor, and of good father Anchises on his son's shoulders.

HARPAGON: That's admirable. I should never have guessed such a thing; and I am very pleased to hear that she has such taste as this. Indeed had I been a woman, I should never have loved young fellows.

FROSINE: I should think not. Fine trumpery indeed, these young men, for any one to fall in love with. Fine jackanapes and puppies for a woman to hanker after. I should like to know what relish anyone can find in them?

HARPAGON: Truly; I don't understand it myself, and I cannot make out how it is that some women dote so on them.

FROSINE: They must be downright idiots. Can any one be in his senses who thinks youth amiable? Can those curly-pated coxcombs be men, and can one really get attached to such animals?

HARPAGON: Exactly what I say every day! With their effeminate voices, their three little bits of a beard turned up like cat's whiskers, their tow wigs, their flowing breeches and open breasts!

FROSINE: Yes; they are famous guys compared with yourself. In you we see something like a man. There is enough to satisfy the eye. It is thus that one should be made and dressed to inspire love.

HARPAGON: Then you think I am pretty well?

FROSINE: Pretty well! I should think so; you are charming, and your face would make a beautiful picture. Turn round a little, if you please. You could not find anything better anywhere. Let me see you walk. You have a well-shaped body, free and easy, as it should be, and one which gives no sign of infirmity.

HARPAGON: I have nothing the matter to speak of, I am thankful to say. It is only my cough, which returns from time to time.

FROSINE: That is nothing, and coughing becomes you exceedingly well.

HARPAGON: Tell me, Frosine, has Marianne seen me yet? Has she not noticed me when I passed by?

FROSINE: No; but we have had many conversations about you. I gave her an exact description of your person, and I did not fail to make the most of your merit, and to show her what an advantage it would be to have a husband like you.

HARPAGON: You did right, and I thank you very much for it.

FROSINE: I have, Sir, a small request to make to you. I am in danger of losing a lawsuit for want of a little money

(HARPAGON looks grave), and you can easily help me with it, if you have pity upon me. You cannot imagine how happy she will be to see you. *(HARPAGON looks joyful.)* Oh! How sure you are to please her, and how sure that antique ruff of yours is to produce a wonderful effect on her mind. But, above all, she will be delighted with your breeches fastened to your doublet with tags; that will make her mad after you, and a lover who wears tags will be most welcome to her.

HARPAGON: You send me into raptures, Frosine, by saying that.

FROSINE: I tell you the truth, Sir; this lawsuit is of the utmost importance for me. *(HARPAGON looks serious again.)* If I lose it, I am for ever ruined; but a very small sum will save me. I should like you to have seen the happiness she felt when I spoke of you to her. *(HARPAGON looks pleased again.)* Joy sparkled in her eyes while I told her of all your good qualities; and I succeeded, in short, in making her look forward with the greatest impatience to the conclusion of the match.

HARPAGON: You have given me great pleasure, Frosine, and I assure you I ...

FROSINE: I beg of you, Sir, to grant me the little assistance I ask of you. *(HARPAGON again looks grave.)* It will put me on my feet again, and I shall feel grateful to you for ever.

HARPAGON: Good-bye; I must go and finish my correspondence.

FROSINE: I assure you, Sir, that you could not help me in a more pressing necessity.

HARPAGON: I will see that my carriage is ready to take you to the fair.

FROSINE: I would not importune you so if I were not compelled by necessity.

HARPAGON: And I will see that we have supper early, so that nobody may be ill.

FROSINE: Do not refuse me the service; I beg of you. You can hardly believe, Sir, the pleasure that ...

HARPAGON: I must go; somebody is calling me. We shall see each other again by and by.

Acting Companies

The French acting companies during the seventeenth century were organized on the sharing plan — women participating equally with men. Plays were accepted or rejected by a vote of the company. Actors specialized either in comedy or in tragedy, with men customarily playing old women's roles. New members of a company learned their roles from the persons whom they were replacing. Spectators sat on the stage, and because the stages were small, there was little room for actors to move about. Usually a long play and a short one were presented on the same bill.

After Molière's death, the state of the French theatre declined. Corneille gave up writing in 1674, and Racine wrote no new plays for public presentation after 1677. Thus, the Golden Age of French drama came to a close.

German Theatre

The most sweeping changes in theatre were occurring in Germany, which, until the eighteenth century, had been a collection of small states and duchies. A generally poor country, it relied for theatre on performances by traveling companies and court productions that featured unbelievable action and violence. Caroline Neuber, an actress who headed her own troupe beginning in 1727, raised the level of acting and drama by insisting on careful rehearsals, high personal morals, and the presentation of plays with higher literary standards than were common. Her work, with that of playwright Johann Gottsched, is considered the turning point in the history of the German theatre; from that time on, drama was more respected.

During the eighteenth century, as the government became centralized and a national awareness and pride began to emerge, there was a trend toward romanticism, one form of which was *Sturm und Drang* (storm and stress), born largely as a result of the writings of Johann Friedrich Schiller (1759–1805). The movement was characterized by a reverence for Shakespeare, a return to nature, and a disregard for the dramatic unities as practiced in France. Romanticism emphasized freedom from the bonds of society, a clear division between good and evil, and a return to man's basic emotions. Schiller's *The Robbers*, which he wrote at age nineteen, was in great part responsible for the beginnings of German romanticism. Its story condemns the social laws of the day and advocates that men should turn away from the law in order to be free.

Johann Wolfgang von Goethe (1749–1832) is best known for his play *Faust* — like Marlowe's *Dr. Faustus*, based on the legend of a man who makes a pact with the devil. The first part of *Faust* was published in 1808. The play is considered the ultimate example of romanticism, although both Goethe and Schiller denied being romanticists.

By the end of the eighteenth century, romanticism was well established in Germany, but did not reach maturity in various other countries until the nineteenth century.

Summary

During the Restoration the most significant dramatic genre was comedy of manners. The most notable playwright was William Congreve whose best play was *The Way of the World*. Most popular during the reign of Queen Anne were sentimental comedy and bourgeois tragedy. With *She Stoops to Conquer*, Oliver Goldsmith made an attempt to return to comedy that was funny. Theatre manager David Garrick introduced a natural style of acting and insisted on closely supervising rehearsals. He used three-dimensional scenery, concealed stage lighting from the audience, and insisted spectators no longer sit on-stage.

Cardinal Richelieu had a theatre built in the Palais and established the French Academy where playwrights adhered strictly to neoclassicism. The most important writers of the Academy were Pierre Corneille and Jean Racine. The most important French playwright was Molière, who introduced literary comedy into France. His masterpiece, however, is *The Misanthrope*, which is closer to comedy of manners.

In Germany, Caroline Neuber, an actress who headed her own troupe, raised the level of acting and drama in Germany by insisting on careful rehearsals, high personal morals, and the presentation of plays with high moral standards.

Questions for Discussion

1. Why do you think the Puritans viewed theatre as sinful?
2. What were the reasons for the increase in audience attendance at the theatre during the latter part of the seventeenth century? How did they influence what was presented? Why?
3. What caused theatrical presentations to sink from comedy of manners to sentimental comedy and bourgeois tragedy?
4. What do you think would cause Garrick in England and Neuber in Germany to change the whole approach to the way plays were presented?

Chapter 15
Nineteenth- to
Twenty-First-Century Theatre

With the Industrial Revolution in full swing and a change from the country to the city as the controller of a nation's wealth, emphasis shifted gradually from romanticism and sentiment to more realistic presentations.

From sentimental comedy and bourgeois tragedy, the pendulum swung in the opposite direction, and it became a playwright's task simply to record life and report it. Yet a swing too far either way lasts for only a time before the pendulum falls again toward moderation.

Throughout the past two hundred years, changes have come faster than at any other time in theatrical history, and innovations have often disappeared just as quickly. Never before have so many dramatic forms and styles existed within such a short period of time. Much of the rapid growth occurred due to the expansion of the railroads, which allowed theatrical companies to travel to many locations where professional theatre had never before been seen on a regular basis.

Romanticism

Even before the storm and stress movement developed in Germany, many of the concepts of Romanticism had already appeared in English theatre. It was easier for Romanticism to gain a foothold in England because neoclassicism had never been so widely adopted there as in other countries. The lure of Romanticism showed that there was a growing distrust of reason and a growing conviction that one had only to follow his or her instincts to do what was right. Hence, humankind could discover truth by examining nature. The subject matter of nineteenth-century Romantic plays often dealt with humankind's need to be free from the restraining forces of society.

Yet Romanticism began to recede in both England and Germany before it gained acceptance in France through the writings of Victor Hugo, who, in the preface to his play *Cromwell*, set forth the doctrine of Romanticism that called for abandoning both the unities and the strict separation of genres.

Melodrama

Melodrama, characterized by a simple and suspenseful plot and a strong emotional appeal, became highly popular during the nineteenth century. The name *melodrama* goes back to the time when musical accompaniments were used to heighten the changes in mood and pace, a device borrowed from opera and then modified.

Melodrama was related to both tragedies and sentimental comedies, which advocated virtue above all else as the solution to humankind's woes. Vice, on the other hand, would ultimately be punished. The genre also was influenced by both Jean-Jacques Rousseau and Immanuel Kant. "Rousseau offered ideas relating to the noble savage, the natural goodness of man, and the equation of evil with inequality; Kant emphasized the individual's right to freedom."[1]

Thus developed a spectrum of nineteenth-century "common" heroes — such as the cowboy, the American Indian, Davy Crockett (the frontiersman), and, in England, Jack Tar (the sailor). Of course, this also led to stereotyping and to later objections by such groups as Native Americans and blacks. For instance, in America the most widely produced nineteenth-century play was *Uncle Tom's Cabin*, based on the Harriet Beecher Stowe novel. There were several dramatized versions, but the most successful was an adaptation by George Aikin, which ran for more than two hundred performances at New York's National Theatre. Until the early part of the twentieth century, touring companies presented "Tom" shows five or more times a year in dozens of communities.

Much of melodrama's popularity was due to spectacle — drawing on new advances in staging and such diverse media as the circus and fantasy novels. Melodrama also was popular in England because it offered a way for music halls to "link songs, dances and spectacular tableaux into sequences illustrating a popular theme with a well-defined beginning, middle, and end ... These shows came to be called burlettas. All that was required to give this

---

1. Glynne Wickham, *A History of the Theatre*, 2nd ed., (London: Phaidon Press Limited, 1992), 184–85.

embryonic type of popular entertainment a shape and quality of its own was a suitable injection of moral, philosophic, and literary animation."[2]

Throughout the century theatre increased in popularity, attracting far more spectators than ever before. Many new theatres were built so as to offer specialized types of entertainment, ranging from variety and burlesque to serious dramas. Shakespeare also drew large audiences.

Settings were now being built for individual plays, and they had to be historically accurate, following the trend begun in Germany just after the turn of the century. In England, Charles Kemble's production of Shakespeare's *King John* in 1823 was the first play in which the costuming was historically correct. It was followed in 1824 by a production of *Henry IV, Part I*, which was scenically accurate. By mid-century, nearly every production reflected the backgrounds and costumes of its period.

Theatre Companies

Until the 1830s, in both Europe and America the most popular type of acting troupe was the **repertory company**, which presented a repertoire of shows for a season. This was followed by the **star system** in which actors who had gained prominence began traveling to various communities with their own companies. Many cities found it difficult to keep a good resident troupe. In America, this system was aided by the rapid expansion of the railroads. The star system then gradually gave way to **combination companies** that traveled for a season to a "combination" of theatres along a route. Generally they presented a single play, although some had a repertoire of several plays. By the beginning of the twentieth century, however, almost all actors were hired only for specific roles in specific plays.

In America, an outgrowth of these changes was the Theatrical Syndicate, formed in 1896 to book touring shows in various communities. The syndicate demanded that local theatre owners work with it exclusively. Since it handled most of the major touring companies, theatre managers were afraid to try to run a season independently. If any did, the syndicate most often brought rival theatres in town to try to put them out of business. The syndicate's monopoly on theatrical booking was not broken until 1915.

---

2. Wickham, 184.

In England, acting was becoming a socially accepted profession. Henry Irving (1838–1905), the first actor to be knighted, was renowned for his presentations of romantic plays and melodramas.

Realism

New dramatic forms slowly replaced the old. Following romanticism and melodrama came their direct opposite — realism, which developed as a result of oppressive political and economic conditions. Playwrights who favored realism felt that Western society was unacceptable and must be changed, thus their task was to reveal social ills and injustices. They emphasized the importance of what could be observed through the senses, for only thus could real truth be known. Playwrights believed that if audiences didn't like the social conditions depicted on the stage, they'd be driven to change them, rather than simply attack the playwright.

Advances in Staging

Perhaps the most significant change in staging in the nineteenth century was the development of gas lights. This innovation made it possible to go from general illumination, which spilled into the audience areas, to specific lighting. Now the designer could control the amount, the intensity, and the direction of the light on-stage. By 1840, most theatres had gas lights. By 1880, electricity was in general use and lighting could be even more effectively controlled from the dimmer board. The use of gas and electricity allowed actors to move Upstage and inside a setting that provided an environment.

The Industrial Revolution placed theatre within the reach of the common person, who demanded more realistic settings and the abandonment of stock or standard sets that previously had been adapted for use in any number of plays.

The development of the realistic movement, which began in France around 1850, was aided by technical advances that made for more believable settings. The **box set**, which was built of flats to represent an indoor location, was developed by 1840 and was in general use by the end of the century. There was a trend toward making stage floors flat, rather than raking them for purposes of perspective.

To facilitate quick changes of scene, elevator and revolving stages were used, as were wagons on which entire sets would be rolled on and off. The ultimate theatre of the period was Steele MacKaye's Madison Square Theatre in New York.

From The Scientific American
April 5, 1884

[The Madison Square Theatre consists] of two theatrical stages, one above another, to be moved up and down as an elevator car is operated in a high building, and so that either one of them can easily and quickly be at any time brought to the proper level for acting thereon in front of the auditorium ...

This immense contrivance is suspended at each corner by two steel cables, each of which would be capable of sustaining far more than the whole load, and these cables pass upward over sheaves or pulleys set at different angles, thence downward to a saddle, to which all are connected. Connected to this saddle is a hoisting cable, attached to a hoisting drum, by the rotation of which the stages are raised and lowered. Practically, only forty seconds are required to raise or lower a stage into position, and four men at the winch are as much as is ever required. This movement is thus easily effected, without sound, jar, or vibration ...

While the play is proceeding before the audience, another scene is ... arranged by the assistants on the upper stage, to be followed, when this is lowered, by similar preparations for the succeeding scene, should this be necessary, on the stage that will then be twenty-five feet below.

Forms of Drama

The Well-Made Play

Realistic dramas had been seen at times before the beginning of the nineteenth century, but did not gain popularity until the last third of the century. When they did, it was largely due to the Norwegian playwright Henrik Ibsen (1828–1906), sometimes called the father of modern drama. Although he began writing in 1850, his early plays were romantic. Not until the 1870s did he shift to a realistic vein and deal with socially significant themes. More than any other playwright of his time, he established realism as an integral part of drama. Among Ibsen's dramatic reforms was a discontinuation of soliloquies and asides. In addition, his so-called thesis play provided a thorough exposition of prior events, presented logically and interestingly. Every element of the production was to contribute to the overall effect, with each character an individual affected both by heredity (or personality) and environment (including experience). Ibsen's plays deal with a variety of social issues, including women's rights — *A Doll's House* — and conscience versus financial success — *The Pillars of Society* and *An Enemy of the People*.

The Slice-of-Life Drama

Next came naturalism which carried realistic drama to its ultimate end. As developed by the novelist Émile Zola, naturalism meant that playwrights should constantly seek the truth through objectivity — that is, their own ideas must not be allowed to intrude upon the facts presented in their writings. Playwrights should be recorders of events, not interpreters. They should select the beginnings and endings of their drama at random. Any attempt to concoct a plot results in a distortion of the truth, since life itself has no real beginnings or endings. This **slice-of-life** technique insists that the dramatist reproduce actual life on the stage. In some naturalistic productions, actors made no attempt to project their voices and turned their backs to the audience at will.

Nineteenth-century naturalism has been criticized for depicting the seamiest sides of life. Still, Zola's ideas spread quickly over Europe and influenced writers and producers everywhere.

The Playwrights

In England, the most important playwright of the late nineteenth and early twentieth century was Irish-born George Bernard Shaw (1856–1950), whose witty plays emphasize social themes and feature believable characters. In his intellectual plays, such as *Saint Joan*, *Misalliance*, *Androcles and the Lion*, and *Arms and the Man*, he preached his own social beliefs. The latter, for instance, is a satire on romantic ideas about war. The following excerpts contrast the views held by the two women with the opinion of The Man (Captain Bluntschli). The second scene picks up after The Man has hidden in Raina's room.

Arms and the Man
George Bernard Shaw

From Act I

CATHERINE: *(Entering hastily, full of good news)* Raina! *(She pronounces it Rah-eena, with the stress on the ee.)* Raina! *(She goes to the bed, expecting to find RAINA there.)* Why, where — ? *(RAINA looks into the room.)* Heavens, child, are you out in the night air instead of in your bed? You'll catch your death. Louka told me you were asleep.

RAINA: *(Dreamily)* I sent her away. I wanted to be alone. The stars are so beautiful! What is the matter?

CATHERINE: Such news! There has been a battle.

RAINA: *(Her eyes dilating)* Ah! *(She throws the cloak on the ottoman and comes eagerly to CATHERINE in her nightgown, a pretty garment but evidently the only one she had on.)*

CATHERINE: A great battle at Slivnitza. A victory! And it was won by Sergius.

RAINA: *(With a cry of delight)* Ah! *(They embrace rapturously.)* Oh, mother! *(Then, with sudden anxiety)* Is father safe?

CATHERINE: Of course! He sends me the news. Sergius is the hero of the hour, the idol of the regiment.

RAINA: Tell me, tell me. How was it? *(Ecstatically)* Oh, mother! Mother! Mother! *(She pulls her mother down on the ottoman; and they kiss one another frantically.)*

CATHERINE: *(With surging enthusiasm)* You can't guess how splendid it is. A cavalry charge! Think of that! He defied our Russian commanders — acted without orders — led a charge on his own responsibility — headed it himself — was the first man to sweep through their guns. Can't you see it, Raina? Our gallant splendid Bulgarians with their swords and eyes flashing, thundering down like an avalanche and scattering the wretched Servians and their dandified Austrian officers like chaff. And you! You kept Sergius waiting a year before you would be betrothed to him. Oh, if you have a drop of Bulgarian blood in your veins, you will worship him when he comes back.

* * * * * * * * * *

THE MAN: A narrow shave; but a miss is as good as a mile. Dear young lady: your servant to the death. I wish for your sake I had joined the Bulgarian army instead of the other one. I am not a native Serb.

RAINA: *(Haughtily)* No: you are one of the Austrians who set the Serbs on to rob us of our national liberty, and who officer their army for them. We hate them!

THE MAN: Austrian! Not I. Don't hate me, dear young lady. I am a Swiss, fighting merely as a professional soldier. I joined the Serbs because they came first on the road from Switzerland. Be generous: you've beaten us hollow.

RAINA: Have I not been generous?

THE MAN: Noble! Heroic! But I'm not saved yet. This particular rush will soon pass through; but the pursuit will go on all night by fits and starts. I must take my chance to get off in a quiet interval. *(Pleasantly)* You don't mind my waiting just a minute or two, do you?

RAINA: *(Putting on her most genteel society manner)* Oh, no: I'm sorry you will have to go into danger again. *(Pointing to the ottoman)* Won't you sit — *(She breaks off with an irrepressible cry of alarm as she catches sight of the pistol. THE MAN, all nervous, shies like a frightened horse.)*

THE MAN: *(Irritably)* Don't frighten me like that. What is it?

RAINA: Your revolver! It was staring that officer in the face all the time. What an escape!

THE MAN: *(Vexed at being unnecessarily terrified)* Oh, is that all?

RAINA: *(Staring at him rather superciliously as she conceives a poorer and poorer opinion of him, and feels proportionately more and more at her ease)* I am sorry I frightened you. *(She takes up the pistol and hands it to him.)* Pray take it to protect yourself against me.

THE MAN: *(Grinning wearily at the sarcasm as he takes the pistol)* No use, dear young lady; there's nothing in it. It's not loaded. *(He makes a grimace at it, and drops it despairingly into his revolver case.)*

RAINA: Load it by all means.

THE MAN: I've no ammunition. What use are cartridges in battle? I always carry chocolate instead; and I finished the last cake of that hours ago.

RAINA: *(Outraged in her most cherished ideals of manhood)* Chocolate! Do you stuff your pockets with sweets — like a schoolboy — even in the field?
THE MAN: *(Grinning hungrily)* Yes: isn't it contemptible? I wish I had some now.

Other important English playwrights were W. S. Gilbert (1836–1911) and Arthur Sullivan (1842–1900). Through their operettas satirizing the upper classes, they hoped to bring about changes in the social structure. Among their best-known works are *H.M.S. Pinafore*, *The Mikado*, and *The Pirates of Penzance* .

Another satirist of the time was Oscar Wilde (1854–1900), who wrote *The Importance of Being Earnest* and *Lady Windermere's Fan*. He, too, was a witty and entertaining writer who satirized the prudery of his day.

One of Ireland's greatest dramatists was John Millington Synge who spent several years observing the Irish peasants. As a result, he wrote six plays that are considered the best among any written in that country. *Riders to the Sea*, generally considered his best, is the story of the sea's claiming the lives of all the men in a family. Yet none of the catastrophe is shown on-stage — only the reaction to it.

In Russia, Anton Chekhov (1860–1904) wrote plays based on contemporary Russian life, presenting sympathetic characters who are defeated by circumstances. Among his best works are *Uncle Vanya* and *The Cherry Orchard*.

In Chekhov's *Uncle Vanya*, the title character has lost all will to manage the estate ever since the arrival of old Serebrakoff and his young wife, Helena. The brother of Serebrakoff's first wife, Uncle Vanya (Voitski) had scrimped to send Serebrakoff as much money as possible. Now he is disillusioned by the retired professor's egotistical and demanding ways and by the fact that he apparently does not love Helena, though she loves him.

Uncle Vanya
Anton Chekhov

From Act I

VOITSKI: There goes our learned scholar on a hot, sultry day like this, in his overcoat and galoshes and carrying an umbrella!

ASTROFF: He is trying to take good care of his health.

VOITSKI: How lovely she is! How lovely! I have never in my life seen a more beautiful woman.

TELEGIN: Do you know, Marina, that as I walk in the fields or in the shady garden, as I look at this table here, my heart swells with unbounded happiness. The weather is enchanting, the birds are singing, we are all living in peace and contentment — what more could the soul desire? *(Takes a glass of tea.)*

VOITSKI: *(Dreaming)* Such eyes — a glorious woman!

ASTROFF: Come, Ivan, tell us something.

VOITSKI: *(Indolently)* What shall I tell you?

ASTROFF: Haven't you any news for us?

VOITSKI: No, it is all stale. I am just the same as usual, or perhaps worse, because I have become lazy. I don't do anything now but croak like an old raven. My mother, the old magpie, is still chattering about the emancipation of woman, with one eye on her grave and the other on her learned books, in which she is always looking for the dawn of a new life.

ASTROFF: And the professor?

VOITSKI: The professor sits in his library from morning till night, as usual —

"Straining the mind, wrinkling the brow,

We write, write, write,

Without respite

Or hope of praise in the future or now."

Poor paper! He ought to write his autobiography; he would make a really splendid subject for a book! Imagine it, the life of a retired professor, as stale as a piece of hardtack, tortured by gout, headaches, and rheumatism, his liver bursting with jealousy and envy, living on the estate of his first wife, although he hates it, because he can't afford to live in town. He is everlastingly whining about his hard lot, though, as a matter of fact, he is extraordinarily lucky. He is the son of a common deacon and has attained the professor's chair, become the son-in-law of a senator, is called "your Excellency," and so on. But I'll tell you something; the man has been writing on art for twenty-five years, and he doesn't know the very first thing about it. For twenty-five years he has been chewing on other men's thoughts about realism, naturalism, and all such foolishness; for twenty-five years he has been reading and writing things that clever men have long known and stupid ones are not interested in; for twenty-five years he has been making his imaginary mountains out of molehills. And just think of the man's self-conceit and presumption all this time! For twenty-five years he has been masquerading in false clothes and has now retired, absolutely unknown to any living soul; and yet see him! Stalking across the earth like a demi-god!

ASTROFF: I believe you envy him.

VOITSKI: Yes, I do. Look at the success he has had with women! Don Juan himself was not more favored. His first wife, who was my sister, was a beautiful, gentle being, as pure as the blue heaven there above us, noble, great-hearted, with more admirers than he has pupils, and she loved him as only beings of angelic purity can love those who are as pure and beautiful as themselves. His mother-in-law, my mother, adores him to this day, and he still inspires a sort of worshipful awe in her. His second wife is, as you see, a brilliant beauty; she married him in his old age and has surrendered all the glory of her beauty and freedom to him. Why? What for?

ASTROFF: Is she faithful to him?

VOITSKI: Yes, unfortunately she is.

ASTROFF: Why "unfortunately"?

VOITSKI: Because such fidelity is false and unnatural, root and branch. It sounds well, but there is no logic in it. It is thought immoral for a woman to deceive an old husband whom she hates, but quite moral for her to strangle her poor youth in her breast and banish every vital desire

313

from her heart.

TELEGIN: *(In a tearful voice)* Vanya, I don't like to hear you talk so. Listen, Vanya; every one who betrays husband or wife is faithless, and could also betray his country.

VOITSKI: *(Crossly)* Turn off the tap, Waffles.

TELEGIN: No, allow me, Vanya. My wife ran away with a lover on the day after our wedding, because my exterior was unprepossessing. I have never failed in my duty since then. I love her and am true to her to this day. I help her all I can and have given my fortune to educate the daughter of herself and her lover. I have forfeited my happiness, but I have kept my pride. And she? Her youth has fled, her beauty has faded according to the laws of nature, and her lover is dead. What has she kept?

The Rise of the Director

From theatre's beginnings, someone always has been in charge of rehearsals and staging. Much of the time, it was the playwright. Then during the eighteenth and early nineteenth centuries, an actor-manager assumed the duties. Yet an increasing dependence on special effects, the desire for historical accuracy, and the desire for accurate and consistent interpretation of plot and character contributed to the necessity of having someone who was responsible for all the elements of the production, with giving each play a proper direction.

The person who generally receives the credit for being the first director was George II, the Duke of Saxe-Meiningen (1826–1914), a small duchy, which now is Thuringia, Germany. In his Meiningen Court Theatre, he refined the concept of **ensemble acting**, in which no one actor is more important than any other, and the effect of the total production is more important than any of its parts. The duke believed that the director should be the dominant artist in the theatre, with complete authority over his actors. He felt that the stage picture should be worked out meticulously, that there should be accuracy in historical detail, and that crowd scenes should be meticulously staged. The company became one of the most admired in Europe.

The Private Theatre Movement

Since plays were subject to censorship in much of Europe, a number of independent theatres were established. That is, they were open only to members and so were exempt from government censorship. The first, organized in Paris in 1887 by André Antoine (1858–1943), was the Théâtre Libre, which produced various types of plays but was largely concerned with naturalism. Antoine believed that the actors' environment determined their movements. He went so far as to bring in people off the streets to act in his plays, so they would appear natural. Once he hung carcasses of beef on-stage to make a butcher shop scene realistic.

Two years later, Otto Brahm (1856–1912) established the Freie Bühne (Free Theatre) in Germany and gave a hearing to new writers, thus contributing to the establishment of modern drama in Germany.

In 1891, J. T. Grein, along with William Archer and George Moore, founded the Independent Theatre Society in London. Its initial production was Ibsen's *Ghosts*. Perhaps most important, the Independent Theatre was responsible for George Bernard Shaw's turning to playwriting.

In Russia, Konstantin Stanislavsky (1863–1938), began to develop his system of acting. With others he founded the Moscow Art Theatre in 1897. The group was dedicated to the ensemble concept and naturalness, clarity, and simplicity.

The Eclectic Approach

Recent theatre is eclectic in its combination of many forms. This approach was given impetus by the work of director Max Reinhardt (1873–1943), who believed each play required a different style of presentation and that the director must control the style. Reinhardt, perhaps more than anyone else, made various movements in the theatre acceptable to audiences. Another person who used a variety of styles was Vsevolod Meyerhold of Russia (1874–1940), who favored a return to such forms as the *commedia dell'arte*, Japanese drama, and Greek theatre. To Meyerhold, the actors were no more important than any other elements of a production.

Many new forms of staging and directing were widely accepted in Europe before they gained a foothold in America.

The new stagecraft was first presented to American audiences by little theatre groups such as the Provincetown Players, which produced many of Eugene O'Neill's plays, and the Group Theatre, responsible for developing the talents of many performers who later became America's foremost actors.

Another form that developed along with realism and naturalism was **symbolism**, which began in France and usually took its subject matter from the past. The symbolists did not believe in realistic scenery, preferring backgrounds that gave a general impression of the mood of the play.[3]

Adolphe Appia (1862–1928), a Swiss theorist and designer, and Edward Gordon Craig (1872–1966), an English producer, actor, and stage designer, sought to create an environment that was fitting for each play. Working independently, they laid the foundations upon which much of modern theatrical practice was built. Craig's settings were designed to capture the feeling of a work without representing an actual place. Appia emphasized the role of light in creating unity for his productions.

Expressionism was another important trend in playwriting. One of the best-known expressionist playwrights was August Strindberg (1849–1912), the first important Swedish playwright. He began writing in a realistic vein, but his later plays, such as *The Ghost Sonata* (1907), were actually forerunners of the new movement. Several important American playwrights, including Eugene O'Neill (1888–1953), wrote expressionistic plays. (O'Neill, considered by many to be America's most outstanding playwright, experimented successfully with a variety of styles.) His *The Hairy Ape*, first presented by the Provincetown Players in 1922, shows what might happen if the rules of the universe are changed and our worst fears become reality.

In the play, Yank, a stoker on an ocean liner, is convinced that he and his co-workers are the only ones who count or "belong," since they run the ship. Then Mildred Douglas, daughter of the shipowner, comes to see the men working. Meeting Yank, whom she calls a hairy ape, so repulses her that she faints. This makes him begin to doubt his humanness, a doubt reinforced when he cannot find acceptance in New York City. He goes to a zoo to claim kinship with an ape, but it crushes him to death.

Similar to the work of European expressionists, the play is highly symbolic in its subject matter and content. Yank is the symbol of man, who has emerged from an animal state but has failed to progress spiritually. Alienated from society, he makes the

---

3. For a discussion of the "isms," see Chapter 3.

ultimate discovery that he does not belong in the world either as a man or as a worker. Despite the symbolism and expressionism in the play, much of the dialog is realistic.

Surrealism developed in the theatre at about the same time as expressionism and encompasses a number of other styles, such as theatre of cruelty and theatre of the absurd. Actually, its roots can be traced back at least to the beginning of the twentieth century in paintings and novels. The word *surrealist*, for instance, was used to describe Alfred Jarry's *Le Surmâle*, a 1902 novel. The movement involves breaking down the barriers between the inner and outer, or conscious and subconscious, worlds, as illustrated, for instance, in the dreamlike paintings of Marc Chagall.

One of the earliest dramatists to write in this style was Luigi Pirandello (1867–1936) with *Right You Are — If You Think You Are* and *Six Characters in Search of an Author*. One of the ideas behind surrealism is that we can never define the true self — because of the many things we are and the many roles we play, which may be altogether different from the inner person.

Epic Theatre

Bertolt Brecht (1898-1956), a German writer and director, developed his concept of "making strange," or distancing, in what is called **epic theatre** or **the theatre of alienation**. Although he agreed with the expressionists' wish to change society, he felt their methods too vague and unworkable. Influenced by Marxism, he believed that many of the world's problems occur as the result of capitalism. He wanted the audience to identify with the social and political issues of plays so they would see the need to change conditions rather than identifying with the characters.

As a result of his new approach, Brecht began using such devices as masks and asides and having the actors add "he said" or "she said" to their lines to provide distancing. He used fragmentary scenery and lighting instruments displayed in full view. Further, he felt that each element of a production should make its own statement rather than contributing to a unified whole, which he called redundant. In the plays themselves, he preferred a loose narrative for the same reasons.

At the same time Brecht wanted to distance audiences from the characters, he wanted to engage them and draw them in before presenting a song, for instance, that again was to have the effect of distancing. This later distancing allowed audience members time to think about the social implications of what they had just witnessed.

With Kurt Weill in 1928, Brecht wrote *The Threepenny Opera*, a satire on capitalism and based on John Gay's *The Beggar's Opera*, which was to be his biggest theatrical success. During the presentation of this opera (and others later), musicians remained on-stage, placards provide the audience with an objective view of the action, and there was a separation of dialog from song.

Two of Brecht's plays, *Mother Courage and Her Children* (1939) and *The Good Woman of Setzuan* (1943), established his reputation as a serious dramatist.

Due to his opposition to Hitler, Brecht fled Germany and lived in Scandinavia and the United States before returning to East Berlin in 1948. Back in Germany, he and his wife, actress Helene Weigel, founded the Berliner Ensemble. Brecht remained a controversial figure since his "moral pessimism" was at odds with the Soviet ideal of socialist realism. He often has been called the most influential person in Western Theatre since World War II.

Theatre of the Absurd

Still another important new form was **absurdism**, which asserts that nothing is good or bad as such — only what human beings attribute to something can make it either moral or immoral. Truth is to be found in disorder and chaos, because everything is equally illogical. Among the forerunners of absurdism were the French writers Jean-Paul Sartre and Albert Camus, the latter of whom saw a parallel between the contemporary human being and mythological king Sisyphus who was condemned to rolling a stone up a hill in Hades only to have it roll down each time he neared the top. In other words, he felt the search for meaning was futile.

Later came Romanian-born Eugène Ionesco, whose first play *The Bald Soprano* (1950) opened in Paris to rave reviews. The play consists of non sequiturs, and at the end the characters are shouting nonsense syllables at each other. The philosophy behind the work is that all human endeavor basically is absurd and thus terrifying. Equally absurd is attempting to use language to communicate.

Irish-born Samuel Beckett's *Waiting for Godot* is often considered to be the archetypal absurdist drama. Produced in Paris in 1952, it helped focus the world's attention on the theatre of the absurd. In the play, the two characters seem to be expecting something to happen that will save them in some way, symbolized by their waiting for someone or something (never identified) called Godot.

Absurdism reached its peak in the 1950s but still continues to influence recent and current plays.

Waiting for Godot
Samuel Beckett

From Act II

VLADIMIR: You again! *(ESTRAGON halts but does not raise his head. VLADIMIR goes toward him.)* Come here till I embrace you.

ESTRAGON: Don't touch me!

(VLADIMIR holds back, pained.)

VLADIMIR: Do you want me to go away? *(Pause.)* Gogo! *(Pause. VLADIMIR observes him attentively.)* Did they beat you? *(Pause.)* Gogo! *(ESTRAGON remains silent, head bowed.)* Where did you spend the night?

ESTRAGON: Don't touch me! Don't question me! Don't speak to me! Stay with me!

VLADIMIR: Did I ever leave you?

ESTRAGON: You let me go.

VLADIMIR: Look at me. *(ESTRAGON does not raise his head. Violently.)* Will you look at me! *(ESTRAGON raises his head. They look long at each other, then suddenly embrace, clapping each other on the back. End of the embrace. ESTRAGON, no longer supported, almost falls.)*

ESTRAGON: What a day!

VLADIMIR: Who beat you? Tell me.

ESTRAGON: Another day done with.

VLADIMIR: Not yet.

ESTRAGON: For me it's over and done with, no matter what happens. *(Silence.)* I heard you singing.

VLADIMIR: That's right, I remember.

ESTRAGON: That finished me. I said to myself, He's all alone, he thinks I'm gone for ever, and he sings.

VLADIMIR: One is not master of one's moods. All day I've felt in great form. *(Pause.)* I didn't get up in the night, not once!

ESTRAGON: *(Sadly)* You see, you piss better when I'm not there.

VLADIMIR: I missed you ... and at the same time I was happy. Isn't that a queer thing?

ESTRAGON: *(Shocked)* Happy?

VLADIMIR: Perhaps it's not quite the right word.
ESTRAGON: And now?
VLADIMIR: Now? ... *(Joyous)* There you are again ... *(Indifferent)* There we are again ... *(Gloomy)* There I am again.

Amid such a diversity of dramatic forms, the eclectic approach became a necessity. The distinctions between forms blurred over time.

American Playwrights

Drama written in a realistic vein continued to dominate American theatre to a great extent between World War I and World War II. It was, however, modified in that it was psychological realism where often nonrealistic devices and scenery were used. The three most important playwrights at this time in America were Eugene O'Neill, Arthur Miller, and Tennessee Williams. The latter two used such devices as dream and memory scenes and symbolic characters. Even O'Neill's later work, such as *Long Day's Journey Into Night* which was highly realistic, used poetic dialog as a buffer against the harshness of the story.

Considered the country's first major playwright and the first to gain an international reputation, O'Neill (1888-1953) wrote in a variety of styles. He started as a realist and then turned to expressionism in *The Emperor Jones* and *The Hairy Ape* and various other styles before turning once again to realism. His work also often is rich in symbolism. His best work debatably is the autobiographical play, *Long Day's Journey Into Night*, which he did not want produced until after his death.

Until the end of World War II there were no other major American playwrights. The first after O'Neill to gain wide critical acclaim was Arthur Miller (1915-2005). His second drama, *All My Sons*, which dealt with the effects of opportunism on a family, pointed the way to his later works aimed at social and political reform. His third play, *Death of a Salesman*, written in 1949 (See synopsis in Chapter 1), moved between realism and scenes in the protagonist's memory. The play won both the Drama Critics' Circle Award for best play of the year and the Pulitzer Prize. His next major work, *The Crucible* (1953), dealt with the Salem witch trials, but as an analogy of the widespread congressional investigation of subversive activities. A more recent play is *Resurrection Blues*, which premiered in 2002.

The other major playwright who had a deep impact on postwar America was Tennessee Williams (1911-1983). His first Broadway success was *The Glass Menagerie*, which won the Drama Critics' Circle Award for best play of 1945. (See Chapter 3 for a discussion of the play.) Williams' drama *A Streetcar Named Desire* won a Pulitzer Prize and often has been called the best American drama written to date. His *Cat on a Hot Tin Roof* won him a second Pulitzer. All three, as well as other plays he wrote, are poetic and symbolic and deal in one way or another with sexual suppression or repression and with the inability to cope with the brutality of everyday life.

Coming to prominence a decade later was Edward Albee with such plays as *The Zoo Story* (1958), *Who's Afraid of Virginia Woolf?* (1962, winner of the Drama Critics Circle Award), and *Three Tall Women* (1994), the latter of which won Albee his third Pulitzer Prize. Later plays include *The Play about the Baby* and *The Goat, or Who Is Sylvia?* Often his settings appear to be realistic, but with an overlay of surrealism. Many of his plays are adaptations from other works. These include *The Ballad of the Sad Cafe* (a novel by Carson McCullers) and *The Lady From Dubuque* (adapted from *Lolita* by Vladimir Nabokov).

Two other playwrights who first became known in the 1960s were John Guare and Sam Shepard, both of whom had work produced at Off-Broadway's Caffe Cino. Guare's early writing was somewhat satirical. In the 1990s, with *Six Degrees of Separation*, his work became much more so in exploring social and cultural issues. Shepard's drama, though more lyrical and poetic, always seems to involve a degree of violence. In *Fool for Love*, May and Eddie have a dangerous overpowering and devouring attraction and need for each other, or else they reject each other completely.

The world's most commercially successful writer of comedy is Neil Simon with such hits as *Barefoot in the Park*, *The Odd Couple*, and *45 Seconds From Broadway*. He later began to write a series of autobiographical plays, the first of which were the trilogy that included *Brighton Beach Memoirs*, *Biloxi Blues*, and *Broadway Bound*, though they, too, contain comedy.

Brighton Beach Memoirs
Neil Simon

It is 1937 in Brighton Beach, Brooklyn. The family is having a bad time financially with Eugene's father forced to work two jobs. As the scene shows, his brother Stan will be fired unless he writes a letter of apology.

This scene occurs early in the play. Until now, Eugene, the central character and narrator, has shown his obsession both with the New York Yankees baseball team and with his cousin Laurie.

STAN: *(In half whisper)* Hey! Eugie!

EUGENE: Hi, Stan! *(To the audience)* My brother Stan. He's okay.

STAN: *(Looks around, lowers his voice.)* Is Pop home yet?

EUGENE: No ... Did you ask about the tickets?

STAN: What tickets?

EUGENE: For the Yankee game. You said your boss knew this guy who could get passes. You didn't ask him?

STAN: Me and my boss had other things to talk about. *(He sits on the steps, his head down, almost in tears.)* I'm in trouble, Eug. I mean, really big trouble.

EUGENE: *(To the audience)* This really shocked me. Because Stan is the kind of guy who could talk himself out of any kind of trouble. *(To Stan)* What kind of trouble?

STAN: I got fired today!

EUGENE: *(Shocked)* Fired? You mean for good?

STAN: You don't get fired temporarily. It's permanent. It's a lifetime firing.

EUGENE: Why? What happened?

STAN: It was on account of Andrew. The colored guy who sweeps up. Well, he was cleaning the floor in the stockroom and he lays his broom against the table to put some junk in the trash can and the broom slips, knocks a can of linseed oil over the table and ruins three brand-new hats right out of the box. Nine-dollar Stetsons. It wasn't his fault. He didn't put the linseed oil there, right?

EUGENE: Right.

STAN: So Mr. Stroheim sees the oily hats and he gets crazy. He says to Andrew the hats are going to have to come out of his salary. Twenty-seven dollars. So Andrew starts to cry.

EUGENE: He cried?

STAN: Forty-two years old, he's bawling all over the stockroom. I mean, the man hasn't got too much furniture upstairs anyway, but he's real sweet. He brings me coffee, always laughing, telling me jokes. I never understand them but I laugh anyway, make him feel good, you know?

EUGENE: Yeah?

STAN: Anyway, I said to Mr. Stroheim I didn't think that was fair. It wasn't Andrew's fault.

EUGENE: *(Astounded)* You said that to him?

STAN: Sure, why not? So Mr. Stroheim says, "You wanna pay for the hats, big mouth?" So I said, "No. I don't want to pay for the hats." So he says, "Then mind your own business, big mouth."

EUGENE: Holy mackerel.

STAN: So Mr. Stroheim looks at me like machine-gun bullets are coming out of his eyes. And then he calmly sends Andrew over to the factory to pick up three new hats. Which is usually my job. So guess what Mr. Stroheim tells me to do.

EUGENE: What?

STAN: He tells me to sweep up. He says, for this week I'm the cleaning man.

EUGENE: I can't believe it.

STAN: Everybody is watching me now, waiting to see what I'm going to do. *(Eugene nods in agreement.)* Even Andrew stopped crying and watched. I felt the dignity of everyone who worked in the store was in my hands. So I grit my teeth and I pick up the broom, and there's this big pile of dirt right in the middle of the floor ...

EUGENE: Yeah?

STAN: ... and I sweep it all over Mr. Stroheim's shoes. Andrew had just finished shining them this morning, if you want to talk about irony.

EUGENE: I'm dying. I'm actually dying.

STAN: *(Enjoying himself)* You could see everyone in the place is about to bust a gut. Mrs. Mulcahy, the bookkeeper, can hardly keep her false teeth in her mouth. Andrew's eyes are hanging five inches out of their sockets.

EUGENE: This is the greatest story in the history of the world.

STAN: So Mr. Stroheim grabs me and pulls me into his back office, closes the door and pulls down the shades. He gives me this whole story how he was brought up in Germany to respect his superiors. That if he ever — *(With an accent)* "did soch a ting like you do, dey would beat me in der kopf until dey carried me avay dead."

EUGENE: That's perfect. You got him down perfect.

STAN: And I say, "Yeah. But we're not in Germany, old buddy."

EUGENE: You said that to him?

STAN: No. To myself. I didn't want to go too far.

EUGENE: I was wondering.

STAN: Anyway, he says he's always liked me and always thought I was a good boy and that he was going to give me one more chance. He wants a letter of apology. And that if the letter of apology isn't on his desk by nine o'clock tomorrow morning, I can consider myself fired.

EUGENE: I would have had a heard attack ... What did you say?

STAN: I said I was not going to apologize if Andrew still had to pay for the hats ... He said that was between him and Andrew, and that he expected the letter from me in the morning ... I said good night, walked out of his office, got my hat and went home ... ten minutes early.

EUGENE: I'm sweating. I swear to God, I'm sweating all over.

STAN: I don't know why I did it. But I got so mad. It just wasn't fair. I mean, if you give in when you're eighteen and a half, you'll give in for the rest of your life, don't you think?

EUGENE: I suppose so ... So what's the decision? Are you going to write the letter?

STAN: *(Thinks.)* ... No!

EUGENE: Positively?

STAN: Positively. Except I'll have to discuss it with Pop. I know we need the money. But he told me once, you always have to do what you think is right in this world and stand up for your principles.

EUGENE: And what if he says he thinks you're wrong? That you should write the letter.

STAN: He won't. He's gonna leave it up to me, I know it.

EUGENE: But what if he says, "Write the letter"?

STAN: Well, that's something we won't know until after dinner. Will we? *(He walks into the house.)*

EUGENE: *(Looks after him, then turns to the audience.)* All in all, it was shaping up to be one heck of a dinner. I'll say this though — I always had this two-way thing about my brother. Either I worshiped the ground he walked on or I hated him so much I wanted to kill him ... I guess you know how I feel about him today.

Other important playwrights include August Wilson (1945-2005) and Suzan Lori-Parks. Wilson, a native of Pittsburgh, set most of his nine plays there. Each is a separate work but also a part of a cycle of ten about African-American life in the last century. With *Topdog/Underdog*, Suzan Lori-Parks won the 2002 Pulitzer Prize for Drama, the first African-American woman ever to receive this award. In addition to the Pulitzer Prize, Parks already had won two Obies for best Off-Broadway plays and a MacArthur Genius grant, as well as another Pulitzer Prize nomination for her 1999 play.

Also of note is Tony Kushner, who wrote *Angels in America, Parts I* and *II* and, more recently, *Homebody/Kabul*, which takes place mostly in 1998 shortly before and after the U.S. bombed terrorist camps in Afghanistan in response to two embassy bombings in Africa. Interestingly, the play was written before the terrorist attacks in New York and Washington but presented afterwards.

Another major playwright is Athol Fugard. Although a South African native, Fugard spends about half the year in the United States, and many of his works have appeared on Broadway. A white man, Fugard has repeatedly attacked apartheid. His plays include *Master Harold and the Boys* and *A Lesson from Aloes*. His later plays are more autobiographical. An example is *Exits and Entrances*, which greatly appealed to the audience.

The response, Fugard said, "came as such a surprise to me ... "

Still, what Fugard hadn't calculated was how his jewel of a play would become a prism through which audiences can glimpse many themes, political and personal, that have kept him in the ranks of the world's great dramatists since [1961 when] his *Blood Knot* defied the apartheid system.[4]

Influences on American Theatre

Theatre in the United States began to come into its own in the early part of the twentieth century. Its forerunners were several specific but diverse types of entertainment: the minstrel show, with its jokes and songs and variety; the circus, which developed on a larger scale in the U.S. than in Europe; the showboat, which provided entertainment for isolated communities; variety shows and vaudeville; and musicals. The Broadway district in New York City became the center of American theatre.

Concepts that developed in Europe also influenced American theatre. An example is the **theatre of cruelty** as advanced by Antonin Artaud (1896–1948). In the twenties and thirties, he advocated capturing a sense of danger in relation to the theatre as an expression of the loss of the spiritual aspect of life. To Artaud, the director became the important theatre artist, more important than the playwright, in using sound, lights, color, objects, and actors. The "cruelty" was not against the performers, but rather in compelling the audience to face itself.

Another influence was Jerzy Grotowski's Polish Laboratory Theatre, which sought to rid the theatre of everything that wasn't necessary. Grotowski (1933-1999) concluded that the only two essentials were the actor and the audience. His group became a powerful force in influencing the development of theatre throughout the Western world.

One avant-garde group was Julian Beck and Judith Malina's Living Theatre, considered by some to be the beginnings of the Off-Off-Broadway movement. From its founding, the group rebelled against the mainstream in all of its facets. There were similar groups, though the Living Theatre was the most radical.

After leaving the Living Theatre, Joseph Chaikin founded The Open Theatre, developing a technique for focusing on the

---

4. Anna Marie Welsh, "Notes from a Native Son," *The San Diego-Union Tribune*, July 20, 2004, E1.

performer, not the role, and on "transformation," in which the actor changed from one character to another in front of the audience. The group began working on ensemble creations shaped by one playwright. Also, Richard Schechner began experimenting with **environmental theatre**, or **found space**, that is, performing in any available space and mingling performers and audiences.

The **happenings**, a specialized form popular in the 1960s, combined a variety of media — film, painting, and theatre. Seemingly unrelated occurrences came together in an almost uncontrolled format. One of the early advocates of this form was John Cage, who wanted each person at his happenings to be aware of what was occurring and to judge it independently. Later, people laid more groundwork for the happenings, even preparing outlines. Here, too, there was little or no separation of audience and performer; the spectator was to become an integral part of the happening. The purpose was to break down any separation of life and art.

An outgrowth of the happening is performance art which often is nonlinear and uses a mixture of media. One of those responsible for the multimedia approach was Robert Wilson, an American director with training in both architecture and painting. In such work as *A Letter to Queen Victoria* (1974) and *Einstein on the Beach* (1976), Wilson collaborated with Christopher Knowles, an autistic adolescent, to create Knowles's atypical manner of patterning perceptions. The resulting work, lacking plot and conventional characters, encompassed a stream of visual and auditory images, often involving massive scenic and lighting effects presented in slow motion.

In recent years the trend has been away from the purely and essentially visual to performance pieces that may or may not be fully planned, but most often involve a single artist who may combine such performance areas as acting, oral interpretation, pantomime, and dance, together with paintings and rapidly changing visual and sound effects using various electronic media.

The performers, more often than not appearing solo, may point up particular themes or social problems, often taking a strong stand on an issue such as AIDS. The form has been particularly successful within the last fifteen or twenty years.

A man who has attracted attention in recent years is Guillermo Gómez-Peña with such works as *New World Border* and *The Temple of Confessions*. In the latter, according to Scott T. Cummings, a "blood-red gallery houses a temple adorned with artifacts, icons, trinkets, memorabilia, printed texts, music, and the recorded voices of previous visitors ... At either end of the gallery two 'techno-confessionals' sit like plexiglass altar-booths ... The temple-keepers encourage visitors to kneel on the prayer bench, don a pair of headphones, and speak into the microphone, which gives them a private, direct connection to the headphoned priest in the booth."[5]

> Provocation is a constant characteristic of performance art, a volatile form that artists use to respond to change — whether political in the broadest sense, or cultural, or dealing with issues of current concern — and to bring about change, in relation to the more traditional disciplines of painting and sculpture, photography, theatre and dance, or even literature. Performance art never settles exclusively on any one theme, issue, or mode of expression; rather it defines itself in each case by responding provocatively. It rarely aims to seduce its audience and is more likely to unravel and examine critically the techniques of seduction, unnerving viewers in the process, rather than providing them with an ambiguous setting for desire. It can sometimes be ridiculous, sometimes grotesque, and now and then frightening.[6]

With increased use of digitized images and computer technology, multimedia presentations in today's theatre are icons of our fast-evolving world.

Postmodernism

Whereas modernism, which came into being with the various "isms," embraced the present and the future, postmodernism redefines art in new and unexpected ways. Rather than coordinating a production into a single style, it combines varieties of styles. Rather than attempting to interpret a play in the way the playwright intended, postmodernist directors say that there is no way of knowing how a writer wanted his work interpreted since words are merely symbols that mean different things to different people.

In other words, postmodernism is an **antirealistic** theatre which is more likely to deal with discontinuity of observable reality. Often it combines styles and elements from various historical periods and

---

5. Scott T. Cummings, "Guillermo Gómez-Peña: True Confessions of a Techno-Aztec Performance Artist," *American Theatre*, November 1994, 52.

6. Rose Lee Goldberg, "The Provocateurs," *American Theatre*, December 1998, 22.

cultures. It makes no effort to find any integrated meaning and stems from various recent movements in theatre. These include absurdism, dadaism, epic theatre, happenings, and performance art. Postmodern artists can choose their own style and can break down boundaries between the arts and between audience and spectator. Further, to the postmodernist performer, there is no difference between high and low art and a blurred distinction between dramatic genres.

Current Broadway Theatre

Broadway tends to stay with the more established dramatic forms. During recent years, revivals of older plays have been highly successful, as have been some based on earlier movies. These include the highly successful *The Producers*, the mega-hit *Hairspray*, and *Throughly Modern Millie*. All were nominated for and received various Tony Awards.

The September 11, 2001, terrorist attacks also have influenced theatre as they have every other facet of life. A large number of plays have been written and produced about the subject. Professional theatre also suffered financial losses due to initial lack of attendance. Most productions, however, managed to survive.

Summary

Throughout the past two hundred years, there have been more changes in form and style than ever before. Romanticism taught that a person has only to follow his or her instincts to know what is right. Melodrama inspired the development of common heroes.

Until the 1830s the most popular type of acting troupe was the repertory company. This was followed by the star system and then the combination company. Realism developed as a result of oppressive political and economic conditions. Henrik Ibsen, the father of modern drama, dealt with socially significant themes and did more than any other playwright of the time to establish realism as an integral part of drama.

After realism came naturalism, carried to its ultimate end with the belief that a playwright's only job was to observe and record events.

The most important playwright of the late nineteenth and early twentieth centuries was George Bernard Shaw. Others of importance were Oscar Wilde and John Millington Synge. In Russia, Anton Chekhov wrote plays based on contemporary Russian life.

Georg II, Duke of Saxe-Meiningen, generally is credited with being the first director. The eclectic approach to theatre received impetus through the work of director Max Reinhardt. Adolph Appia and Edward Gordon Craig sought to create an environment that was fitting for each play.

One of the best-known expressionist playwrights was August Strindberg of Sweden. Expressionism was advanced in American theatre largely through the work of Eugene O'Neill. Developing at the same time as expressionism was surrealism. Epic theatre was established by Berthold Brecht who developed a theory of distancing to point up social problems.

The forerunners of absurdism were Jean-Paul Sartre and Albert Camus, while Eugéne Ionesco began writing absurdist drama. However, Samuel Beckett's *Waiting for Godot* is considered the archetypal absurdist drama.

Eugene O'Neill became America's first important playwright. Arthur Miller and Tennessee Williams, the two most important postwar playwrights, wrote psychological realism. Coming to prominence a decade later was Edward Albee.

Theatre in the United States began to come into its own in the early part of the twentieth century. Important influences on American theatre were Artaud's theatre of cruelty, Jerzy Grotowski's Polish Laboratory Theatre, and the Living theatre of Julian Beck and Judith Malina, and later Joseph Chaikin's The Open Theatre.

Postmodernism, which combines a variety of styles, became popular during the late twentieth century. Another trend was toward performance pieces, or solo works often dealing with a social issue.

The September 11, 2001, terrorist attacks affected theatre financially and subject-wise. Along with such plays, Broadway theatre also has in large part stayed with established forms. In recent years musicals based on earlier films have been particularly successful.

Questions for Discussion

1. Why do you think styles of writing and production changed so much during the past two hundred years?
2. In what ways do you think electric lights and the box set helped advance theatre?
3. Why do you think there were no internationally recognized playwrights in America until Eugene O'Neill?
4. Explain what you feel is the reasoning behind the eclectic approach to production.
5. What do you think are the most important influences on theatre today?

Glossary

Absurdism or theatre of the absurd: A movement of the 1950s and 1960s in which playwrights dramatized the absurdity and futility of human existence. Generally, absurdist drama is nonsensical and repetitive.

Acting area: The staging area used by the actors during a performance. Most often, it is divided to make the blocking and movement more easily explainable.

Actors' Equity Association: The professional stage actors' and stage managers' union.

Aesthetic distance: The detachment that allows us to appreciate the beauty of a work of art.

Amphitheatre: Originally, the theatre of ancient Rome; now used to refer to any outdoor theatre.

Antagonist: Opposes the protagonist; the antagonist can be a person or persons, society, a force such as a flood or a storm, or a conflicting tendency within the protagonist.

Apron or forestage: The area of a proscenium stage that extends in front of the grand drape.

Archon: Master of revels in ancient Greek festivals.

Arena stage: The type of stage in which the audience surrounds the playing area.

Aristotle's elements: The six elements Aristotle felt were essential for tragedy are plot, character, thought, dialogue, melody, and spectacle.

Aside: A speech delivered directly to the audience by a character in a play; supposedly, the other characters on-stage are unable to hear what is said.

Asymmetrical balance: Making mass, shape, and color differ from one side of the stage to the other, but keeping the total weight or mass the same so that there is a feeling of balance.

Audition: An actor appearing before a director or casting director to try out for a production. Auditions may consist of memorized pieces, cold readings of the script to be used, an interview, improvisation, or a combination of any of these.

Automatism: Visual or verbal gag that is repeated many times.

Auto Sacramental: Spanish drama akin to medieval mystery and miracle plays in subject matter, yet similar to morality plays in the use of allegorical characters.

Backdrop or drop: Theatrical canvas or muslin that stretches across the stage, is weighted at the bottom, and is painted with scenes.

Backstage area: The area of the stage usually hidden from the audience's view. It includes the wings and the back wall. It is used for storage of scenery and props, for actors to await entrances, and so forth.

Ballad opera: Burlesqued Italian opera; satirized the current political situation. An example is John Gay's *The Beggar's Opera*.

Battens: Pipes to which drops (or other scenery) are attached to be raised and lowered in a theatre with fly space.

Black box: Flexible theatre space that allows for various staging and seating areas with temporary seats that can be moved according to the way a production is staged. The staging area can be anything from a thrust stage to an arena stage to a modified proscenium stage.

Blackout: Dimming or turning off the lighting to leave the stage in complete darkness.

Blocking: The planned movement or business in a play; the stage directions for the actor.

Border: Short horizontal curtains that hang behind the teaser or downstage horizontal curtain.

Bourgeois tragedy: Characterized by false emotion and sentimentality over the misfortunes of others; unlike sentimental comedies, the plays ended unhappily when the leading characters yielded to temptation.

Box set: A setting that generally represents an indoor location and is constructed of flats.

Broadway: The main commercial theatre district of New York City.

Burlesque: Derisive imitation; also a type of low comedy that relies on beatings, accidents, and vulgarity for its humor; later came to refer to striptease performances.

Burlesque farce: Popular during the 1700s, this form of drama poked fun at the sentimental drama of the time.

Business: Physical action taken by the actor.

Callbacks: The stage of the audition process when certain actors are asked to return for a second audition.

Catharsis: The purging of emotions; the release of emotional tension.

Character comedy: A play whose humor directly involves the actions and eccentricities of the central character.

Character inconsistency: Comedy that results from a trait that does not seem to fit with a character's personality.

Character makeup: Makeup that makes an actor appear different from normal.

Choregi: Wealthy citizens chosen by the archon or master of revels to pay for the training, costumes, and room and board for the chorus in ancient Greece. Each year one choregus was chosen per playwright.

Chorus: A group of actors or oral interpreters in ancient Greek theatre. They most often performed in unison. A chorus sometimes appears in plays of other historical periods and as singers and dancers in musicals.

Circular structure: A type of organization in which the action of a play shows no real progression from one point to another, but ends as it began.

City Dionysia: In Athens, the major festival honoring the god of wine and fertility, Dionysus, and at which plays were performed.

Classical drama: The plays from ancient Greece and Rome. Also used to denote any outstanding drama from any historical period.

Climax: The high point of the plot; the moment when an irrevocable action occurs that determines the outcome of the play.

Color scrollers: A device that attaches to the front of a stationary stage lighting instrument. It scrolls a roll of different colored filters in front of the instrument, stopping at a pre-selected color.

Combination companies: In the nineteenth and early twentieth centuries, theatre companies that traveled (that is, visited a "combination" of theatres) for a season presenting a single play. At first, combination companies usually presented only road shows of current New York hits.

Comedy of manners: A play that deals with the foibles or amoral characteristics of the upper class.

Commedia dell'arte: Professional acting troupes who traveled throughout Western Europe from the mid-fifteenth to the mid-sixteenth centuries. They improvised from outlines called scenarios, thus making their work adaptable to changing locations and situations. An actor continued to play the same stock character so long as he or she remained with the company.

Comic devices: Techniques that playwrights use in establishing a comic frame of reference. They include exaggeration (intensification and enlargement), incongruity (unlike elements appearing together), automatism (the running gag), character inconsistency (an inconsistent personality trait), surprise (the unexpected), and derision (poking fun at people and institutions).

Comic relief: Comic elements in a tragedy or serious play to relieve the tension, so that it will build more completely once the comic scene ends.

Complication: Change in direction of the dramatic action in a play.

Conflict: Opposition; antagonist and protagonist engaged in a struggle to triumph over each other.

Concert performances: Musicals centered around a musical group and usually using little scenery.

Constructivism: Including in the setting only those elements that are necessary to the action of a play.

Conventions: Writing and theatrical practices, devices, or processes agreed upon and accepted by both theatre artist and audience to further the progression of a play.

Corrales: Open courtyards in northern Spain where plays were presented during the Renaissance period.

Counterweight system: A system of ropes, cables, pulleys, and weights used to fly scenery in a theatre with a fly system.

Cue: The final line or action that signals that it is time for an actor to begin the next action or speech.

Cue sheet: Written instructions giving information about prearranged signals for any changes in lighting, sound, scenery shifts, and so on.

Cycle plays: In the medieval period, a series of plays presented one after the other, though not necessarily related structurally, and dealing with Biblical subjects.

Cyclorama: Usually a circular curtain surrounding the sides and rear of the acting area in exterior scenes, providing the illusion of distance.

Denouement or falling action: The final portion of a play in which all the loose ends are tied up, and all the questions answered.

Deus ex machina: A machine or crane used to fly in the gods to address human problems in ancient Greek drama; in current usage, a derisive term applied to a playwright's having fate intervene in solving the protagonist's problems rather than having the character solve them.

Derision: Making fun of people or institutions for the purpose of social reform.

Dialog: The conversation between or among characters in a play; the lines or speeches of the characters in a play.

Dichroic color filters: Thin layers of chemical on a sheet of glass that reflects selective wavelengths of light when viewed from different directions.

Dimmer board: The panel containing switches to raise and lower the intensity of stage lighting.

Dionysus: The god of wine and debauchery in Greek mythology; hymns of praise called "dithyrambs" in his honor are at the root of Western theatre.

Director or artistic director: The person responsible for interpreting a script, planning blocking and movement, and rehearsing the actors. The director generally oversees all the aspects of a production.

Dithyrambs: Hymns of praise to Dionysus, delivered by a chorus of fifty men.

Domestic tragedy: Sentimentalized tragedy about common people and involving in some way the protagonist's disregard of virtue.

Downstage: In a proscenium theatre, the area closest to the audience.

Drama: All written plays, regardless of their genre or form.

Dramatic action: Everything that occurs in a play and advances it toward a conclusion; the motivation and purpose of a play; the physical, spiritual, psychological, and emotional elements that hold a play together.

Dramatic time: The amount of time represented by a play; an hour on-stage may represent any amount of time, although more time usually is represented as having passed than the actual two hours or so it takes to present a play.

Dramaturg: A relatively new position in America, though long-established in Europe. The dramaturg's duties vary from theatre to theatre, but may include historical research about a play, acquainting potential audiences with the writer and the period, and helping with the script's interpretation.

Dress rehearsal: The final stage of rehearsals when all the technical elements, costumes, and makeup are added to a production. The dress rehearsal should be as polished as the production before an audience.

Drolls: Comic excerpts from familiar plays, presented at fairs in England during the seventeenth century.

Dutchmanning (dutching): Applying a strip of fabric to scenery flats, those that are hinged together, to cover the cracks between them.

Ekkyklema: A stage device in ancient Greece somewhat like a wheeled cart or platform in which "bodies" of fallen warriors could be brought on and taken offstage.

Elevator stage: Stage which is an elevator; can raise and lower entire sets.

Emotional memory: Remembering how one felt in a particular set of circumstances and then relating those emotions to similar circumstances in a play.

Empathy: Emotionally relating to or identifying with a character, a theme, or a situation in a play.

Ensemble acting: The concept that no one actor is more important than any other, and the effect of the total production is more important than any of its parts.

Environmental theatre or found space: The production of plays in any available space large enough to accommodate theatre artists and audience members. In environmental theatre, there was a mixing of audience and actor and blurred lines between acting and audience areas.

Epic theatre or theatre of alienation: A style of theatre, advocated by Bertolt Brecht, in which the audience is asked to identify with the overall social problem rather than with individual characters. Generally, the style of the drama is episodic.

Epilogue: The concluding scene of a play, occurring some time after the major conflict has been resolved; in Greek tragedy, it usually involved a shift in mood or tone, and often the inclusion of a *deus ex machina*.

Episodic structure: A series of loosely related events to make up a play.

Exaggeration: Humor through overstatement and intensification.

Exodus: In Greek tragedy, the departure of the chorus at the end of the play.

Exposition: Any background information necessary to the understanding of a play; it may be presented through dialogue, setting, and properties.

Expressionism: A style that presents the inner reality of the major character; the audience witnesses the workings of the character's mind.

External approach: Concerned with the technique of acting, or which outward signs of a particular emotion can be used to portray that emotion.

Falling action or denouement: The part of a story play that occurs after the climax. It shows the results of the climax.

Federal Theatre Project: A federal program of the 1930s. Like other Works Progress Administration projects, it was geared toward work within specific communities and to provide employment for out-of-work actors, playwrights, and other theatre artists.

Flashback: A theatrical convention in which the audience, through the eyes of a character in a play, is able to see scenes from before the time in which the play exists.

Flat: Scenery frame constructed of one-by-three boards, covered with canvas, painted, and used most often for interior or exterior walls of a building in a stage setting.

Floodlights: Non-focusable lighting instruments used for general illumination.

Floor plan: A drawing of the setting as seen from above.

Fly space: The area behind the top of the arch of a proscenium stage.

Focal point: The area toward which the audience's attention is directed. This can be accomplished by actor placement, lighting, costuming, and so on, or through a combination of these elements.

Formalism: Using the physical appearance of the stage rather than a designed setting; using only what is absolutely necessary. For example, ladders represent houses in *Our Town*.

Fourth wall: The imaginary wall that exists between the actors and the audience in a representational play; through this "wall" the audience sees the action of the play.

Framework: Prescribes all the conditions of the world and universe of a play.

French scene: Begins with the entrance and ends with the exit of an important character.

General lighting: Lighting that provides visibility on the whole stage.

General manager: The person who oversees a production's budget and financial operation.

Genre: A way of classifying plays into types such as tragedy, comedy, farce, and so on.

Given circumstances: The background information provided about a character or the play as a whole. Actors take the given circumstances as a beginning in establishing a character.

Grand drape: The heavy front curtain in a proscenium theatre.

Greenroom: The waiting area for actors before a show or their entrance and at intermissions.

Hand props: Articles that are handled or carried by the actors.

Happenings: A type of unstructured theatre presentation, generally involving the audience, in which there was little planning; the purpose was to break down the separation of life and art.

Heroic tragedy: Popular during the Restoration period in England, heroic tragedy was written in rhymed couplets. It nearly always dealt with themes of love and honor.

High comedy: Humor through verbal wit that appeals to the intellect.

House: The auditorium or seating area; a "good house" refers to a responsive audience.

Immediacy: The quality of a work of art that makes it important or relevant to the time in which it is presented to the public.

Impressionism: A style in which the designer and director determine what they wish to emphasize most and apply this element to the setting; the style deals with the design exclusive of the script.

Improvisation or improvisational theatre: Building a scene or a play on the spur of the moment with little preplanning and no script.

Inciting incident: The point of a play at which the initial balance is upset and the plot begins to build.

Incongruity: Humor through showing differing or opposing elements together, such as tennis shoes worn with a formal gown.

Independent Theatre Movement: A movement that began in the late nineteenth century to counteract censorship of plays by opening private playhouses.

Instrument schedule: An instrument schedule is a supplement to the lighting plot. It resembles a spreadsheet that presents all necessary information about each lighting instrument, such as its color, channel, and dimmer hookup, etc.

Interlude: A scene or presentation not related to the play and usually presented during intermissions. Also, in medieval England, a short morality play.

Intermezzi: A series of short scenes or plays, with singing and dancing, presented between the acts of a neoclassic tragedy.

Internal approach: Seeking within oneself the emotions and experiences to portray a character in a play.

Kabuki theatre: Secular Japanese theatre involving female impersonation.

Lazzi: Stage business in *commedia dell'arte*.

Lenaia: The winter festival in Athens where comedies were presented.

Lighting plot: A plan view of the permanent stage lighting positions that shows the locations of all general and specific lighting instruments as they will be hung for a specific production. Generally, an instrument schedule accompanies the lighting plot.

Liturgical drama: A play presented in conjunction with a church service, such as the "tropes" or playlets presented in the Middle Ages throughout Western Europe.

Low comedy: Humor that relies on physical actions.

Ludi romani: Roman games at which theatrical performances were given.

Managing director: The person responsible for financial matters in a nonprofit theatre.

Mansion or sede: One of several specific locations in medieval theatre used as the starting point for playlets that then moved to the platea or unlocalized playing area.

Mask: To conceal areas (such as backstage) and objects (such as lighting instruments) from the audience's view. The word also refers to face or head coverings used by actors to alter appearance.

Masque: A dramatic form presented in England during Cromwell's time and featuring spectacular staging and costumes. Written by Ben Jonson, masques told allegorical stories honoring well-known persons or occasions.

Melody: The rhythm and flow of the language in a play; should reflect the emotional content of the situation.

Mime: A short play, usually comic and often improvised; a particular favorite in ancient Roman theatre and one of the few types of theatre in which women appeared. The word currently refers to a performer who uses actions without words or props.

Mimetic instinct: The human need or desire to imitate; through the mimetic instinct we acquire much of our learning.

Minstrel shows: The minstrel show consisted of white men with blackened faces presenting comedy, music, and dance interspersed with dialect conversations and, finally, the "stump speech" — a lecture on a current topic, but filled with puns and malapropisms.

Miracle play: A medieval drama that dealt with the lives of saints and martyrs, but could include topical scenes involving family troubles.

Monolog: A long speech delivered by a character in a play, either to the audience or to other characters.

Morality play: A form of medieval drama concerning moral instruction, particularly the attempt to save a person's soul. All the characters were allegorical, and the central figure usually was called Everyman. Such characters as Virtue and Vice fought over his soul.

Motivation: The reason for taking any action; why the protagonist in a play attempts to reach a certain goal.

Motivational base: Same as the inciting incident, the point at which the conflict is introduced.

Motivational unit: The occurrence of a new scene when something slightly alters the direction the protagonist takes in attempting to reach the goal or solution to the problem.

Musical: Any play that includes a substantial amount of singing and dancing, more recently as an integral part of the plot.

Mystery play: In medieval Europe, a play depicting episodes from the life of Christ.

Naturalism: A theatrical style that attempts to duplicate life, or, in effect, to transfer actual life to the stage.

Neoclassicism: A style popular during the Italian Renaissance, with a strict five-act format and a completely unified production.

New comedy: The form of Greek comedy popular in the time of Alexander the Great and associated with the playwright Menander. It dealt with middle-class citizens and character types.

No or Noh theatre: A form of classical Japanese theatre that was temple-centered and used rigid production conventions.

Off-Broadway: Professional New York theatre outside the Broadway district, mostly in Greenwich Village. At its inception in the 1950s and into the 1960s, it was synonymous with experimental drama. Presently, however, it's more akin to Broadway in terms of union contracts and theatre capacities.

Off-Off-Broadway: New York theatre that usually is nonprofessional and generally experimental. It developed in the 1970s to combat the commercialism of Broadway and Off-Broadway theatre.

Offstage: Out of sight of the audience.

Old comedy: The form of Greek comedy, as written by Aristophanes, which lasted from 454 to 404 BC and is characterized by its emphasis on an idea rather than on a cause-to-effect relationship of events. The plays have many episodes, which often seem unrelated to each other, but do build in comic intensity.

Orchestra: In Greek theatre, the area where the chorus appeared. In contemporary theatre, the seating area closest to the stage in a proscenium theatre.

Pace: The overall rate of speed in handling lines and business.

Pageant wagons: In medieval theatre, wheeled platforms on which plays were mounted and which usually moved from location to location.

Pantomime: A form of Roman entertainment in which dancers performed accompanied by music. In eighteenth-century England, as presented by John Rich, pantomime featured dances and mimicry to musical accompaniment, presenting both comic and serious scenes with elaborate scenery and effects. In today's usage, pantomime is the same as mime — performing actions without words.

Paradoi: The space on either side of the orchestra and between the skene and seating area in the Greek theatre; used primarily for the chorus's entrances and exits.

Platea: The unlocalized or central acting area near the mansions in medieval theatre.

Plot: The progression of a story from the point of attack through the climax and denouement.

Point of attack: The place in a story where the writer decides to begin.

Postmodernism: Redefines art in new and unexpected ways in drawing on a number of sources for any particular production.

Practical: Refers to something on-stage that actually works, rather than simulating an object. For instance, a "practical" window in the set actually opens.

Presentational style: A broad category of theatrical style that is audience centered; the actors, director, and designer make open acknowledgment of the audience.

Preview: A public performance of a play before the official opening.

Producer or producing organization: The person, group, or institution providing the financial backing for presenting a play.

Properties: Articles that can be moved or carried in the course of a play. Set properties include such objects as curtains and paintings; hand props include anything that the actors use or carry.

Proscenium or proscenium arch: A picture-frame stage; the framing device that isolates the stage area and provides the focal point for the action. The audience views the action through an imaginary fourth wall.

Promptbook: The director's record of blocking, business, movement and technical cues, and any other information necessary for running the show. The stage manager uses a promptbook to call the production.

Protagonist: The major character in a play; generally, the protagonist tries to reach a certain goal and is opposed by the antagonist.

Raked stage: A stage that slopes upward from front to back.

Realism: A style that attempts to present life as it is, but selectively; not all details are presented — only those that are essential for the audience's understanding of the play and for the establishment of the mood.

Repertory company: A theatrical company that alternates a series or repertoire of plays.

Regional theatre: Professional, nonprofit theatre existing in various locations across the country; also called resident theatres.

Rehearsal: When the actors, under the supervision of the artistic director, ready a show for performance. The process begins with an interpretation of the script and individual characters, progressing to blocking followed by a period in which concentration is more completely on developing character and on line delivery. Then come run-throughs and finishing rehearsals. See *technical rehearsals* and *dress rehearsals.*

Restoration comedy: Beginning in 1660, when Charles II was restored to the English throne, there developed a particular type of comedy marked by witty dialogue and addressing the foibles of the upper class. This form was known as a Comedy of Manners.

Representational style or representational theatre: A broad category of style that is stage-centered; the actors make no acknowledgment of the audience, but try to duplicate life.

Revolving stage: A circular portion of the stage floor that rotates, taking from view one setting and revealing another.

Rhythm: The flow of the lines; the speed with which the actors pick up their cues.

Rising action: The building or intensification of the struggle between the protagonist and the antagonist.

Ritual: A repeated pattern of behavior, which may have its basis in religion, pageantry, or individual behavior. It originally meant a controlled sequence of action to achieve a supernatural goal. Now it also refers to a type of play structure in which a pattern of action is repeated.

Role playing: Changing one's ways of behaving in different situations; modifying behavior to fit the situation.

Romantic comedy: A comedy whose humor lies in the complications the hero and heroine face in their love for each other.

Romanticism: A style characterized by freedom, gracefulness, and a belief in humankind's basic good.

Run-through: A rehearsal that includes the entire play from opening line to ending, ideally without any stops.

Rural Dionysia: A festival honoring Dionysus and held each year in December in ancient Greece.

Satyr play: A ribald form of comedy in ancient Greece presented along with a playwright's three tragedies. A satyr was half goat and half human.

Satire: Gentle mockery for the purpose of reform.

Schematics: In regard to theatre makeup, outlines of the head with the face divided into areas, showing the color or type of makeup to apply to each area.

Scrims: Semitransparent cloths usually serving as backdrops; when lighted from the rear they are semitransparent, and when lighted from the front they are opaque.

Selective visibility: Providing focus through lighting.

Sense memory: Remembering and portraying anything sensory.

Sentimental comedy: Characterized by false emotions and sentimentality over the misfortunes of others. The plays were referred to as comedies not because they were funny, but because they ended happily.

Set dressing: Articles such as draperies or paintings that are attached to the walls of the set.

Set props: Articles that stand within the setting, including furniture, trees or bushes, and rocks.

Setting: The environment or physical background for a play; the visual symbol of a play.

Sightlines: The line of vision for the audience watching a theatrical production. A designer considers sightlines in relation to how well the audience can see all of the action from any part of the seating area.

Situation comedy: A comedy whose humor derives from placing the central characters in a comedy in unusual situations.

Skene: The scene house in ancient Greek theatre. Used at first for storage and then as a place for actors to change costumes, it became a background or scenery for the action.

Slice-of-life: Refers to a movement, extremely naturalistic, in which a playwright was to be a faithful recorder of life, transferring it directly to the stage as observed. As a slice of life, it should have no manufactured beginning or ending.

Soliloquy: A theatrical convention in which a character, while alone on-stage, thinks aloud, revealing his or her innermost thoughts.

Specific lighting: Lighting for special effects, such as to suggest sunlight or to set the mood.

Spine or superobjective: The major goal of a character in a play.

Spotlights: Focusable lighting instruments customarily used for specific illumination.

Stage directions: Blocking, movement, and scene descriptions written into a published script.

Stage Left (or Left Stage): In a proscenium theatre, the area that is on the actors' left as they face an audience.

Stage manager: Second in command after the director. After the opening, this person calls the show.

Stage Right (or Right Stage): In a proscenium theatre, the area that is on the actors' right as they face an audience.

Stock characters: Character types in which certain traits, such as miserliness, are highly exaggerated.

Story play (or cause-to-effect play): A form of drama that has a plot and builds in intensity from an inciting incident to a turning point and climax.

Street theatre: Literally taking to the streets to bring theatre to the people, usually in support of a political or social cause.

Straight makeup: Makeup that accentuates an actor's natural features.

Subplot: A secondary or subordinate story or plotline accompanying the major thread of a play.

Subtext: The meaning behind the actions and spoken words in a play or script; the ideas, message, and motivation beneath the surface and often more meaningful than the text itself.

Summer stock: Theatre companies that perform only during the summer season. They include resort and tourist area theatres and outdoor theatres.

Surprise: Humor through the unexpected.

Surrealism: A movement begun in theatre in the 1920s and characterized by a blurring of lines between the conscious and the subconscious.

Symbol: One thing that stands for another. In the theatre the setting and lights, for instance, represent a background or environment for the action, while the actors symbolize the characters in the play.

Symbolism: A style that presents life in terms of allegory; it depicts subjective or internal reality, determined by the playwright.

Symmetrical balance: Giving either side of a setting exactly the same elements in the same relationship to each other.

Teaser: The short front or horizontal curtain that helps mask the fly space. All other horizontal curtains behind the teaser are called borders.

Technical director: The person, usually in resident and educational theatres, who is responsible for overseeing all the technical aspects of a production and for carrying out the director's plan for the production.

Technical rehearsal: One of the finishing rehearsals in which all the technical aspects — lights, sound, scenery shifts, etc. — are added to a production.

Theatre of cruelty: A theory of theatre's purpose and execution developed by Antonin Artaud in which the goal was to confront the violent impulses in the subconscious mind through sensations rather than a plot.

Theatricalism: A treatment of a play in which audience members are constantly reminded that they are in a theatre; the fourth wall is broken down, and the audience uses its imagination in the matter of setting.

Theatron: Literally "seeing place"; used in ancient Greek theatre to mean the audience area.

Thematic structure: The organization of a play unified around a particular idea or theme.

Thesis play: A subgenre of the well-made play; it attempted to teach a moral lesson.

Thespian: Synonym for actor; derived from the name Thespis, a man who is credited with being the first to step forward from the Greek chorus and deliver dialog as an individual.

Thrust stage: A stage that juts into the seating area, with audience seating on three sides.

Timing: The use of pauses in delivering lines.

Tormentors: The first set of vertical curtains hung at either side of the stage to mask the backstage area. (Other vertical curtains hung behind the tormentors are called legs.)

Tragoidia: Hymns of praise to Dionysus sung by the ancient Greek dithyrambic chorus dressed as satyrs (half goats); goat songs.

Trope: A liturgical playlet that was a part of medieval church services in Western Europe.

Turning point: The moment in a plot when the action can go no further without something irrevocable happening.

Unity: A harmony in the way all the elements of a play combine.

Unities: Neoclassic ideal stating that a play must observe the three unities of time, place, and action. That is, they should occur in a single day, at the same location, and should not mix genres.

Universality: The trait of having meaning for everyone in all places and times.

Upstage: The area closest to the back wall in a proscenium stage.

Upstaging: Actors drawing attention to themselves to the detriment of the production.

Vaudeville and variety shows: Presented as a series of unrelated acts in a single program. These could be dancing, singing, recitations, animal acts, and so on.

Wagon stage: A platform on casters that can be wheeled on and off the stage.

Well-made play: In current theatre, refers to a play with a plot; historically, a play that presented a particular social problem for which the playwright offered a solution.

Willing suspension of disbelief: The audience's willingness to accept theatrical conventions and allow themselves to be transported into the world of the play.

Wings: Flats that stand independently and are placed a short distance apart from the front to the back of a stage; also the areas to the right and left of the playing area in a proscenium theatre.

Zanni: The comic servants in the *commedia dell'arte.*

Selected Bibliography

Part I

The American Theatre Planning Board, Inc. *Theatre Check List: A Guide to the Planning and Construction of Proscenium and Open Stage Theatres.* Middletown, CT: Wesleyan University Press, 1969.

Aristotle. "The Poetics," *European Theories of the Drama.* Barrett H. Clark, ed., newly revised by Henry Popkin. New York: Crown Publishers, Inc., 1965.

Baker, George Pierce. *Dramatic Technique.* Boston: Houghton Mifflin Company, 1919.

Bentley, Eric. *The Life of the Drama.* New York: Atheneum, 1964.

———. *In Search of Theatre.* New York: Alfred A. Knopf, Inc., 1953.

———. *The Theatre of Commitment and Other Essays.* New York: Atheneum, 1967.

———. *The Theory of the Modern Stage: An Introduction to Theatre and Drama.* Baltimore: Penguin Books, Inc., 1968.

Bloom, Martin. *Accommodating the Lively Arts: An Architect's View.* Lyme, NH: Smith and Kraus, 1997.

Boyle, Walden P. *Central and Flexible Staging.* Berkeley: University of California Press, 1956.

Brown, Catherine R., William B. Fleissig, and William R. Morrish. *Building for the Arts: A Guidebook for the Planning and Design of Cultural Facilities.* Santa Fe, NM: Western States Arts Federation, 1984 and 1989.

Burris-Meyer, Harold, and Edward C. Cole. *Theatres and Auditoriums,* 2nd ed. New York: Reinhold Publishing Corporation, 1964.

Carlson, Marvin. *Places of Performance.* Ithaca, NY: Cornell University Press, 1989.

Cogswell, Margaret, ed. *The Ideal Theatre: Eight Concepts.* New York: The American Federation of Arts, 1962.

Condee, William Faricy. *Theatrical Space: A Guide for Directors and Designers.* Lanham, MD: The Scarecrow Press, Inc., 1995.

Driver, Tom F. *Romantic Quest and Modern Theory: History of the Modern Theatre.* New York: Delta Books, published by Dell Publishing Co., Inc., 1970.

Elder, Eldon and Michele Larue, associate writer. *Will It Make a Theatre?* New York: ACA Books, 1993.

Fergusson, Francis. *The Idea of a Theater.* Princeton, N.J.: Princeton University Press, 1949.

Izenour, George. *Theater Technology.* New York: McGraw-Hill Book Company, 1988.

Jones, Robert Edmund. *The Dramatic Imagination.* New York: Meredith Publishing Company, 1941.

Kaye, Deena, and James Lebrecht. *Sound and Music for the Theatre.* New York: Back Stage Books, 1992.

Leacroft, Richard and Helen. *Theatre and Playhouse: An Illustrated Survey of Theatre Building from Ancient Greece to the Present Day.* London: Metheun London, Ltd., 1984.

Lewis, Allan. *American Plays and Playwrights of the Contemporary Theatre.* New York: Crown Publishers, Inc., 1965.

Mackintosh, Iain. *Architecture, Actor, and Audience.* New York: Routledge, 1993.

Reid, Francis. *Designing for the Theatre,* 2nd ed. NY: Theatre Arts Books/Routledge, 1996.

Willet, John, ed. *Brecht on Theatre.* New York: Hill and Wang Inc., 1964.

Woolworth, George. *The Theater of Protest and Paradox: Developments in the Avant-Garde Drama,* 2nd ed. New York: New York University Press, 1971.

Part II

Archer, William. *Play-Making: A Manual of Craftsmanship.* New York: Dodd, Mead & Company, 1928.

Bates, Brian. *The Way of the Actor: A New Path to Personal Knowledge and Power.* London: Century, 1986.

Benedetti, Jean. *Stanislavski and the Actor.* New York: Routledge/Theatre Arts Books, 1998.

Bennett, Susan. *Theatre Audiences: A Theory of Production and Reception,* 2nd ed. New York: Routledge, 1997.

Black, David. *The Magic of the Theater: Behind the Scenes with Today's Leading Actors.* New York: Macmillan Publishing Company, 1993.

Blau, Herbert. *The Audience.* Baltimore: The Johns Hopkins University Press, 1990.

Boleslavsky, Richard. *Acting: The First Six Lessons.* New York: Theatre Arts Books, 1933.

Bradley, David, and David Williams. *Directors' Theatre.* London: Macmillan Publishers Ltd., 1988.

Burdick, Elizabeth et al., eds. *Contemporary Scene Design U.S.A.* New York: International Theatre Institute of the United States, Inc., 1974.

Cassady, Marsh. *Acting Games: Improvisations and Exercises.* Colorado Springs, CO: Meriwether Publishing Ltd., 1993.

———. *Acting Step by Step.* San Jose, CA: Resource Publications, Inc., 1988.

———. *Characters in Action: A Guide to Playwriting.* Lanham, MD: University Press of America, 1984.

————. *Characters in Action: Playwriting the Easy Way*. Colorado Springs, CO: Meriwether Publishing Ltd., 1995.

————. *Playwriting Step by Step*. San Jose, CA: Resource Publications, Inc., 1985.

Chaikin, Joseph. *The Presence of the Actor*. New York: Atheneum, 1972.

Chapman, Gerald. *Teaching Young Playwrights*. Portsmouth, NH: Heinemann, 1991.

Chekhov, Michael. *To the Actor on the Technique of Acting*. New York: Harper & Row, Publishers, 1953.

Cohen, Robert. *Acting Professionally: Raw Facts About Careers in Acting*, 4th ed. Mountain View, CA: Mayfield Publishing Company, 1990.

Cole, Susan Letzler. *Directors in Rehearsal*. New York: Routledge, 1992.

Cole, Toby, ed. *Playwrights on Playwriting: The Meaning and Making of Modern Drama from Ibsen to Ionesco*. New York: Hill and Wang, Inc., 1961.

Crawford, Cheryl. *One Naked Individual: My Fifty Years in the Theatre*. Indianapolis: The Bobbs-Merrill Company, Inc., 1977.

Egri, Lajos. *The Art of Dramatic Writing*. New York: Simon and Schuster, 1946.

Field, Shelly. *Career Opportunities in Theater and the Performing Arts*. New York: Facts on File, 1992.

Frommer, Myrna Katz, and Harvey Frommer. *It Happened on Broadway: An Oral History of the Great White Way*. New York: Harcourt Brace & Company, 1998.

George, Kathleen E. *Playwriting: The First Workshop*. Boston: Focal Press, 1994.

Grotowski, Jerzy. *Towards a Poor Theatre*. New York: Simon and Schuster, 1968.

Gruver, Bert. Revised by Frank Hamilton. *The Stage Manager's Handbook*. New York Drama Book Publishers, 1952 and 1953; new material copyright 1972.

Hays, David. *Light on the Subject: Stage Lighting For Directors and Actors—and the Rest of Us*. New York: Limelight Editions, 1989.

Henderson, Mary C. *Theater America: 250 Years of Plays, Players, and Productions*, new updated edition. New York: Harry N. Abrams, Inc., 1996.

Hull, Raymond. *How to Write a Play*. Cincinnati: Writer's Digest Books, 1983.

Ingram, Rosemary, and Liz Covey. *The Costume Designers Handbook: A Complete Guide for Amateur and Professional Costume Designers*. Englewood Cliffs, NJ: Prentice Hall, 1983.

————. *The Costume Technicians Handbook: A Complete Guide for Amateur and Professional Costume Designers*. Portsmouth, NH: Heinemann Educational Books, Inc., 1992.

Izenour, George. *Theater Technology*. New York: McGraw-Hill Book Company, 1988.

Jackson, Sheila. *Costumes for the Stage*. New York: New Amsterdam, 1988, © 1987 by Sheila Jackson and published by arrangement with The Herbert Press Ltd., London.

Jeffri, Joan, ed. *The Actor Speaks: Actors Discuss Their Experiences and Careers*. New York: Greenwood Press, 1994.

Jones, Margo. *Theatre-in-the-Round*. New York: Holt, Rinehart, and Winston, Inc., 1951.

Jones, Richard. *Great Directors at Work: Stanislavsky, Brecht, Kazan, Brook*. Berkeley: University of California Press, 1986.

Kaye, Deena, and James Lebrecht. *Sound and Music for the Theatre*. New York: Back Stage Books, 1992.

Kerr, Walter. *How Not to Write a Play*. New York: Simon and Schuster, 1955.

Langner, Laurence. *The Play's the Thing*. New York: G. P. Putnam's Sons, 1960.

Lawson, John Howard. *Theory and Technique of Playwriting*. New York: Hill and Wang, Inc., 1960.

Lord, William H. *Stagecraft 1: A Complete Guide to Backstage Work*, 2nd ed. Colorado Springs, CO: Meriwether Publishing Ltd., 1991.

Leiter, Samuel L. *The Great Stage Directors: 100 Distinguished Careers of the Theatre*. New York: Facts on File, Inc., 1994.

Luere, Jeane, ed. *Playwright Versus Director: Authorial Intentions and Performance Interpretations*. Westport, CT: Greenwood Press, 1994.

Luere, Jeane, and Sidney Berger, eds. *The Theatre Team: Playwright, Producer, Director, Designers, and Actors*. Westport, CT: Greenwood Press, 1998.

Markowitz, Charles. *Alarums & Excursions: Our Theatres in the Nineties*. New York: Applause, 1996.

Matthews, Brander, ed. *Papers on Playmaking*. New York: Hill and Wang, 1957.

Nelson, Richard, and David Jones. *Making Plays: The Writer-Director Relationship in the Theatre Today*. Boston: Faber and Faber, 1995.

O'Neill, Brian. *Acting As a Business: Strategies for Success*. Portsmouth, NH: Heinemann, 1993.

Payne, Darwin Reid. *Computer Scenographics*. Carbondale, IL: Southern Illinois University Press, 1994.

Reid, Frances. *Designing for the Theatre*. London: A & C Black [Publishers] Limited, 1989.

Schechner, Richard. *Environmental Theatre*. New York: Hawthorn Books, Inc., 1973.

Smiley, Sam. *Playwriting: The Structure of Action*. Englewood Cliffs, NJ: Prentice-Hall, Inc., 1971.

Straczynski, J. Michael. *The Complete Book of Scriptwriting*. Cincinnati: Writer's Digest Books, 1982.

Sweet, Jeffrey. *The Dramatist's Toolkit: The Craft of the Working Playwright*. Portsmouth, NH: Heinemann, 1993.

Sponberg, Arvid F. "Producing," *Broadway Talks: What Professionals Think About Commercial Theater in America*. New York: Greenwood Press, 1991.

Stern, Lawrence. *Stage Management*, 5th ed. Boston: Allyn and Bacon, 1995.

Stanislavski, Constantin. *An Actor Prepares*. Trans. by Elizabeth Reynolds Hapgood. New York: Theatre Arts Books, 1936.

Sweet, Harvey. *Handbook of Scenery, Properties, and Lighting, Volumes 1 and 2*, 2nd ed. Boston: Allyn and Bacon, 1995.

Swinfield, Rosemarie. *Stage Makeup Step-by-Step*. Cincinnati: Betterway Books, 1994.

Williams, Bill. *Stage Lighting Design 101*. Online at http://www.mts.net/~william5/sld.htm. 1997-1999.

Williams, Tennessee. *Where I Live: Selected Essays*. New York: New Directions, 1978.

Wolf, Thomas. *Presenting Performances*. New York: ACA Books, 1991.

Part III

Arnott, Peter D. *Public and Performance in the Greek Theatre*. New York: Routledge, 1989.

Artaud, Antonin. *The Theatre and Its Double*. Translated by Mary Richards. New York: Grove Press, 1958.

Berkowitz, Gerald M. *New Broadways: Theatre Across America: Approaching A New Millennium*, revised ed. New York: Applause, 1997.

Berthold, Margot. *A History of World Theatre*. New York: Frederick Ungar Publishing Co., Inc., 1972.

Bieber, Margarete. *The History of the Greek and Roman Theater*, 2nd ed. Princeton, N.J.: Princeton University Press, 1961.

Bigsby, C. W. E. *Modern American Drama, 1945–1990*. Hampshire, England: Macmillan Publishers Ltd., 1992.

Birringer, Johannes. *Theatre, Theory, Postmodernism*. Bloomington: Indiana University Press, 1991.

Bordman, Gerald. *American Theatre: A Chronicle of Comedy and Drama, 1869-1914*. New York: Oxford University Press, 1994.

———. *American Theatre: A Chronicle of Comedy and Drama, 1914-1930*. New York: Oxford University Press, 1995.

———. *American Theatre: A Chronicle of Comedy and Drama, 1930-1969*. New York: Oxford University Press, 1996.

Bradby, David, and David Williams. *Directors' Theatre*. Hampshire, England: Macmillan Publishers Ltd., 1988.

Brandon, James R., ed. *The Cambridge Guide to Asian Theatre*. Cambridge, England: Cambridge University Press, 1993.

Brockett, Oscar G. *History of the Theatre*, 7th ed. Boston: Allyn and Bacon, Inc., 1995.

Cheney, Sheldon. *The Theatre: Three Thousand Years of Drama, Acting, and Stagecraft*, revised ed. New York: Longmans, Green & Co., Inc., 1972.

Clurman, Harold. *The Fervent Years: The Story of the Group Theatre in the Thirties*. New York: Alfred A. Knopf, Inc., 1945.

Cohn, Ruby. *New American Dramatists, 1960–1990*. Hampshire, England: Macmillan Publishers Ltd., 1991.

French, Warren, ed. *Sam Shepard, Arthur Kopit, and the Off-Broadway Theater*. Boston: Twayne Publishers, 1982.

Gillespie, Patti P., and Kenneth M. Cameron. *Western Theatre: Revolution and Revival*. New York: Macmillan Publishing Company, 1984.

Grose, B. Donald, and O. Franklin Kenworthy. *A Mirror to Life: A History of Western Theatre*. New York: Holt, Rinehart, and Winston, 1984.

Guicharnaud, Jacques. *Modern French Theatre from Giraudoux to Beckett*. New Haven, CT: Yale University Press, 1961.

Harris, Andrew B. *Broadway Theatre*. New York: Routledge, 1994.

Hartnoll, Phyllis, and Enoch Brater. *The Theatre: A Concise History (World of Art)*, 3rd ed. New York: Thames and Hudson, Inc., 1998.

Hewitt, Barnard. *Theatre U.S.A., 1665–1957*. New York: McGraw-Hill Book Company, Inc., 1959.

Jacobsen, Josephine, and William R. Mueller. *Ionesco and Genet: Playwrights of Silence*. New York: Hill and Wang, 1968.

Mantzius, Karl. *A History of Theatrical Art in Ancient and Modern Times, Vol. I, The Earliest Times*. New York: Peter Smith, 1903; reprinted 1937.

Meserve, Walter J. *An Outline History of American Drama*. New York: Feedback Theatrebooks & Prospero Press, 1994.

Mylryne, J. R., and Margaret Shewring. *Shakespeare's Globe Rebuilt*. New York: Cambridge University Press, 1977.

Nicoll, Allardyce. *The Development of the Theatre: A Study of Theatrical Art from the Beginnings to the Present Day*, 5th ed, revised. New York: Harcourt, Brace, and World, Inc., 1966.

Wainscott, Ronald H. *The Emergence of the Modern American Theater, 1914-1929*. New Haven: Yale University Press, 1997.

Watt, Stephen. *Postmodern/Drama: Reading the Contemporary Stage*. Ann Arbor: The University of Michigan Press, 1998.

Wickham, Glynne. *A History of the Theatre*, 2nd edition. London: Phaidon Press Limited, 1992.

———. *The Medieval Theatre*. London: St. Martin's Press, 1974.

Permissions Acknowledgments

and in any form, are strictly reserved and none of these rights can be exercised or used without written permission from the copyright owner. Inquiries for stock and amateur performances should be addressed to Samuel French, Inc., 45 West 25th Street, New York, NY 10010. All other inquiries should be addressed to Gary N. DaSilva, 111 N. Sepulveda Blvd., Suite 250, Manhattan Beach, CA 90266-6850.

Neil Simon: Excerpt from *Broadway Bound* © 1987 by Neil Simon. Professionals and amateurs are hereby warned that *Broadway Bound* is fully protected under the Berne Convention and the Universal Copyright Convention and is subject to royalty. All rights, including without limitation professional, amateur, motion picture, television, radio, recitation, lecturing, public reading and foreign translation rights, computer media rights and the right of reproduction, and electronic storage or retrieval, in whole or in part and in any form, are strictly reserved and none of these rights can be exercised or used without written permission from the copyright owner. Inquiries for stock and amateur performances should be addressed to Samuel French, Inc., 45 West 25th Street, New York, NY 10010. All other inquiries should be addressed to Gary N. DaSilva, 111 N. Sepulveda Blvd., Suite 250, Manhattan Beach, CA 90266-6850.

August Wilson: Excerpt from *Joe Turner's Come and Gone* by August Wilson, copyright © 1988 by August Wilson. Used by permission of Dutton Signet, a division of Penguin Group (USA) Inc.

About the Author

Marsh Cassady is the author of more than fifty books including novels, true crime, biography, collections of plays, short stories and haiku, and books on theatre and storytelling. His plays have been widely performed in the United States (including Off-Broadway) and in Mexico.

A former actor/director and university professor, he has a Ph.D. in theatre, is a member of Actors' Equity Association and the Dramatists Guild, and has worked with more than a hundred productions. In addition, Cassady has taught various creative writing courses at UCSD and elsewhere. A former small press publisher, he also has been editor of three magazines. Since the early 1980s he has conducted all-genre writing workshops in San Diego and in Playas de Rosarito, Baja California Norte, Mexico, where he has lived since 1997. While teaching at Montclair State in the 70s, he started a playwriting program that included classes, workshops, and individual projects. He has won regional and national awards in the U.S. in playwriting, fiction, nonfiction, and haiku.

Cassady writes editorials, a column and occasional articles for *The Baja Times*, and his digital art and ceramic sculptures are exhibited in several galleries. He continues to write books in various genres.